I Am Shakti

Reclaiming Women's Innate Power to Heal Themselves and Restore Balance, Health, Prosperity, and Joy for All Beings

What People Are Saying About

I Am Shakti

I have read scores of books that touch on yoga, ayurveda, and even social justice, but I have never read anything so beautiful and profound. I'm in awe. I now understand why Maya's teachings can so easily take up residence in the hearts and minds of women everywhere, including my own.
Linda Sparrowe, former editor of *Yoga Journal, Yoga International,* and author of several books on yoga and women

Maya's book, *I Am Shakti,* is a story of how her Shakti has shaped her amazing life. And it is much more. It is an invitation for all women to reclaim their innate power to heal themselves and restore balance, health, love, and joy for all beings. In this eloquent exposition, Maya demonstrates that we are all Shakti.
Vandana Shiva, Indian scholar, environmental activist, food sovereignty advocate, ecofeminist, and anti-globalization author of 20 books

I Am Shakti is more than a book – it is a celestial hymn to the forgotten pulse of the divine feminine, resonating deep within the cosmic tapestry of life. Maya Tiwari's words unfold like a sacred dance of wisdom, drawing us into the rhythmic heartbeat of Shakti. In this masterpiece, she stitches together the ancient and the modern, the personal and the universal, to guide us on a profound journey toward healing, balance, and collective restoration. With poetic precision and the tender ferocity of a sage, Maya calls us to reclaim the Shakti energy that resides in every woman and man. She invites us to transcend the binaries that have divided us for millennia and to remember our origin

as beings of both Shakti and Shiva – intertwined, inseparable, and infinitely powerful. Maya's own story of transformation from suffering to strength is not merely an inspiration; it is a map for those of us seeking to restore the primordial feminine energy, and in so doing the sacred balance within ourselves and in the world. Every page of *I Am Shakti* vibrates with life, offering the reader both a challenge and a promise – the challenge to embrace the fullness of our feminine power and the promise of healing and wholeness that follows. This is a book for seekers, healers, warriors, and nurturers alike – a profound manifesto that will guide generations to come. In Maya's words, we find not only the truth of Shakti's power but also the courage to rise and embody it.
Dr Vijay Murthy, PhD, Director of The Murthy Clinic, Functional Medicine Practitioner, Ayurvedic Doctor & Naturopath, London, UK

Words are holy magic, and books appear when our souls and our world are ready. *I Am Shakti* has been summoned into being by the Goddess. In her service and ours, Maya Tiwari has unrobed her heart, offering her inspiring story, her wisdom, and the way home to the primordial, divine feminine power from which all things arise. With this compelling, brilliant, and deeply healing manifesto, Maya Tiwari reveals the light ready to be born from within us all.
Phyllis Curott, Wiccan Priestess, attorney, internationally best-selling author of *Book of Shadows*, and vice-chair of Parliament of the World's Religions

I Am Shakti

Reclaiming Women's Innate Power to Heal Themselves and Restore Balance, Health, Prosperity, and Joy for All Beings

by Maya Tiwari

BOOKS

London, UK
Washington, DC, USA

First published by O-Books, 2026
O-Books is an imprint of Collective Ink Ltd.,
Unit 11, Shepperton House, 89 Shepperton Road, London, N1 3DF
office@collectiveinkbooks.com
www.collectiveinkbooks.com
www.o-books.com

For distributor details and how to order, please visit the 'Ordering' section on our website.

ISBN: 978 1 80341 997 8
978 1 78904 409 6 (ebook)
Library of Congress Control Number: 2024949635

A CIP catalogue record for this book is available from the British Library.

Design: Lapiz Digital Services

UK: Printed and bound by CPI Group (UK) Ltd, Croydon, CR0 4YY
Printed in North America by CPI GPS partners

Table of Contents

Foreword

In the spring of 2009, I found myself in Australia attending a transformative global conference that attracted nearly a thousand attendees, including health professionals, holistic health seekers, and advocates for sustainable living. The conference focused on exploring health beyond medicine, and touched on philosophy, purpose in life, world peace, and natural approaches to well-being. Among the luminaries was Maya Tiwari, who delivered the keynote address with an elegance that spoke of worlds both ancient and eternal, a voice filled with wisdom drawn from the sacred wellsprings of feminine power. She spoke not just to the audience, but to the very soul of the cosmos, weaving the threads of Shakti – the primordial feminine force – into the very air we breathed.

After her speech, amidst a sea of attendees, Maya's gaze found me. There was something immediate, almost fated, in her attention. She approached me with the simplicity of a question, "What's your name, and what do you do?" I introduced myself as the head of the faculty of Ayurveda, expecting the usual nod of acknowledgment, but Maya's reply was anything but conventional. With a mischievous smile, she said, "You're too young to be head of anything," and, in that moment, the ice of formality cracked. A natural connection was born – one that would deepen with time and shared journeys.

In the years that followed, I had the honor of traveling alongside Maya on her World Peace Mandala projects in New Zealand and Australia. These peace pilgrimages were not mere trips but spiritual sojourns, journeys that reflected the profound work Maya does in the world. Her World Peace Mandala projects, like her teachings, are more than a restoration of ancient wisdom – they are a living blueprint for the healing of our fractured world. This connection I share with Maya goes beyond professional admiration. It is rooted in our shared understanding of the ancient, of Shakti's grace, and the call to restore balance. In this, her latest work, *I Am Shakti*, Maya once again reminds us of this sacred duty. Her words, much like the keynote address that first drew me to her, pulse with the energy of the divine feminine. This book is not just an exploration but a call to reclaim the essence of Shakti in each of us — woman, man, and all who walk between.

I Am Shakti is more than a book — it is a celestial hymn to the forgotten pulse of the divine feminine, resonating deep within the cosmic tapestry of life. Maya Tiwari's words unfold like a sacred dance of wisdom, drawing us into the rhythmic heartbeat of Shakti. In this masterpiece, she stitches together the ancient and the modern, the personal and the universal, to guide us on a profound journey toward healing, balance, and collective restoration. With poetic precision and the tender ferocity of a sage, Maya calls us to reclaim the Shakti energy that resides in every woman and man. She invites us to transcend the binaries that have divided us for millennia and to remember our origin as beings of both Shakti and Shiva — intertwined, inseparable, and infinitely powerful.

Maya's own story of transformation from suffering to strength is not merely an inspiration, it is a map for those of us seeking to restore the primordial feminine energy and, in so doing, the sacred balance within ourselves and in the world. Every page of *I Am Shakti* vibrates with life, offering the reader both a challenge and a promise — the challenge to embrace the fullness of our feminine power and the promise of healing and wholeness that follows. This is a book for seekers, healers, warriors, and nurturers alike — a profound manifesto that will guide generations to come. In Maya's words, we find not only the truth of Shakti's power but also the courage to rise and embody it.

Dr Vijay Murthy, PhD, Director of The Murthy Clinic, Functional Medicine Practitioner, Ayurvedic Physician & Naturopath, London, UK
September 10, 2024

Acknowledgments

First off, my deep gratitude to the immutable grace and divinity of the universe, whose presence in dark and light times continually reminds me that I am woman, worthy, and whole. I would like to thank my friend, mentor, and agent, Linda Sparrowe, without whom this book would not have been born. Her immense investment of time, space, and literary wisdom, notwithstanding her outreach to garner invaluable feedback from seasoned editors, has shaped these pages. My profound thanks and appreciation to Aimee Ellis, my editor, whose magical pen and innate penchant for the word have sharpened otherwise rough drafts into polished gems. My deep thanks to my publishing team at O-Books and my editors, copy editors, and marketing pros for their immediate and instant embrace of *I Am Shakti*. Gratitude to the wonderful artist, Marnie Mikell, for her fine hand in refining my line drawings.

A shout-out to Kamala Asher for her many years of service to my work at large and for referring me to Aimee. Eternal thanks to Patricia Peluso, a friend who has been a steadfast mentor alongside many long years of traversing the world with my work on women's empowerment and the content of this book. My immense love and respect for all women — those who will read this book and those who will not — all are goddesses close to my heart space. Deep love and encouragement to all men who recognize the galactic need to reclaim their primordial masculine power and protect the feminine force. First, last, and always, my eternal gratitude to my mother, Kalyai, who has recently reached her ninetieth year and whose precious embodiment of compassion and love is earthed within my soul.

Part I
We Are Broken

Chapter 1

Mining the Cavernous Depth

We are half of the world's population. We are the womb of Mother Earth. We gave birth to the human world. We are women.

All my life, the Divine Feminine — Shakti, the Goddess and Mother of all creation — has guided, guarded, and led me ever closer to her. Shakti's powers are infinite. She is the primordial feminine force of creation. As the primordial feminine energy, she is the root source on which all else depends for survival, nourishment, and thriving. She exists in every iota of life, each life form, and in all genders, albeit only women carry her power in its awakened form. This concept is rooted in the idea that women are the repository of both creative and destructive power, reflecting the dual nature of feminine primordial power. In Hinduism, women's inheritance of Shakti is used to empower them, to resist patriarchy and reclaim their inherent divine power. By recognizing and honoring the sacred feminine, women can tap into their inner strength and potential, leading to greater balance and harmony in their lives and the world around them. Shakti is the Mother of peace, nourishment, nurturance, love, compassion, and endurance. When necessary, she arms herself, transmogrifying her presence into the fierce protector of her creation. Shakti has revealed herself to me through study and prayer, steered me when my steps have faltered, and surged through my body to set my soul aflame in moments of heart-opening love. Yet it is through suffering most of all that I have truly come to know her; the suffering we all must endure as children of Mother Earth, who endures all. To deeply discern Shakti is to see that she is powerful beyond measure, pulsing at the heart of every living creature and gravid with the seed of all creation; it is also to realize that she is in a state of violent imbalance in our world today. Driven by a primal fear of the Mother and her Mother Earth, the fragile yet tenacious patriarchy has striven for centuries to plunder her cosmic light. The balance of cosmic energy between Shakti and her Divine Masculine counterpart, Shiva, is the fulcrum on which all life hinges. The imbalance of that divine energy is the core cause of humanity's miseries, affecting the health of our bodies, minds, spirits, relationships, society, and the Earth itself. It falls to us — the daughters, vessels, and wielders of Shakti — to restore this balance and heal our world.

My Sojourn to Shakti

As is often the case with spiritual journeys, my path to Shakti had been winding, onerous, and riddled with blessings — generated from ancestors, previous karmas, and the stoic lessons of this life. We all bear a myriad of wounds, some propelling us further along our paths, others holding us back. At this stage of my journey, I often find myself on bended knees, humbled by devotion to the divine, which has a million forms and names in my tradition of birth. Yet I store memories deep within, shaped by the arduous experiences of my forebears, who were knuckled on bended knees not because they were awed by the glories of the Goddess or their Brahminical heritage but because they were broken into little pieces by their noxious, colonized circumstances. Broken. Pieces, lodged like a bone in an unknown crevice of my body, perhaps in my soul, a visceral suffocating feeling amid otherwise fluent moments. Hauled like bales of cotton and packed like sardines in dank seafaring transports, my great-grandparents were exported from North India as indentured serfs by British prospectors of human life. They traveled 12,000 nautical miles across the vast oceans from Port Kolkata to British Guiana (now Guyana). Although, as a child, I was not fully aware of my grandparents' and parents' experiences, I had an intuitive sense of their emotional pain. By the age of 6 or 7, I had a strong impression that my own innocence and heritage had been violated, even though my people never spoke of their past. Somewhere within me, I carried an unconscious memory of the atrocities endured by my elders — a wound that continued to fester. This wounding manifested in many forms and diseases during an early odyssey with ovarian cancer and throughout my life. While I am privileged with a strong intellect, joy, and purpose and perennially rescued by the sheer grace and exquisite beauty of nature surrounding me, I am not surprised to find this woundedness continues as an ellipsis to the present.

My cancer diagnosis was a wound that doctors believed would prove fatal. At age 23, exhausted from their painful, wounded ancestral karmas, my ovaries and womb screamed, "I want out!" Through 13 major surgeries, chemo, radiation, and a complete hysterectomy, I forfeited the mysterious organ and the promise of birthing a child. While I was acutely aware of the dissonant rhythm in the underbelly of my beautiful femininity, I was too young to know the full impact this loss would have on my life. Reflecting on my youthful self, I felt only relief from losing my womb: no more bleeding, I thought. And what of my womanhood and marital bliss? Like a young prospector, sensing lost treasures to scavenge, I cast aside these considerations to delve into the intensive training of a Vedic monk, the rarefied field of my powerful male ancestors.

That was 50 years ago. My five-year-long cancer sojourn and the lingering psychic and emotional vulnerability it engendered launched an otherworldly journey that deeply mined the roots of my being. Beyond my youthful years, and through ancient ancestry, tears of the fragile crones, and angst of the fathers, I discovered a cavernous depth within me, the soul of my soul I understood to be the Shakti, my primeval feminine power. This discovery shaped the way I became familiar with my vulnerabilities, wounds, angst, and fears. It pummeled me time and time again into the abyss where darkness co-existed with light, fears with hope, bitterness with love, and betrayal with trust. In retrospect, it effectively stripped me of the false persona I had established to hide my insecurities and fears while navigating the treacherous waters of white, male-dominated America as a woman, an immigrant, and a person of color. Had I not been pummeled, I could not have emerged from my trauma forged and tempered. Had I not been stripped of my pretenses and laid bare, I could not have donned the mantle of the Divine Mother's infinite love, wisdom, and forgiveness.

***

In October 1977, I lay on the cold gurney at Mount Sinai Hospital in New York, awaiting what was to be my final surgery. The raw, antiseptic odor and the cacophonous clatter of stainless steel equipment made me almost despair again. Though I had become a famous New York fashion designer by then, I was alone. My family had only recently immigrated to Canada following the heinous racially promoted civil war in Guyana that broke out after it became independent from British rule. My people were forced to relocate with barely their lives intact. While cancer raged within me, war waged mercilessly in Guyana – violence within and without. The disease of cancer and the imperium of patriarchy, anarchy, and military atrocity had engulfed my reality. By November 1977, my doctors had determined that my cancer was fatal. The prognosis was six months to live.

In my loneliness, I drew on my father's Shiva-like protection – we were very close, and he exemplified the powerful and impressive masculine characteristics we attribute to the primordial male Shiva energies. I slipped back to when I was

2 years old, and he cared for me through a bout of diphtheria. His rich tenor voice still called to me, keeping me alive with his persistent love. Loosely hinged between the physical world and the ethereal, I experienced numerous out-of-body journeys. During one of his many visits during my cancer, my father read me scriptural passages from the third chapter of the *Bhagavad Gita* that reveal the true nature of karma yoga — the path of selfless service. Karma, he explained, holds both positive and negative consequences for us. The universal law of cause and effect impels us into countless rebirths to address and undo the negative results of previous actions. The results of all actions are in accordance with the divine, and all should be seen as blessings — dharma. "This, too, you will survive," he consoled. "Trust the Goddess Mother." Trust. Divine Mother. Goddess. An eternal journey, I'd discover.

With the shadow of a death sentence, I left the hospital and medical care and instead sought refuge in a friend's ski cabin in the winter white of Vermont. After three months of subsisting with an enduring hardwood fire burning bright and a cast iron pot of whole grain and root vegetable soup simmering on a wood stove, I settled into waiting. Waiting to die. Being unhinged from my physical body seemed like a blessing. I felt as light as air, floating about with little or no pain. I wept, yet somehow felt a deep stillness inheriting the smoldering embers of my soul. I was unhinged and hanging, suspended in the imperceptible reality of near death. I saw light beams and rainbows streaming through the windows, with crystal refractions everywhere I turned. Erratic dreams and storms of tears and rawness prevailed. One morning, the comforting crackling sounds of a herd of deer rambling on the dry underbrush drew me outdoors. Early winter mornings in the Vermont forest were heavenly; virgin sunlight streaking through the tall cedars and pines in dancing infractions upon the thickly quilted snowfield. I found myself basking in the solace of raw-some nature. In this place, the Mother Goddess answered my unspoken prayers. Death released me.

I was 28 years old and weighed only ninety pounds, with barely enough fat and muscle to buffer me from the frenzied pace of life in Manhattan. My hands and head shook involuntarily, and a fierce coldness permeated every vein and limb. The ends of my nerves were frayed. And yet, in a strange and inexplicable way, I was jubilant. I felt free. Having withdrawn from the fashion industry due to my illness, I didn't have to work at constantly reinventing my history or persona to succeed in that frenetically glamorous fashion world. I was able to breathe without worrying thoughts. I began to explore the loosely woven fabric of my life and of my illness, which had been stitched with threads that tied me not only to my childhood but to the lives of my ancestors. To find my way out of the confusion that my cancer and my people's upheaval had caused, I had to untangle the knots in those threads and look closely at their colors and textures before I could begin to weave myself anew.

This unraveling led me to the profound traditional studies of self-knowledge and self-healing: Ayurveda. Vedanta. Sanskrit. I was passionately driven to learn how the ancient Vedic Rishis approached humanity's healing from despair, chaos, and disease. I was instructed in this ancient education by my guru, His Holiness, Swami Dayananda Sarasvati, under whose keen wit and brilliant tutelage I would spend the next 20 years studying the greater Vedas. I was further instructed by the depth of my near-death experiences. The gems I began to uncover in my miraculous recovery from cancer were as brilliant as the sunlight reflecting on the undifferentiated white of nature's wintry welkin.

The transmission of Vedic studies seemed to be linked to my paternal ancestors, most of whom were Vedic priests, scholars, and gurus. A kinship with this tremendous knowledge, my past endurance, and present awakening surfed alongside my studies.

In 1989, I participated in an initiation as a Brahmacharini, a dedicated Vedic protege. As I stood in the Holy Ganges River in Rishikesh during that ritual initiation, I felt the spirits of my ancestors released into the early dawn fog. A sudden scud of chilling winds crashed upon the jagged edges of the waters, gleaming with rime as the sun broke out. I remember feeling the regale of fragile freedom. Tenderness in my heart. I was connecting with my ancestors.

Having garnered immense privilege and purpose from my erudite studies, I spent the next three decades as a teacher of holistic ways of living and being. Like its precursor, yoga, the work of Ayurveda that I introduced to the Western world took root. I traveled the globe and helped thousands of women heal from reproductive disorders, cancers, distress, and domestic abuse. I was sought after by the media and publishers. It seemed I was sailing along seamlessly through the smooth and salient riverbed of my calling. The Mother's grace was with me.

Pleasing my father, I decided to dive even deeper into the ancestral fire. Each year, I would return to the holy river at Rishikesh for the annual observation of *Sivaratri*, the celebration of the God Shiva, and to spend time with my guru. This was the time when he would bestow the title of *Saṃnyāsa* – a Vedic monk in the erudite lineage of Veda Vyasa – upon students he deemed fit for the journey of the robes, and in February 1996, he presented me with mine. I received the bright orange raiment and the spiritual nomenclature, "Her Holiness, Swami Mayatitananda." "Being a dedicated student and doing such good work in the world, you are well suited to this destiny," he declared. Knowing my ambitious vision for restoring Ayurvedic science to its global destiny, he threw me a carrot: "You will be among the very first women to be offered this honor in this ancient lineage of Veda Vyasa." His unuttered thought was, "Having lost your womb, you should have far fewer challenges on this well-traversed ancient path of the male guru." Though

I was well aware of the challenges I would face in this male-dominated field, my purpose was pure, and my future seemed to beckon with boundless potential.

The Pearl in the Shadow-Self

The two decades following my initiation as a full-fledged Vedic monk were a shocking antithesis to my prior quarter century of reconciliation, success, and applause. My long and arduous years in orange robes unfolded with endless impediments, obstacles, and slighting from my dear community, family, friends, and strangers alike. My three-book contract with a top publishing house was dropped, sales for my published works dropped radically, and media interest in my growing and thriving work in Ayurveda education in the United States desisted. There was no apparent reason, yet it held a logic all the same: the path of a renunciate naturally renounces material privileges. It seemed like the universe herself was stripping me of the buffer that protected my ego, notoriety, and equanimity.

As both father and guru would say, "See every disadvantage as a blessing." A very Shiva/Masculine Divine point of view, I might point out, easily uttered when the Shakti Force pays the dear price for all such becoming. Nevertheless, I attempted to do just that as I returned to the world on the major stage of health and spirituality conferences. I began to carve out the feminine face of Ayurveda by restoring long-lost lunar, seasonal, and solar rhythms to my therapies, practices, and principles, especially those that guide women's wellness. My studies pelted me into a man's world where the patriarchal mindset flourished. Vedic scholarship and monkhood retained barely a glint of the practicing feminine energy even though India boasts more than a million goddess shrines. While learning and chanting the Sanskrit mantras, especially those for the Goddess, my inner goddess fired up. Experiencing the brunt of emotional conflicts that naturally came with the terrain of being female in a tightly knitted male-oriented system, I chose to live away from the primary monasteries in the United States and India. Instead, I created a non-profit school in the mountain forests of Asheville, North Carolina. Living away from the ashram kept the spirit of condescension and competition with my male peers to a minimum. However, it did not entirely safeguard me from jealousy, misunderstanding, and abuse for being a successful woman in robes. When *Ayurveda: A Life of Balance,* my second book, was published, my Vedanta colleagues rendered kind and beautiful reviews on my restoration of the Earth-based intelligence of the ancient Ayurveda that modern clinical Ayurveda had lost. However, the comments I received from the ashram's senior power gurus were quite the opposite: "No one except a sage can restore these ancient works," or worse yet, "Ayurveda is a dead vidya," meaning Ayurveda has become so defunct in India and lost to the world that it could not be brought back to life. With the global popularity of Ayurveda today, these same gurus now see themselves as its promoters and sponsors.

The cut got deeper still — I became aware that the brilliant orange robes of a Vedic monk had indelibly stamped me as Hindu. After centuries-long colonized rule, this identity had become stigmatized by the prejudices of Western academia that continue to promote misunderstanding, fear, and distrust of Hinduism. In reality, the Hindu Vedic system has always been a thorn in the side of modern power structures, colonizers, and intelligentsia who seek to diminish or appropriate its rich spiritual history and Earthly treasures. (India's rare and priceless gems can still be found in crowns and museums throughout Europe — most recently, the glistening wonder of India's 105.6-carat Koh-i-Noor twinkled regally from the coffin of Queen Elizabeth II as her funeral procession moved through the streets of London.) The Vedic system — comprising cosmic sciences such as astronomy and cosmology, Earth sciences such as mathematics and physics, and healing sciences such as Yoga, Ayurveda, and Vastu, or cosmic architecture – explicates the most ancient wisdom humans possess through an immense repository of knowledge that neither Western academia nor any single extant religion or culture can rival. Yet these magnificent Vedas – the very works helping to heal my ancestral scars and redefine my life's trajectory – had simultaneously branded me with an indelible "otherness."

Western wariness of Hinduism and the Vedic system is wholly unfounded. Vedic knowledge, though transmitted to humanity by the Vedic sages, is not restricted to Hindus; it has always been available to anyone who seeks its wisdom. Indeed, the eponym for Hinduism is *Sanatana Dharma*, meaning a universal way of life belonging to all humanity. It was never an organized religion. Compared to the vastness of the Vedic sciences, its religion plays a very small role. In all of history, the Hindus have never attempted to conquer another country or religion, forbade people from practicing whatever their ancestral calling was, or attempted to change or convert a single person to their faith or way of life. Ironically, India's insurmountable rise in patriarchy did not occur until after numerous foreign invasions, colonization, and violations of her material and spiritual treasures. Before these foreign-power invasions, there was barely a glimmer of the group violence, dissent, or competition that plagues modern patriarchal India. Nevertheless, despite its benign and benevolent history, Western suspicion of this venerable tradition largely prevails.

Nothing could have prepared me for the disrespect and danger the orange robes would subject me to. I was continually taunted and slighted when out and about in the community. Traveling through US immigration also became a tedious process. The orange robes worn by an ethnic person were like wearing a Taliban red flag. I was stopped, questioned, and searched at every orange-clad trip. Before becoming a monk,

I had subsisted peacefully for 20 years in an idyllic, sparsely populated valley in the oxygen-filled forest of Mount Pisgah, where I established the Wise Earth School of Ayurveda. When I donned the orange robes, a slew of barbaric intrusions suddenly eclipsed my tranquil forest and home. By this time, most of the local elders, craftsmen, and craftswomen who had helped me build my sanctuary and kept a watchful eye out for me had passed away, and the few remaining were in nursing homes. A rush of unauthorized activity began on my property, the retreat I spent years building according to Vastu principles, consisting of a gushing spring from the mountain tops, with 15 acres of unfelled forest where the Cherokee people's ginseng and sassafras continued to thrive, alongside my lush organic gardens. There were nightly noxious activities wherein my organic gardens were trampled and sprayed with toxic chemicals. Trespassed by local hunters, new developers who had just moved into the area, and unidentified locals on the hire, I endured numerous break-ins to my home and compound. Intruders repeatedly desecrated my sacred altars indoors and out, and did immense structural damage to my home. Precious pieces of jewelry were stolen. My antiques and finely handcrafted furnishings were vandalized. A new neighbor's hunting dog was deliberately and repeatedly let loose to hunt the innocent herd of deer who had taken to sitting in the fields, attentively tuned in to my morning meditation and chanting practice. When I called the Sheriff's office, I received no help or protection other than lubricous advice: "When you catch them, give us a holler," and, another time, "Set some bear traps in the forest."

The violations continued. Blessings from the prolific spring reservoir on my property were overcast with the shadows of developers who had moved to the top of the ridge above my forest. They stripped a part of my forest and installed pumps and underground conduits from my private reservoir to supply their new housing developments in the vicinity, all the while flooding my forest. For the last six months I was in my forest home, these illegal activities were conducted under cover of nightfall, with a few surrounding neighbors coerced or bribed to stand guard and keep mum. Seeking help to get the wrongdoings stopped and rectified, I called in a local geologist, a groundwater expert, and the county water and forest authority, all to no avail. Shocked and awed by the audacity of lies, deceit, and corruption, I was forced to accept that my once serene sanctuary had morphed into a prison camp of agony and injustice simply because the absence of law enforcement — at least for me — made it so easy and convenient for men with big machines and big bucks to bulldoze and oust the little Indian woman from her home.

History repeats itself. Almost two centuries ago, in 1838, the Native Cherokee people who were the rightful inhabitants of these forests were savagely uprooted from their ancestral lands and marched off on foot to walk hundreds of miles away and forced into interments in Oklahoma. This journey of savage eradication of Native people and their intelligence, now known as The Trail of Tears, resonated with a deep ache in my chest. On the surface, much appears to be improved, but deep down, we are still being manipulated, controlled, and bullied by a new breed of greedy patriarchal offspring.

I have been an outlier all my life, criticized, shunned, or marginalized for my varied pioneering accomplishments, but even this paled in comparison to the discrimination I endured when I became a monk. Ironically, when I first relocated my school from New York City to Pisgah Mountain, I was well-received by the local gentry, elders, farmers, and kind folks, many of whom had never flown in an airplane or traveled great distances outside their locale. They taught me their ancestral building techniques and how to live in mountain forest terrain. They lent their expertise on many fronts along the way. We traded their wisdom of the land and farmers' calendar in exchange for Ayurvedic herbal remedies and Vedic food preparation and gardening techniques. They loved Earth medicine and preferred it to modern chemical drugs. But those serene days of retreating to my forest sanctuary after my world tours and teachings ended abruptly. It was not until I took the initiation of a Vedic monk and became a robed person that I realized that the jealousy, erasure, and marginalization I kept encountering was not because I am an outlier but because I am a woman and a dark-skinned immigrant, lit by ancestral largesse who somehow understood the paradox of reality and the balancing measure that paradox gives to truth. My light can help heal the suffering world and often exposes the darkness that this world of imbalances tries to hide. These experiences show me how vulnerable the Shakti energy in our world has become.

After a decade of walking in robes, I began to recognize that I was losing vital energy, not from the tiredness of my tours but from a feeling of uneasiness that was getting more palpable. While I felt at home in complete confidence on the master stage, I felt deeply vulnerable offstage, where the earth beneath my feet would begin to tremble. My inner space of serenity was shrinking; I was losing a sense of compassion with the student body I was training to become Ayurveda practitioners. In 2008, after fainting in the sweet grass meadow at my school's compound, I was diagnosed with uranium and other heavy metals in my blood. Traces of uranium, lead, and cadmium were also found in my spring reservoir.

As serious as this illness was, I sensed that my feelings of vulnerability and dejection were from more than the heavy metal poisoning. These physical signs were the material symptoms of an inner layer of toxicity: separation from my sacred state of the Shakti-Divine Feminine energy. Ironically, while doing the profound work of bailing out ancestral grief and defending the noble tradition of the Vedas, I found myself sinking deeper into dark patriarchal waters. Now, I would have to rise above this oppressive immersion to reconcile my despair, this dwindling sense of opulence, and what was becoming a derisory existence.

As I was recovering from the uranium poisoning, I realized I had not given much thought to my femininity in years. I used to delight in dressing in beautiful, unique, feminine fashion of my own design. Even then, though, I don't recall having sensed my immense femininity. I only knew I was young and beautiful, with a powerful body that I loved to dress up and flaunt. In contrast, the simplicity of monastic life has no room for frills, and although it was austere, I had come to love it. In some strange, subtle way, I was becoming more tuned in to my femininity while walking a monk's journey. Indeed, simplicity is a mature, Shakti-endowed quality. Being a monastic began to awaken my forgotten sense of the feminine, that largess I had stored away after marching on full speed away from my cancer years. Pondering this, I began to choose a special shade of orange shawl for my orange wardrobe; I redesigned the sari into a two-piece that was easy to wrap and wear, and I loved feeling the Gandhi hand-loomed khaki against my skin. I adorned my feet with exquisitely simple sandals and blessed my throat with the finest pearls and crystals. I reveled in the simplicity of the original Zen and Vedic spaces and still live on tatamis on the wooden floors of my rooms. I thought fondly of my elderly aunt's *kutya,* a mud cottage on the lush rural Corentyne Coast, daubed weekly with organic cow dung. These abodes exuded the smell of sanity and sentiency — astringent protection that wise women used to ward off predators, diseases, and even drunken husbands while keeping their minds pristine. The ultimate grace, I learned, is to live simply and gently in the form of the Earth Shakti. My burgeoning femininity infused my every action and aspiration: to live and let live, to be kind, to use only what we need, to be conscious of nature, to connect myself and others to our inner beauty, and to seek harmony.

Twenty-five years of this arduous monastic journey revealed secret caverns within me that beckoned exploration, spaces where the exquisite essence of my feminine felinity, my womanhood, was hiding, cowering, and recovering. My womb space, now sanctified by loss, offered up the quantum mystery of the Divine Feminine force. The physical organ was gone; in its place, I found the Goddess. The journey of healing and helping other women heal gifted me with thousands of children, many of them mischievous, neglected, guileless souls whom I would have loved to have suckled and nurtured.

From Suffering to Seraph

In 2010, I renounced my role as a renunciate and gave up my monastic life and titles. It became clear that the ashram environs could not nourish the peaceful inner weaponry I would now need to finish restoring and safeguarding my Shakti force. My mission was to rebuild my life around the healing presence of the Divine Feminine. Following my cancer years, she sent me back to my native Indian soil to rescue my ancestral spirits. Job done. Her next set of clear and trenchant instructions was for me to embody my womanhood fully. To reclaim this largesse, I would need to put to rest all my deeply scarred ancestral wounds. But changing journeys do not just happen from the process of mind. The heart intervenes at every crossroads.

I set aside my brilliant orange uniform and began wearing light pink, though the dresses still resembled flowing robes. I had a prescient sense that my life was about to change forever and change it did. On a mid-September afternoon at the Atlanta airport, en route from San Francisco to another event on my Peace Mandala World Tour, I was surprised to find my luggage lost upon arrival – and stunned by what I found in its place. There he was, standing at baggage claim and gazing into my soul: "My Shiva!" my heart thundered. "This cannot be," answered my mind. I had been celibate for almost 40 years with rarely a sexual stirring. Yet, I ceased to doubt when I felt my heart trail his sandaled footsteps out of the baggage area. I remained rooted to the spot for interminable moments, heart pounding and air forced from my lungs. Eventually, I took refuge in the lost baggage kiosk and scribbled some words in a daze, waiting for my luggage and composure to return. This tall, handsome man with piercing blue eyes bore a stark resemblance to the portrait of a seraph I had embroidered 45 years earlier. I felt as if the doors to my heart were wrenched wide open. A memory flooded my senses and transported me to the burnished grass meadow of Pisgah Mountain, where I chanted with cows and meditated with the deer, a nearby field of golden wisps floating around me. My breath stood still, exuding barely a whisper like the glistening wings of butterflies as they glided in the dawn light across an ethereal sky. As I left the airport, everything around me shimmered with a vague scent of sandalwood, the aroma that inherited my heart as it reached out to claim this new, utterly transforming feminine emotion.

I had no idea at the time how significant and revelatory this isolated encounter would become for me, but I did have a sense of knowing this man beyond the limits of time-bound life. His was the face I had been seeing in the fragmented images of my colonized past. I sensed the potency of his archetypal male energy, and so I christened him "My Shiva." He reminded me of the first great man in my life, my father, whose vigorous masculine energy had helped me heal from cancer. This meeting felt serendipitous. I was still very vulnerable from my recent experience of being poisoned – was this cosmic messenger, the primordial Shiva energy, coming to my rescue again? The experience felt like a fairytale; the timing felt like a miracle. As I began my journey to stand tall and poised in my Shakti energies, I had no idea where my path would lead me. But I sensed now with the awkward opening of my feminine heart that while there were ancestral wounds still to be healed, I had finally summoned the power to heal them.

Had I known how formidable that brief, heart-awakening moment in my life would be — the impact it would have on my thawing heart, the reprieve of divine love that would blossom inside of me, and the conduit it would open to the Goddess herself — I would have dropped my shyness and run after him, grabbing him into my arms and abandoning myself to the longing to behold and to be held. But life has its own plans; it rarely plays out as we had hoped. Afterward, I prayed the Divine Mother would pave the way to unrobing my heart. This time around, I leaned into my life's gentler, softer nature. She had positioned herself at every turn of my arduous journey. When she first rescued me from the odyssey of ovarian cancer, I recalled my *sankalpa*, sacred intent, was to serve her however she guided me to. The hairpin twists of my path had thus far led me to destinations that pleased and lauded my father, guru, and ancestors. However, this journey as a monk was not divergent from the path; it prepared me for my next step and honed me in ways my beloved ancestors would be proud of. I hope my learning and sacrifices helped them move the angst and agony they endured into a space of resolve, untethered now from the world of the living and the dead. I sense they are floating freely in this magnificent cosmos, beyond the long reach of scars. Having completed that stage of my journey, I stood again at the crossroads, and again, I stoically pledged to Her the devotion of my newly awakened feminine heart.

Healing the Sense of Separation

As I journeyed further from the monastic path and ever closer to Her, I experienced a longing for my womb and fleeting thoughts of embracing all that my feminine heart would bring to me. I realized the Goddess was directing me to reclaim the feminine energies that had lain still and forlorn within me or been violated by external forces; the wounded women of my past with broken hearts pouring tears, the misogynistic slights and dismissals, the agony of hate crimes in my forest sanctuary, and the feminine longing after years in the monastery. The odyssey of life in the last decade had cleaved my sacred relation to my personal Shakti. As women, we must recognize the supreme challenge of wounds that we naturally bear. Weakened from the long years of endless battle while trying to keep harmony, we've become tired. We've become angry. With dimming awareness and shallowing breath, we are losing consciousness. In truth, we are not alone – both genders are suffocated by doubt, ambivalence, false beliefs, apathy, and distrust. In this fractured reality, we find ourselves trapped in a state of disharmony that affects the health and well-being of all beings, though women are at greater risk. Now more than ever, we must restore Mother Earth's sanctity, which reflects our own. Awareness and healing of these wounds are part of the rite of passage to the primordial feminine. The first thing we must remember is this: we are the womb of Mother Earth. We gave birth to the whole human world. We carry its heavy burdens. We are women. We are Shakti. Perhaps the critical question to ask ourselves is this: do you believe you can heal the vast chasm of hurt and disappointment you and generations before you have experienced as women, especially when the transgression of trust against the very fiber of our primordial nature, the Shakti, has served only to elide our grace and power? I believe we can. The Shakti genesis story I tell in this book is to help you delve into a profound space of understanding – a space that hardship had made brittle in my own life. This phase of my journey demanded a wide openness of mind and spirit beyond the binaries of tradition, scholarship, and accomplishment. Beyond societal norms. Little did I know that the Goddess's grace would be the sole buffer for the arduous events that awaited my beautiful soul. Finally, after I survived the journey and rose again, I recognized that this depth of darkness, the terrifying abyss into which I was continually thrown, was required to bring forth the immutable light I can now share with you.

I am rising now beyond the physical longing for love into a sublimation of trust. Trust that my new life will unfold precisely as it is intended. In truth, the universe always has a greater plan for us than we envision. It is a plan that is destined to fulfill our purpose, whatever that may be. I am purposed to the perennial path of Shakti's service and healing our humanity in need. Perhaps the emotions of my womanly love and longings are arming me for the next stage of my growth and purpose as I awaken further into my womanly heart. Having once been fully armored as a goddess-warrior, I sense I am being disarmed for my vigil, divested of an unnecessary burden as I stand in strength and friendship with 3.8 billion human goddesses on Mother Earth. It took a host of horrifying experiences to draw me closer to Shakti, yet I would never trade my path for another's. When Shakti smiles, my lips widen; when she breathes, my lungs open; when she closes her eyes, I fall asleep.

Chapter 2

Shakti: The Primordial Feminine Power

> *Women are the embodiment of Shakti. To preserve the progress of creation, its joys, sentiency, nurturance and peace for humanity she must be loved, respected and treated as auspicious.*
>
> Devi Upanishad

To restore the sacred balance in ourselves, our relationships, and our world, we need to understand Shakti, the primordial feminine principle that is at work at the core of all existence. Her prana, or life force, has infused breath into life on Earth for billions of years. Though she graces all her children with the gift of consciousness, she endows her cosmic blueprint to women alone, honoring them with the blood that brings forth new life. Look closely at the skin that covers your womb. There, you will find her *Sri Yantra* indelibly imprinted into the navel, the sacred design marking all women as her own. In the silent umbilicus of her creation, she stamped the magical seal of her Red Bindu into the reproductive memory of all female species. This Red Bindu is a drop of her Shakti Prana that imbues each womb with the life-giving force that keeps Shakti's primordial memory vibrant in the feminine cellular body. It is the origin of creation and life, of consciousness and vitality.

In the Tantric works, the union of Shiva and Shakti is seen as the union of consciousness and energy. Shakti is the primordial, active, and dynamic feminine energy of creation, derived from the Sanskrit root "shak," meaning "to be able," "to do," or "to act." This concept is personified in the form of Kundalini Shakti, the divine creative power. The Kundalini, derived from the Sanskrit word Kundala, is the powerful feminine force within the body that produces "awakening." In reality, the Kundalini is the body's energetic chakra system chartered by Para-Shakti, the universal power aspect of Shakti that transcends all relationships, even her counterpart aspect with Shiva. As Para-Shakti, she gives birth to her creation while simultaneously containing and transcending it.

As Shakti force within the Kundalini rises, consciousness rises. Her primary goal is to enjoin Shiva, ultimate consciousness, in the crown chakra. The two primordial energies that underpin all of life are Shiva and Shakti. The cosmic energy of Shiva and Shakti is infinitely vast and inherent in each person and every gender. In Vedic thought, Shiva-Shakti transcends the binary principle: their cosmic energies are inseparable yet limitless. As we explore these primordial energies within and without, let us shift awareness from a dualistic perspective to the fundamental reality of Shiva-Shakti by creating a sense of balance of our innate primordial energies.

As the feminine force, she expresses herself as Para-Shakti in the greater universal field and as Kundalini Shakti in the individual energy-body. As in the microcosm, so too the macrocosm. Kundalini Shakti charters individual evolution as she traverses the major energetic pathways of the seven main chakras within the body en route to the crown chakra. Her journey stirs the inner awakening into consciousness and is reflected in the greater universe through a progression of global awareness that appears as consciousness-awakening behavior. In other words, our personal enlightenment spurs social enlightenment. At the same time the alignment of the planets in the rarest of configurations, the mounting unease so many of us feel, and the awakening of awareness in a significant percentage of humanity forecast a radical overhaul that supports feminine justice — a key occurrence for restoring the Earth's intelligence. At this pivotal junction in our history, women, in particular, are becoming more sensitized to their

Shakti prowess. We are shifting perspective away from an outmoded and ineffective model of femininity and how it's been misunderstood in the past, where so much has been about copying what men are doing. Instead, we are creating a new vision by redefining feminine power for the new generation through the deep exploration of the Shakti principle. As we shift awareness from the old feminist model that never truly worked for women and stop emulating the inured patriarchal model, we forge forward with a new and ancient beacon to restore feminine power. At the same time, we light the way for women, men, and all genders to fuel and facilitate the non-binary and non-dualistic agenda in harmony with universal justice that we are seeking.

Fortunately, the ground for reclaiming our sacred right of the Shakti is ripened and fertile. Standing at a major crossroad of consciousness where we feel the palpable, visceral energy of Para-Shakti, women are galvanized to reclaim their primordial feminine power. In so doing, we regain the balance that has been blown asunder by our masculine counterparts. We can greatly influence the present masculine-dominated spheres by bringing Shakti's prowess to the fore. We can also inspire our men to awaken to their primordial Shiva nature. We not only need their help to accomplish this palpable shift of consciousness in our world, but we need to help them find their own exquisite masculine balancing force. The primordial masculine energy is naturally protective, stoic, and well-balanced, a needed counterpart for Shakti's mission to successfully effect the necessary shift in awareness and operating modes. Our primary task is to reincorporate the Goddess's intrinsic rights and rites into our living structure — cultural, social, economic, scientific, ecological, and spiritual.

At this time of social and individual evolution, a rapidly growing percentage of humanity, women and men and all genders, is already experiencing a new quiet surge of awareness. At the same time, we are witnessing the breakup of old, rote, anarchical, ancestral, social, and political patterns. The reins of patriarchal control are wearing thin and taut. We are sensing the emergence of a vast sweep of consciousness affecting every being on Earth. *I Am Shakti* could not be written at any other time. This luffing of consciousness moves my fingers and thoughts in a sanguine motion on the page. Fresh conscientious impetus to support the awakening of awareness is being disseminated through quantum physics, yoga, holistic medicine, ancient spiritual practices rooted in indigenous cultures, teachings by spiritual luminaries, and through books and online portals. We are experiencing a vast communal synchronicity steeped in both extremes of challenge and illumination: the paradox of the deep dark cavern of Earth and, simultaneously, the brilliant sunlight of the open sky. We are awakening through evolution and revolution; each of us has the potential to do so. The critical mass theory of convolution – wherein a group of people might band together to propagate and act on a message of hatred and violence – postulates that as soon as that mass reaches 10 percent of a population, their noxious activities begin to spread like wildfire. However, this critical mass theory likewise applies to the awakening that is happening. More than 20 percent of the world's population is leaning toward the unshakeable understanding that we are self-aware consciousness and children of Mother Earth. The major difference between the mass of humbugs and the mass of humanity is that the latter requires awareness, the gift that arises from deep struggle; one who truly possesses humanity is bowed by experience yet stands tall through mighty storms that inscribe the heart with the inner poise of calm. Be still for a moment. Listen. At the personal level, the light of awareness is beckoning each of us to claim our most authentic selves. Let us not fail to take advantage of the cosmic timing after enduring such a long and painful history.

As the Power, So the Vulnerability

> *With your gentle form that moves through the three worlds and with your surpassingly terrible ones, protect us and also the Earth.*
>
> Devi Mahatmya 4.26

Shakti is not an immense clump of iron muscles, nor can she be lived through emulating patriarchal agendas and modes of existence. As we embody Shakti, we experience freedom, liberation, self-generating intelligence, and intuitive guidance from the Goddess herself. We are reclaiming her patterns of love which are indelibly inscribed in the cellular memory of our DNA. We are rebuilding her nutritive healing force within. We cherish the power that can create or destroy. We reclaim the non-dual oneness we share as a human family. However, nowhere on Earth, in nature, or in the heavens is there such a thing as equality in and of itself. We are each diverse and unique in our individual karmas and rights; we are unique within the Shakti and Shiva forces. No two leaves on the maple, oak, or elm tree are alike or equal in size or shape; no twins are truly identical in structure. In competing in the patriarchal territory, women soldiers, heads of corporations, or women entrepreneurs, for example, are not equal to any male. Yet, neither is any male equal to those women or any other male. Not only can women be better warriors, leaders, and inventors, but when we work from our Shakti nature, we also fight for justice, compassion, fairness, kindness, cooperation, love, and nourishment for all. We do not share the same untidy value system as the present male power structure. Working in these male-oriented structures can never give us true equality, and fighting for it may earn us a clump of muscles that ache for the return of our feminine touch.

We may emulate numerous instances of the Goddess Shakti in her warrior forms of Kali and Durga, armed with weapons and righteous rage as she rides her Ghatokbahini Singha, a tiger and lion hybrid, into battle to fight for and protect the gods from the demons. Often, the gods of the Hindu pantheon would find themselves in a predictable mess generated through masculine power-ego struggles. In such instances, they would call upon the Goddess Parvati, or Shakti, for help. When Durga-asura, a demon, was misusing the power bequeathed him by the gods to destroy the Earth, the Goddess Shakti came to the gods' rescue. Assuming her terrifying form, she sprouted eighteen arms, each fitted with a specific goddess weapon. At first, seeing her, the demon jeered. She attacked him, and the demon fell but rose again. Now, taking the Goddess's threat seriously, he used all his weapons and skills to fend her off. Aiming her trident with great precision, she punctured his chest, and he fell dead. The name Durga was given to the Goddess by the gods to mark this historic victory. In single-handed battle, with her battalion of arms, Tantric literature relates countless victories over the asuras where Durga defended the gods and celestial realm, among them: Madhu, Kaitabha, Mahishasura, Dhumralochana, Chanda, Munda, Raktabija, Nishumbha, and Shumbha. Shakti can be formidable in defending her own. Indeed, women can become even more competitive and vindictive than their male counterparts, especially when plunged into the dark lower parts of their nature.

Though women are equally formidable, we must seek not equality with men but harmony. Even when we gather our gallant enchantment of women warriors and do fierce battle for restoring the Goddess's power and her overarching rights that uplift humanity, we will find no equality, nor should we wish to. Equality implies a sameness that does no justice to our potent femininity. Harmony, on the other hand, celebrates and balances our male and female energy. In a state of harmony, we work for equality of justice, equality of opportunity in all spheres, equality of access to nature's resources such as food, shelter, and safety, equality of rights in social structures for all beings, and equality of economic freedom.

With her immense power, Shakti perennially defends her Earth, the feminine force, her human charges, and even the often-defenseless gods. In safeguarding her universe and its foundational laws, her actions can be bloody and violent when required. The connotation of the feminine here is not the same as the inchoate demeaning darkness depicted by the patriarchal culture. Her tenacious force, when used, is always in the interest of humanity's evolution. She stomps out the destructive forces that threaten harmony within and without. Like a seed breaking its shell, enduring the violence of sprouting through the dense black earth to reach sunlight, her destructive force eliminates obstacles that block spiritual vision and self-awakening. All perceived darkness and mystery in the Goddess's nature exist solely to bring justice and keep the balance of her creation.

The Portal of Birth

I do not fear death; it is life that I fear the most.

Recognizing the vast expanse of vibrational energy and immutable power contained in the shaktified seed of human life, the Vedic people conceived a specific syllabus to add sentiency and inspire the gestating fetus. Through Sanskrit mantras, music, prayers, sacred intentions, and prescribed rituals for the wellness of mother and child, the mother would continually imbue her body, mind, and spirit with healthful thoughts and nutrition to instill well-being, courage, and other prized human values in the auric formation of her child. Bearing, rearing, and nurturing her child through its developmental years express a woman's sense of connectedness with all living things. This primordial feminine trait is not fully developed in the male.

Human beings experience a yonija birth, meaning all genders enter the world through the vagina, or yoni, of our mothers. Yoni is sacred. It is the gateway to human mortality. Vedic natives imposed no shadows of shame or embarrassment on the private sanctums of either the male or female. In ancient Hindu temples, women statues stood tall and displayed their vaginas for devotees – symbolic of the one and only portal that can transport the coexistence of seed and ovum through its passage to Earth. A yonija birth brings both the pleasure of life and the pain of death. That is why the inner sanctum of the Hindu temple is referred to as womb-house, *garbha griha*. The temple, as a whole, is seen as her cosmic form, the spread-eagle feminine being who gives shelter to the male deity in her body.

The Shiva lingam is also revered in Hindu temples as half of a balanced whole. The masculine primordial *lingam*, or male phallus, as it is known, is anything but a mere sexual organ. The lingam relates to the God Shiva and the Masculine Divine principle. As an essential symbol of pleasure, desire, and seed-giver, the lingam transports fertility, vitality, and energy. Here, the lingam represents the static absolute, and the yoni represents the dynamic energy, the universe's womb. The lingam and yoni are anatomical indicators of the greater universe's potent passages and trajectories for human evolution into consciousness.

At a physiological level, the lingam is the penis, and the yoni is the vulva. As the projectile energy that ferries and delivers its seed to the ovum, the lingam is an organ of procreation. In Hinduism, *kama*, encapsulating pleasure and desire, is an indispensable element in the four paths to consciousness. Pleasure is manifested through the phallus. Tantric philosophy considered the vulva, the phallus, and the bodily fluids essential to fertility rites. The divine ecstasy, which comes from the union of the lingam/phallus and the yoni/vulva, is part of the ecstatic development of human consciousness. Sexuality, in the context of consciousness transformation, is not merely about sexual activities; the union of Shiva-Shakti is fundamental to this transformation.

At the metaphysical level, the lingam is a projectile in the unification principle of Shiva-Shakti. At the spiritual level, it is the bearer of *ananda,* divine ecstasy. The primordial masculine's unique largesse transforms awareness, carrying it beyond to the *ananda* state, giving way to non-attachment and enlightenment. The bliss of Shiva-Shakti, the unified one, is demonstrated through the merging of yoni and lingam. Ancient native cultures kept life's vital physical/sensual and psychic/spiritual elements in unison. While they observed the universal values and timing for cohabitation, they did not isolate sensual or sexual functions as moral or immoral, shameful or respectable, per modern societal etiquette. The epidemic of sexual aberrations we are witnessing today is largely due to the primal purpose and function of human coitus being pushed into the shadows.

Sexuality is an intrinsic part of our divine anatomy in masculine and feminine forms. In a more profound sense, as we dedicate this union to its divine origins, we merge *dehi,* spirit and matter, with *deha,* mind and substrate, lingam being the *dehi* while the yoni is *deha.* Our ancestral light bearers tell us that only through the eternal love embedded in the human soul, and demonstrated through unraveling each sheath of our human anatomy – physical, psychic, spiritual – can opposites bind to each other, a necessary feat to raise consciousness. At the most sublime level, the merging of Shiva-Shakti can occur without sexual activity. Through pranayama and meditation, we can sublimate this energy within the individual and send it upward via the Kundalini's coiled force to enjoin the crown chakra. This phenomenal sublimation process of the inner merging of the masculine and feminine is the ultimate aim of raising consciousness to its absolute state within the human anatomy. As we integrate Shiva-Shakti energy within, we are strengthening sentiency. We influence the progression of consciousness in humanity at large. This understanding is demonstrated by the Shiva-Shakti principle. Now is the time to reclaim our human right to live the unified way. Bob Randall, a native aboriginal leader who grew up in Australia as one of the "stolen children," espouses through his Kanyini teachings, "A new world is being birthed through compassion in action for all life and we are the ones we have been waiting for."

As the Shakti force re-awakens on Earth, we can feel her prana, her breath, growing stronger in our bellies, her heartbeat resounding with a sonorous cadence in our breasts. Shakti energy is more than the power to procreate or give birth to children. She has endowed us with the immutable lunar force that feeds our cells and tissues to nourish, nurture, and heal the good Earth and all of nature by continually invoking nourishment, creativity, wisdom, arts, and light. Mother Earth invites us to walk as goddess emissaries beside her. We are co-creators and co-defenders of nature.

Looking at present conditions around us, we begin to reflect on our past and see how far we have diverted from the infinite grace of the Goddess. As women, we carry multiple barriers, obstacles, and burdens, yet we survive. Sometimes, it feels like we are carrying the mountain on our backs instead of just climbing it. And yet, these tribulations we suffer are almost always baptismal processes. Within them are the shaktified lessons that show us the way back to the inner mother. These lessons force us to acknowledge how tired we had become, weary from years on the treadmill performing the same manufactured routines over and over with predictable, unsatisfactory results. Painful junctures often bring about a conscious awakening within us. As we breathe into new life and gather ourselves, we can make sense of enervating experiences and see the fearsome tunnels for what they are. Each journey we survive makes us worthier and brings us closer to claiming our great purpose.

Consolatory words from the Saundarya Lahiri proclaim, "Oh, Goddess, who is the consort of Shiva, let the darkness of our mind be destroyed by the crowning glory on your head which is of like the forest of blooming blue lotus flowers, soft, and lush that shine with luster."

Forging Shakti's Primordial Energy

Shakti is more than our etheric or spiritual reality. She is the dynamic empowerment, the inner motility of Shakti Prana that is continually coursing through the cells and memory of our psycho-physical being. In its upward mobility to consciousness, her energetic force holds the cumulative karmic imprints of our individual lives from previous births. These ancestral traits hold all the expressions of our lives. Shakti's transformative force of ascendence within our central nervous system is what we know as the Kundalini. In our lifelong journey, each individual is meant to transcend the various stages of the seven chakras aligned in the subtle spinal conduit. (In the Bhagavad Gita, the subtle body refers to the combined mind, intellect, and ego.) The Kundalini shapes both the primordial masculine and feminine journeys for each and every person. The name Kundalini, meaning coiled energy, refers to its serpentine alacrity, the reservoir of cosmic energy residing at the base of the spine. We visualize this force as a coiled serpent curled three and a half turns in the nerve center at the bottom of the spinal column, known as the root chakra, *Muladhara*. As she rises, the Kundalini awakens each successive chakra. We arouse this energy from its sleeping state through deep meditative practices and karmic imprints. Through the force of Shakti Prana, we vibrationally ascend the central column of the spine, transiting through the seven major chakra centers until we reach the crown chakra, *Sahasrara,* where Shiva resides. Kundalini's ascension into the crown chakra foments our inner awakening to consciousness.

Tantra Vidya informs us that the upward-rising Kundalini force marks Shakti's primeval ascendence into Shiva. This taut connective force generates various levels of consciousness as she moves through the chakra centers. Here, Kundalini is *Parashakti*: creator, sustainer, and dissolver of the universe. She exists simultaneously on all levels of creation, the beginning, middle, and end: manifestation, evolution, and dissolution. She alone returns us to the eternal. Through her illimitable force, she unravels the mysteries of each chakra, impelling us through various stages of growth and maturity in our human life. The merging of Shakti with Shiva in the crown chakra dissolves her creative forms into the fold of consciousness, thereby unifying the primordial masculine and feminine; that is to say, the Shiva-Shakti as the unified, non-binary one that creates universal balance. Shakti's primordial feminine force ferries us beyond duality, divisiveness, and conflicts — the forces ripping humanity apart.

Every move we make is Shakti moving through us. She is both our origin and destination. The ultimate enlightenment, *nirvikalpa samadhi,* can only be attained through the movement of the Kundalini as she pierces through into the core of the crown chakra. Depending on the call of our inner energetic state, the Kundalini returns to specific chakras to inspire change or to take rest. Our progress along Kundalini's energetic axis depends on our circumstances, where we are in our life's journey, and the type of emotions or reality we generate. Consciousness development depends on Shakti's transcendent force as she ferries us through her vast terrain of manifestation within. Our human destiny is shaped by this passage through the scree of duality, the division of opposites: darkness and light, right and wrong, negative and positive, hope and despair, love and hate, good and bad, sacred and profane, honor and dishonor, truth and falsehood, loyalty and betrayal. These binaries keep humanity in a fluctuating state of enduring ignorance — the seat of all conflicts. Kundalini Shakti completes her ultimate journey when she returns to *Sahasrara,* the crown chakra, and remains contentedly coiled there. Shakti absorbed in Shiva. This cosmic absorption symbolizes the final emancipation from worldly dualistic existence. At the cosmic level, when Shakti merges into *Sahasrara* and is absorbed into Shiva, she effectuates the dissolution of the world.

The stories and insights I share in this book hold the lessons of feminine circuity – the cadence of intuitive knowing, continually arriving at points we have visited before. This instinctive ability allows us to scumble harsh realities into kinder forms of awareness. When in despair, the Goddess comes to our rescue to safeguard the sanctity of our body, mind, heart, and womb. We must call upon her grace, especially when we feel alone and forgotten. Her Shakti is not just the ability to be poised, beautiful, and strong or to dance, drum, or nurture children, or do Shakti yoga. At the core, her primeval energy imbues us with the power to survive arduous battles and thrive in inimical situations. Women's wounds are not loathsome scars but cosmic insignia marking the imprint of her Red Bindu. More than survivors, we are goddess warriors. We are Shakti. Divine feminine power. Nurturance. Love.

Bhramari Mudra – Humming Breath & Sound

Bhramari Humming Breath practice restores Shakti's vibrational energies within us. It is a potent primordial sound and breath practice named after the Goddess Bhramari who took the form of the precocious bee. The Sanskrit verbal root *bhram* literally means "bees" and refers to the resonant hum of buzzing bees that awakens inner awareness. Surrounded by a bevy of bees, the Goddess Bhramari reverberates the body with higher vibrations that reinforce feminine primordial power. The Vedic scientists, through meditation and pranayama, in exploring the inner realm understood that the act of humming creates spatial awareness between the mind and the nervous system. As a result, when we hum, we dissolve the thinking process. As we breathe into making a buzzing sound, we project prana deep within by extracting it from the universal astral network. Buzzing sounds support *ajna chakra,* the sixth chakra located in the mid-brow, the point where mind merges into consciousness. It also energizes the rise of consciousness from the root chakra to the crown chakra and therein produces a profound vibrational experience whilst purifying the centrifugal force of Shakti Prana that circulates the womb space. As we deepen this practice, the Kundalini energy rises from the base of the spine up into the ajna chakra, arousing intuition and a deep sense of joy.

Bhramari Humming Breath is done in conjunction with the Bhramari Mudra. Mudra is considered one of the most highly developed forms of consciousness harnessing. Mudra means "seal," and refers to meticulously designed hand gestures that draw prana energy into the body to create and fortify a seal of unity and harmony. Our hands comprise the cosmic five elements, which course through our fingers and connect our gestures and actions to the universal mind. Devising innumerable shapes and forms that represent the patterns of divine love, Vedic seers recognized that human beings need the help of visible, tangible forms to help them penetrate the intangible, infinite Spirit and gain access to the astral energies. Therefore, they conceived the formation of yantras, mudras, mandalas, and countless other ceremonial arts to enliven our memory of sacred practice.

Mudras, in various forms, utilize the elemental energy of our hands to invoke wellness, memory, balance, tranquility, and joy. This mudra of the bee is an important gesture in classical Bharata Natyam dance. This exquisite breath and sound practice, which is a personal favorite, fortifies Shakti force and helps to dissolve traumas held in our cellular body. This practice is a worthy investment in keeping the mind in a state of ease and equanimity. Bhramari practice has numerous other benefits. It balances the immunological and nervous systems and strengthens the prana breath that sustains the heart and brain by lifting resonant vibration in the cellular body.

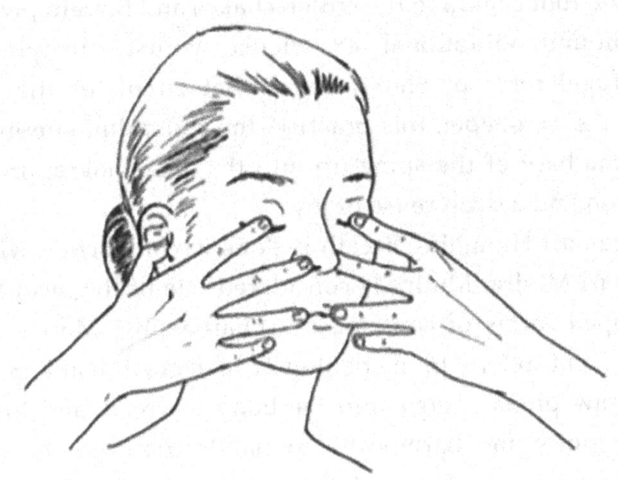

Fig. 1. Bhramari Mudra

The Practice: Bhramari Mudra, Humming Breath and Sound

- Sit in a comfortable posture with a straight back in a quiet space.
- Release stale breath from your body with a forceful exhalation through the nostrils.
- Inhale by taking a deep, leisurely breath and lock all the apertures of the face by using the fingers of both hands

to gently close your eyes, nostrils, ears, and the mouth, as shown in the diagram below.

- As you exhale, begin to vibrate the vocal cords by making an audible humming sound until you run out of breath.
- As you hum out, feel the titillation of the humming penetrating deep into your tissues, connecting you to the Goddess Bhramari.
- Continue this practice of humming out your breath for 10 minutes or so.

Chapter 3

Earth Intelligence

समुद्रवसने देवि पर्वतस्तनमण्डले ।
विष्णुपत्नि नमस्तुभ्यं पादस्पर्शं क्षमस्वमे ॥

Oh Mother Earth, You Who have the Ocean as Your Garments, and Mountains as Your Bosom, O Goddess, Salutations to You; Please Forgive the touch of my feet on the Earth that is Your Holy Body.
Rig Veda

The Earth is alive, and we breathe with her. She is intelligent, and we dismiss her wisdom. As we destroy her, we unwittingly destroy ourselves. Her genesis in the universe began over 12 million years ago in an explosion of cosmic light – a light that still shines today. This light is the source of Earth's intelligence, just as it is the source of our power to think, intuit, reflect, contemplate, and know. The Vedas see this light not as an external force but as the inner radiance through which we are able to see, hear, smell, feel, and remember. Our capacity for awareness is a reflection of this light. Through this consciousness, we can light up every object with the mind, remember our timeless journey, and therefore experience the world, making it visible, audible, and familiar.

For thousands of years in ancient India, Asia, Africa, Egypt, Greece, and Rome, societies built their spiritual beliefs and traditions around the Earth Goddess. Her ecological legends flourished, a repository of human experience and wisdom from lost civilizations that maintained a shared sense of communal spirit and harmonious relation among themselves. They shared a palpable sense that the nucleus that holds our mysterious dance in consort with the rain, clouds, moonlight, forests, rivers, animals, and sunrise is and will forever be Shakti, the potent power of Earth.

Though we have strayed from these beliefs and traditions, we continue to live in the magnificence of the Earth Mother every minute of our lives. Our journeys are seamlessly tied to the mystery and miracle of our Mother, the Earth. As the enduring witness to her eight billion human children, she roars with glee when we are in balance and weeps with us when we are hurting, the cooling balm of her tears our primeval nourishment. While healing from cancer in that snowy welkin, I heard the sounds of the deer scattering the snow-laden brambles to forage for sprouts or pine nuts on the ground. That crunchy sound invigorated me from the warm, cozy cabin outdoors into the brilliant sunshine that day. Nature had called me into the graffiti light of the forest to tell me that I would live again. Through prayers, stillness, meditation, or tears — in whichever way we choose to commune with Her — Mother Earth sends us the answers through signs and symbols and often sounds her signals and sirens so we can hear her call. She makes flexible our limbs and surrenders us to her sacred ground, when necessary through arduous experiences. I've been fortunate to walk a long and deep journey tethered to her. I began to see that the answers to the most painful questions were tucked inside her vast, timeless intelligence. She challenged or redirected me at every turn as I traveled the world with my healing work and peace tours. Her message was simple: surrender. Whatever the problem — pain, agony, despair, disease, or torture, "Surrender to me" was her solution. She is vast. She is merciful. Her sacrificial nature is infinite. I can only viscerally touch upon her reality through the magic of my journey and being rescued by her countless times. I cannot cast into words this deep, abiding love I have received from her and feel for her. Scriptures put it this way: love is the Earth's para-dharma that is embedded within the human soul.

When awakened, it shapes the greatest purpose in life — that of achieving a kindred spirit of harmony.

I have taught holistic wellness for the Earth and body under my brand "Wise Earth" for almost 40 years, educating students that our vast terrain within contains nature's untapped inner medicine. The Earth, our healer, heals; therefore, we heal. Our body is the microcosmic mirror of 510 million square kilometers of her territory. To inherit her balm of healing, we listen, we take pause. We sit in the solace space of our hearts. The best doctor is within. We sit still. Still, on a quiet morning, you can hear the whistling of her nature, the trees, wind, streams, and musical chimes made by the rustling foliage. Automatically, these sonic nuances regulate the heartbeat, refueling our vital prana. Living in the bliss of nature, I feel her palpable Shakti Prana oscillating with my body. Every speck of nature thrives on love. She is the heart guru within and without. In times of physical illness and emotional vulnerability, I run to her embrace, drawn from madness into her miracles, her sunshine lightening my heart, her breezes whispering loving notes into my ear. Her healing balm keeps my psyche strong. Earth's love is mother love. It is inviolate. Her epic tale belongs to each of us. Through its storied presence, we become conscious. Earth's love is not a science. It is not tethered to the will of the sky or her open spaces. It is the deer gliding across the ancient forest of spirit. It is not a sexual force. It is the soul of Shiva-Shakti dancing in alignment with purpose. It happens not in the past or the future. It exists only as a presence in the present. Through immense sacrifice, the Earth, our Mother, is continually restoring herself to maintain harmony and balance so that we can imbibe her love.

Earth's Life-force

The Earth is vast and magical beyond human comprehension, and the enormity of the Earth's Shakti force within us is equally astounding. We are magnetically connected to her cosmic dance, much like the celestial bodies in the universe are to each other; the Earth's pull keeps the moon in orbit, and the sun's pull keeps the Earth in orbit. The Earth is the abode of boundless *prana*, the kinetic life force energy that promotes the Earth's creation and recreation. The *Prashna Upanishad* informs us that prana controls everything that exists in the three worlds. The universe protects, sustains, and nourishes her Earth through prana, the sole carrier of our sentiency. Beyond the operations of the body and mind, prana mobilizes awareness, creating the consciousness that is our immutable reality.

Prana is distributed throughout the body by *chakras* – spiritual energy centers – and *nadis* – their conduits. The cosmic anatomy imprinted within the human body has 72,000 nadis and 114 chakras. In addition to the 7 major chakras recognized in the yoga field, there are 21 minor chakras and 86 micro chakras. Two of the micro chakras are said to reside outside the human body. The human body contains 16 special junctures called *adharas*, a Sanskrit word that means "foundation" (and also refers to Shakti as the foundation of Shiva, which we will return to later). These adharas are the cistern-like areas where prana is continually revitalized and transformed.

Prana is the intrinsic aspect of the breath, which controls an individual's quality of life and longevity. The Vedic sages developed the science of breath, *pranayama*, which means "manifestation of ultimate cosmic energy," by studying the cyclical cadence of the Earth's prana and replicating it for use in the human body. Here, we are told that life is defined not by the number of years a person stays alive but by the number of breaths we are given for our journey. Since the Earth's prana is the breath of the soul, a bridge between body and mind, breathing practices nourish our sacred heart and heal our most grievous wounds.

Prana has a direct impact on our oxygen levels. Indeed, the Earth has not always been oxygen-abundant. Science informs us we owe our existence to cyanobacteria, microscopic creatures that helped to radically transform Earth's atmosphere about 2.4 billion years ago by pumping out oxygen as waste and filling the skies with it. This miraculous evolution is all in a nanosecond's work for the Shakti, whose power to balance and rebalance stasis in her creation is supreme. With the depletion of natural resources and the resultant impairment of prana, we are facing an oxygen-scarce Earth once again. According to recent studies, atmospheric oxygen levels are slowly decreasing due to burning fossil fuels, which consumes oxygen, and deforestation, which reduces oxygen production. The Earth's atmosphere contains 21 percent oxygen. This gas makes it possible for humans, animals, plants, and each infinitesimal iota of life to thrive and survive. The very source of our consciousness and Earth's intelligence is at risk. Vitiated prana has a devastating effect on nature as a whole: our food, breath, and sound vibration, the three pillars that nourish and protect life on Earth. Scientists are finding that part of the upper atmosphere is progressively contracting in response to rising human-made greenhouse gas emissions. According to MintPress News, the US military is the world's biggest polluter, utilizing almost 21 billion liters of fuel annually and emitting more than 25,000 kilotons of carbon dioxide by burning them. Our armed forces create 750,000 tons of toxic waste every year in the form of uranium, oil, jet fuels, pesticides, defoliants, lead, and other chemicals. Byproducts of the military-industrial complex are a major contributor to the estimated 50 million metric tons of electronic waste dumped on Mother Earth each year. Patriarchal fear, violence, greed, and destruction have escalated in gargantuan proportions in the twenty-first century, vitiating prana at unprecedented levels. This violation of the Earth's prana is responsible for a host of horrors, including global warming, ocean acidification, loss of biodiversity, and a massive escalation of environmental disasters such as wildfires, landslides, tornadoes, drought, tsunamis, and volcanic eruptions. These disasters bring to mind a story from the Puranas, which relate the adventures of Hindu folklore heroes and heroines. In the story, the unquenchable greed of Hiranyaksha, a sole exploiter of gold, led him to rampage the Earth in such a vile way that it destabilized her floating position and caused her to plummet into the Garbhodaka Ocean that covered half the universe.

Goddess at the Feet of Earth

> *If we surrendered to Earth's intelligence, we could rise up rooted, like trees.*
>
> Rainer Marie Rilke

In Vedic cosmology, Vastu is the cosmic being stretched across the breadth of the universe. Vastu is also the science of Earth's cosmology, which dictates that the Earth's head is at the peak of the Himalayas while her feet are in the Amazon Rainforest. Mystery and magic abound in the Himalayan ecosystem and the Amazon rainforest as they stretch across the Earth in a head-to-toe operation, managing Earth's ever-generating nourishment. (I have often reflected on the sheer synchronicity of my birthplace and that of my paternal ancestors. I was born in Guyana, where the portion of the Amazon rainforest that lies in her outback is closest to the equator, and my grandfather came to Guyana from the Himalayan region. "You were born at the foot of the Vastu," my guru once noted.) My journeys to Vastu's head and feet have been profound experiences that imbued me with an abiding awareness of my embodied alignment with Earth's intelligence.

In Vedic cosmology, the profound science of Vastu represents Earth's pivotal points and energy flow, sort of the energetic meridian junctures of the planet's infrastructure. More than a science of direction, Vastu combines the five elements of nature and the cosmos: space, air, fire, water, and earth, ultimately keeping stasis between Earth's lifeforms and the material world. Earth is the third of eight planets in our solar system and the only one where life is known to exist due to the presence of the five elements. This unique Earth science unifies the five elements to set the conditions for Earthlings to breathe, think, and manifest joy, vibrancy, and well-being. Earth's energy is essentially emanated by two forces: the five elements and the electromagnetic energy generated by its rotation. Vastu science is represented by the figure of a cosmic being situated diagonally across the vast expanse with its head to the north and feet toward the south, signifying the two magnetic poles of the human body. The head, as the north pole, holds our positive charge, and the feet, the south pole, hold our negative charge.

The Amazon rainforest at Vastu's feet provides and regulates a substantial percentage of the world's oxygen. This rainforest plays an important part in processing prana and regulating the world's oxygen and carbon cycles. It acts as a carbon sink by readily absorbing large amounts of carbon dioxide from the atmosphere. The Amazon is the most extensive rainforest on Earth and is at great risk of disappearing due to profiteers' egregious crimes against her. Half of the planet's rainforests have already disappeared. This calamity has had a devastating impact on our oxygen-rich Earth. In the last 50 years, Brazil began to colonize its rainforest. It has since destroyed nearly a fifth of its forest cover — more than 275,000 square miles. Matt Sandy, reporting for *Time* Magazine, writes, "Today, logging yards, cattle enclosures, and soy farms sit on the fringes of a vanishing forest. Powered by murky sources of capital and rising demand for beef, a violent and corrupt frontier is now pushing into indigenous land, national parks and one of the most preserved parts of the jungle."

Twenty years ago, I took a long-awaited journey into the Amazonian timelessness. I was awed and bewildered by the sights, smells, and sounds of this seemingly endless forest of 390 billion individual trees and the countless unique animals and insects contributing to its diversity. The most peculiar species here are undoubtedly the tiny black pebble toads that are believed to predate dinosaurs, but there is also the ancient ancestor of the ant called the "ant from Mars" living in the soils of this region. Also on the list of anomalies are the one and only vegetarian piranha, the translucent fish, the flying monkey cat, the Jesus lizard that can run along the surface of the water, the glass frog that is entirely transparent so you can see its internal organs and heart pumping away, carnivorous pitcher plants, and awesome ancient orchids. The list is nearly unfathomable. One can't help but feel the ancient Goddess's profound power here as she first gave rise to the Earth.

In these indescribable moments of being held captive by the other-worldly exquisiteness of the forest, I wondered about the Earth's capacity to regenerate. Assault after assault, the Earth had healed herself for millennia before human destructiveness began to outpace her natural ability to repair damage. Destructive agents of human ignorance and greed have long threatened her forests. As climate change accelerates, her ecosystem is more prone to damage by droughts, ice storms, fires, hurricanes, and earthquakes. The Earth is losing 137 species of plants, animals, and insects daily to deforestation, and a horrifying 50,000 species become extinct yearly. This unnatural extinction is occurring 2500 times faster than natural extinction, which affects only an estimated 2000 species each year. About 72 billion land and sea animals are slaughtered each year globally, with over 25 billion butchered in the US alone. We are destroying Earth's intelligence through manifold layers of violence. To satiate our voracious appetites, we are creating an indelible rift within our sacred Earth, body, and mind. Through the internal violence of consuming the bloodied fodder we have made of the Earth's magnificent flora and fauna, we tamp out inner intelligence.

At the Heart of Earth

Remember our ways, in the crescent of the moon, the fullness of her belly; the ciphers of the waters, the zephyr carried by the wind, the secrets of the elements, the poetry of the trees and starry nights, the lunacy of love, our mores and stories. Remember the mantle of grace that is our Earth.

As I flew over Mount Roraima, the highest of the Pakaraima chain of tepui plateaus in South America, I saw the lost world of awe-inspiring sandstone table-top mountains that are among the oldest geological formations in the world, dating back over 1.6 billion years. These structures are called *tepui,* which in the native Pemón language means "House of the Gods." The indigenous Pemón Amerindians honor the tepui, believing them to be inhabited by nature deities. Here, waterfalls abundantly spill with eager anticipation to kiss the feet of Mother Earth, untouched by humankind. Guardian clouds commune with the deities of nature and transport messages to the deeper space beyond heaven's realm. The flanks of the tepui are carpeted in algae and moss of dark forest green, with veins of quartz crystal glimmering through the blanket of white mist at the summit. While hovering over these majestic plateaus, I heard a subtle, shimmering sonic nuance — a sound that has stayed with me since, influencing my words, expressions, humor, wit, and sense of joy. The Earth is composed of vibrational fields that sustain life and consciousness. We can hear Earth's pulsating resonance when we stand amid mountain ranges, in open landscapes across the oceans, or in vast fields where winds can ride her sonic melodies across endless expanses. Our subtle human bodies are entirely conscious, sentient instruments made from the Earth's cosmic vibrations and pranic energies. The profound rainbow aura and sonic nuance of the untraveled lands of the Pemon

Aborigines catapulted me into my breath force. Enraptured, I reflected on the Goddess's breath, word, and vibration and could hardly wait to begin scribing my journeys with her.

Sound, vibration, and breath bring forth sentiency through our voices and words, which echo cosmic vibrations and resonate in our deeper selves. I recall hearing my father's mellifluous voice chanting Sanskrit mantras from the impressionable age of 4. As I grew up, I was fascinated by his oratory prowess, his use of words, and his love for inspirational communion. He bowed to the presence of the Supreme Goddess. He worshipped Mother Earth. His forebears, the Vedic seers, received their mission and inspiration from Her. They shared their powerful insight into why the spoken word comprising sheer vibration is of unparalleled importance to humanity's abundance, happiness, and health. Vāk is the Vedic Goddess that personifies speech, the vocal aspect of Shakti. It is her voice that is channeled through the cosmic vibration to inspire poets and visionaries. Considered "Mother of the Vedas," she is the originator of the cosmic sound. As the consort of Indra, the Vedic Lord of the Firmament, she inspires all forms of creative expression. In post-Vedic literature, she is identified with Sarasvati, the Goddess of knowledge. The oldest of Vedas, the *Rig Veda,* cites, "When, uttering words which no one comprehended, Vāk, Queen of Gods, the Gladdener, was seated, The heaven's four regions drew forth drink and vigor: now whither hath her noblest portion vanished?" Ahh. Where has her noblest portion vanished? This question asked some 9000 years ago remains.

Women, goddesses, and girls: remember, you are Vāk, your word is your shield, truth is your most effective weapon, truth defends Earth's intelligence, it is your goddess power. I take the liberty of changing the gender in Thomas Merton's timeless words, "Guard the image of women, for it is the image of the Goddess." Let us call upon our goddess power, Earth's body, and Earth's intelligence, all of which are replenished only by her love. The Mother Love. That is the Shakti energy that observes, witnesses, and heals the womb of creation and the heart of humanity. As Earth conduits, we absorb Earth's blessing from head to toe, continually replenishing nourishment, wisdom, and sustenance. This is no small gift.

Goddess at the Head of Earth

Sprawling majestically at Vastu's head, the Himalayas are vital to the ecological security of the Indian landmass, providing forest cover, feeding perennial rivers that are the source of drinking water, irrigation, and hydropower, and conserving biodiversity for more than 70 million people. On one of my first pilgrimages to the holy sites of the Himalayas, I left the group of young monks I was traveling with and ventured out alone up a steep hill to a large overhang where I could see the entire vista of Bander Poonch peak glistening like silvery night caps floating above the golden lace of the sunrise. A hawk-eagle with a 10-foot wingspan glided out from the glinting mist and circled above me. As it spiraled in closer, I noticed it was carrying its prey, still alive, wriggling to be set free. My heart stopped for a moment; it was an awe-inspiring sight. I accidentally slipped into a thicket of thorny bush and bruised my arms. For a split second, I no longer saw the grandeur of the hawk-eagle in the serene innocence of the infant morning but felt the terror of the prey. No escape. Even if my prayers were answered and the bird released its captive, it would free-fall down to certain death. Murder slipped into the sylvan scene, a sobering reminder that death, like dead trees in a forest, is necessary for the progress of structural complexity and biodiversity. Death and predation are essential to maintain nature's balance. The cosmic struggle of life and death is much like a pilgrimage where we put ourselves through a test of physical, emotional, and spiritual endurance, hoping that as we burn away unwanted karmas, we will find our spirit freely soaring like the Himalayan hawks. Later that afternoon, my fellow pilgrims and I arrived at Kedarnath, swelled by abiding silence, hamstrings cramped from riding the obliging mules. They tittuped to the sacred destination as though they had built-in GPS's. Nearly too tired to think, I marveled at the stamina I had summoned to walk and ride along miles of deeply creviced paths, rough with stumps, stones, and trodden stories. Blessings I had received from Ganesha in a dream the previous night had aroused a profound awakening in me, rendering me barely aware of the aches and pains in my body as we progressed. This powerful vision had stirred a pulchritudinous memory. The scent of the Earth we traveled was so familiar.

The next day, I awoke at dawn. The air was crisp as a skein of golden eagles glided across the cloudless sky. Their color matched the cerulean gold-gilded dome of Kedarnath Temple, which I could see from a distance as we departed. We headed to our next destination — Badrinath, where the great Vedanta scholar, Adi Shankara, once arrived on foot from his birthplace in Kaladi in Kerala, some 1500 miles away. The scent of sandalwood, rose, and myrrh from the street stalls effused my ancient soul with far-beyond memories. As I stared at the awing edifice of the imposing Nilkanth Peak, I experienced an astounding realization: I had been there before.

Years earlier, in meditation, I had seen three monumental statues of Ganesha, the elephant-headed god, each as big as the towering Nilkanth Peak. Ganesha, son of Shiva and Shakti (Parvati), the beloved spiritual archetype of hope and abundance loved by millions of people, is known for removing obstacles from the path of his disciples. The first vision of Ganesha was a large Irish-green idol; he lay still like Nilkanth. In the second vision, he was sindur-red in color. In the third image, he was glistening in pearlescent white. In all three visions, Ganesha was sleeping. Was I witnessing his sudden awakening at Nilkanth

Peak? On that day, in the translucent welkin 17,500 feet above the flat lands, Ganesha's presence propelled me deeper into the portal. I pondered the immense obstacles faced by Ganesha's followers today – and indeed all humans. How had we become so divided, I wondered? So constantly at odds with ourselves, with each other, and with Mother Earth? When had we become so entrenched in the binary realities of us and them, good and evil, right and wrong, bad and good? Like a pilgrimage that requires hard work to reach your destination, the journey through these questions would be even more priceless than their answers.

My last pilgrimage to the Himalayas was a transformative experience. A pilgrimage provides the essential embrace of nature's elements wherein we can dive deeply into reflective memory. The solid ground and massive rocks of mountains provided stability, the unusually soft mosses I trod on the path opened my mind, and the running streams of glistening crystalline water sparkled in my mouth and quenched my pain. The endless fields of heritage wildflowers and winds luffing across the vast expanse of Earth felt so close to the sky I could almost touch heaven. Here, I could feel the miracle of the sun's energy, arriving fresh from its 93,000,000-mile, eight-minute journey across the solar system to warm my face. Imbibing this purified atmosphere, I sensed that the entire Himalayan range, Vastu's positive north, was throbbing with compassion for my burdened heart, which had been aching from the stream of poisoning I had endured on Pisgah Mountain. It was now possible to release the harrowing experience of being poisoned along with other even more profound abuses I had survived and to come to terms with the idea that, at junctional times in our lives, we have to suffer parts of ourselves to die – those parts that made us feel unworthy, ugly, shamed, diminished, or guilty. Ironically, we can only slough those parts after extrapolating their harsh lessons.

Poisoning had taken its toll on my body. I found myself catapulted once more into that sublime space of floating in light with a weightless body and having many out-of-body visions. In a dream, I saw a velvety veil of twinkling purple lights lining the pre-dawn skies in a high desert. My guru walked stealthily up the steep, arid hill and waited for me to catch up to him. As I bowed in greeting to touch his lotus feet, I noticed another pair of beautiful male feet, strapped in handmade leather sandals, standing beside him. I looked up. The bright purple lights funneled into a spotlight shining all around him. Slowly, I stood up, squinting. The lights had formed an orb framing the newcomer's face. Bit by bit, his face became clear, like a polaroid developing. It was The Christ. His body soaked in translucent white light, he turned to my teacher and bid him forward toward the lower hills. They did not invite me to join them. My heart fell, and I cried, "What about me?" He stopped, turned slightly to meet my eyes, and responded in a low, resonant voice, "You go and tend to Mother Earth!" A stunningly typical Masculine-Divine commandment, even my dreaming mind noted. I stirred and awoke from a deep sleep, but the purple haze remained in the room.

Tend to Mother Earth. This dream vision stayed with me, urging me to reflect on the endless revolution of violence imposed upon her: she has been dumped on, poisoned, bludgeoned, and razed, yet she rises. Each time, a quintillion times, she has risen, rebalanced, and restored her Earth. After each calamity, she renews her massive internal cleansing, gutting, purging, and discharging in an infinite cycle of sacrifices. Goddess. Mother. Shakti. Earth. Even the most extraordinary measure of personal pain is not a scintilla in the ocean that is the Earth's burden. In the depths of this reflection, I was forced to reexamine my own long sojourn of being poisoned by heavy metal.

My ordeal of being poisoned and otherwise defiled by ignorant haters highlighted the parallel – albeit through my human experience — with how Mother Earth has been egregiously violated and poisoned. Bitter despair brought me closer to understanding Mother Nature's epic struggles. My immunological health was ravaged, teetering on the brink from the uranium poisoning. For over a decade, I had completely lost my sense of balance and suffered a systemic breakdown of my vital organs — my heart, lungs, digestive, nervous, and circulatory systems were in dire disrepair. Having spent long and austere years restoring my good health after cancer while serving the well-being of the world community, I realized I would once more have to take that deep dive into Mother Earth's medicines within and without. However, this time around, I was nearing my sixtieth year and was acutely aware that my seemingly endless stamina had been progressively waning. The recovery journey ahead was perilous, but I kept hearing nature's melodies, soft and serene, around me in the vibrant stillness of my forest. I would sit in my gardens, and suddenly, the red-tailed hawks would come circling above me in the oxygen-infused azure, blue skies. The Earth continues to heal the illimitable damage we do to her, and she responds to each egregious act by reminding us that we, too, can and must heal. She shows us how her forests can recover after massive fires by germinating the seeds stored in her deep ground. After massive oil spills, nature produces oil-consuming microbes in the water whose population grows in proportion to the need. The Earth itself is a lesson in endurance, resilience, and resourcefulness in response to devastating events.

Keenly aware of the toxins in my own body, I reflected on the poisons that we wield against the Earth and all her inhabitants today — the product of thousands of years of patriarchal "progress." From the use of deadly chemicals derived from plant extracts documented as far back as 4500 BCE, poison has evolved from a targeted tool for hunting individual prey into weapons of mass destruction. The evolution of poison has been driven by patriarchal agendas, most expressly in its military goals to control humanity and the Earth's resources. Although humans have employed crude chemical warfare in many parts of the world for thousands of years, it was not until the expansion of industrial chemistry in the nineteenth century that mass production and deployment of chemical warfare agents in war became a possibility, originating with a German attack on Belgium in April 1915 using chlorine gas during World War I. This was followed by Earth-damning nerve gases including Lewiscite, the G and V series of nerve agents, and the Novichok nerve agent. While these gases were designed to damage the nerves, poison the blood, and choke, blind, and blister enemy soldiers and civilians, they have left a devastating imprint on the Earth herself as well.

Considering recent technological advances, easy access to raw materials, the ready availability of technical information on the internet, increasing crime and corruption, and state-sponsored terrorism and globalization, it is not difficult for terrorists to use chemical weapon agents to achieve their inhumane goals. In the meantime, the primary recipient of this gigantic, impossible-to-recycle pile of toxic swill is Mother Earth. Moreover, humanity has created an unintentional artillery of poisons as byproducts of the industrial complex. These poisons and other modes of human destruction have cost human and Earth intelligence dearly. Every day, the immense damage that patriarchal greed, ignorance, and profiteering schemes mete out to her, progressively erodes her self-generating prana, her oxygen, her breath, and her life force. Earth's intelligence is being devalued and diminished. This miasma directly impacts the current erosion of human intelligence and nature's sentience.

The Christ vision and instruction opened my eyes to an inimitable truth: by shifting my perspective to see my pain as sharing the Earth's immense burden, I was gifted a container of purpose to bear my grief. My pain was no longer personal;

it was now empathetic to Mother Earth's grievances. Our grief, distress, and despair, however considerable they may be, are but a speck of what the Great Mother always carries. I do not surrender my sorrows and suffering to the Earth; I bear them, knowing that our Mother bears an $M = 5.9722 \times 1024$ kg burden. In this way, I deepen my sorority to her destiny and align myself to her deliverance, hoping it might relieve a modicum of the crisis and chaos humanity has foisted on her.

The Christ directive gifted to me by Earth's intelligence has also helped me to fathom the unfathomable pain I have endured, and now feel almost privileged to suffer. As women – breathing pieces of the Divine Feminine – we are called to the blessing of the broken; our hearts continually broken, trust continually betrayed, truth continually quashed. These are the harsher reality of our Shakti liberality, and she asks us to befriend these predictable circumstances. In this way, we learn and relearn our strength. This is part of our inherent Shakti power. As this power awakens in me, I become a conduit for the evolutionary lessons of living and dying, resurrection and rebirth. I am continually awed by the subtle, invisible wisdom of the Earth. Nothing is ever still; her massive matter is merely light energy in the form of vibration. At its most fundamental strata, the Earth and everything she comprises is purely vibration manifesting in different ways. Consider how each one of us contains her mysterious vastness within our hearts.

In the many years I have walked as an ascetic – a path of devotion to the magnificent Earth – and the many people I have helped along the way, I have been mindful of keeping my actions aligned with her cadence to unify, resolve, and keep the common ground. In so doing, I forged forward with the dynamic energy of her love pouring into my body. In Ayurveda, this love is the shield of our immunity. We call it "ojas," the Earth's loving essence within us. Ojas is the magical substance that promotes virility and vitality. It plays a large role in upping our positive vibrations and inner luminosity that support the state of Shiva-Shakti balance. The act of love is the most powerful way of generating ojas. In demonstrating gratitude to her in every way we can – from the smallest act of love to the greatest – we preserve her para-dharma that keeps us remembering our sacred nature and purpose: generating harmony and healing for all. At the present time of chaos and confusion, it is imperative that we transcend the state of me-ness and otherness and merge into the higher plane of love-consciousness. The perishing Earth is in desperate need of the vibration of love. We must strive to go beyond the subjective reality of mundane actions and transform each and every action into celestial love that fosters a sense of well-being and positivity. What are three ways you can express your abounding love for the Earth today?

Chapter 4

The Mother Wound

You cannot do a kindness too soon, for you never know how soon it will be too late.

Ralph Waldo Emerson

Humanity bears an innate wound contained in the seed of life. We transport this wound to our children, the girls and boys who become women and men. At the surface, this "mother wound" may be seen as a progressive set of traumas to the child's psyche received throughout their development, often as a result of the mother unconsciously living through and working out her own wounds. But, as you will see, this wounding goes much deeper; it is inscribed in our DNA, the bedrock of ancestral memories that defies the arc of time.

The mother wound is inherited from conception when the Shakti Prana – the potent life force – is impaired. During this process, a mother who has not addressed her own wounds unconsciously bequeaths them to her progeny. These wounds are etched on our mitochondrial DNA, which depends on Shakti Prana for sustenance and upkeep, allowing them to be passed on to offspring. Mitochondrial DNA is imprinted with cellular memory that is informed by the mother's experiences and her matrilineal forebears' depository of experiences. These memories are passed on to the offspring through biological, psychological, and spiritual mechanisms. Mitochondrial DNA in humans is maternally inherited – passed on from mother to child – because an egg cell has many more mitochondria than a sperm cell. Males do not play a big part in the mitochondria equation even though they contribute an equal number of genes to offspring.

The mother wound is so called not only because mothers are the vehicle through which we inherit it but also because they are the only ones who can heal it. Through the process of birth, women ferry this wound from generation to generation; at the same time, women are the carriers of its healing because they are the primordial carrier of life along with all its gifts and griefs. As we will see, this life-giving force, this Shakti energy, holds the key to healing humanity's inherent wounds.

Each gender expresses this vitiation in different lifeways. A woman's core power lies in her spirit of nourishment, creativity, vivacity, and remarkable foresight, and these are the first Shakti qualities that tend to get invalidated and vitiated in the expression of her wounds. A wounded woman shows up with low self-esteem, shame, indecisiveness, eagerness to please, introversion in professional or social settings, addiction, depression, eating disorders, tolerance for being treated poorly, emotional excess, competitiveness with other women, self-sabotage, frigidity or overt sexuality, rigidity, passive-aggressiveness, self-loathing, and so on.

Men express the mother wound differently than women. Each man expresses or hides his pain in similar and dissimilar ways. Our world culture glorifies the hero who fights a war and scales the ladder of ambition and material achievement but derides the man who expresses his vulnerability and grief. A man's core strength lies in his immutable sense of consciousness, awareness, safeguarding, and penchant for noble deeds. These are critical areas in his make-up that become impinged when a man is wounded. His primary wound shows up in his relationships with himself, his spouse, and other men, as well as through his sense of potency and his overt or covert misuse of sex. In drawing on a naturally ascending energy of consciousness innate to the masculine primordial force — his Shiva energy — men are meant to excel in their wholeness. However, when this primal energy is tamped down into its lowest extreme, his genitals, he sabotages himself. He suppresses the flow of consciousness, burying it in the wounds of his manhood. Men tend to hide their shame and cover it up under many ignoble guises: untoward behaviors, social excesses, unabridged ambitions, narcissism, dishonesty, passive-aggressive behavior, sexual aberrations, bullying or demonizing women or weaker men, violence, fierce competition, and so on.

It may surprise you to hear that the mother wound in men is far more entrenched than in women. One reason for this is that men are heavily influenced by a primordial fear of the feminine, an emotion that is fastened in their gut by their paternal forebears. Men are compelled to be part of the competitive economics and binaries of patriarchal power. The patriarchal lifestyle has increasingly dehumanized life and nature, creating an ever-deeper abyss, especially for the male gender (though all genders participate in the competitive drive for power). As Milton Friedman puts it: "The central values of civilization are in danger. Over large stretches of the Earth's surface the essential conditions of human dignity and freedom have already disappeared. Even that most precious possession of Western Man, freedom of thought and expression, is threatened by the spread of creeds which, claiming the privilege of tolerance when in the position of a minority, seek only to establish a position of power in which they can suppress and obliterate all views but their own..."

The mother wound is constantly at play between the genders. We wound each other — men wounding women as engendered in the patriarchal setup, and women responding by wounding men and inflicting wounds on themselves. Almost as though we have been programmed to do so. The truth is, we have been. Gender domination plays a cardinal role in propagating the mother wound. When patriarchal philosophies of the Far East replicated themselves deep into the mores of Western civilization, they helped to imprint the biased ideology into the future of modernity. With the advent of Judea-Christianity, the

Divine Feminine fate became more compromised, not least by the depiction of Eve as the temptress who seduced Adam into sharing the forbidden fruit. Not so long ago in Europe, a woman healer could be killed for making herbal potions from the forest or burnt at the stake for her midwifery skills or any other feminine prowess that flew in the face of male domination. This reality, when examined, encapsulates the wounded male ego.

Men and women experience the mother wound through one common filter: sexuality. We can use our primeval sexual nature to either cultivate wholesome Shiva-Shakti unification or to diminish it. The historical breakdown of the Shiva-Shakti alliance, the wedge that promotes its separation, is the primordial fear of the Divine Feminine.

Both genders have been entrained to fear the power of the Shakti. Men's fear of the primordial feminine force has borne a devastating impact on women. Through her empathetic nature, she has willingly allowed herself to be commanded to fear, participating in fear conditioning to remain invisible, to keep the peace, to support the male members of her family or community, and to align with their agenda. Women, even powerful women, allow themselves to be coerced by the masculine agenda for fear that their independence and individuality are seen as divisive or disrespectful. In compromising ourselves and our feminine values, we betray our intuitive sense of trust, we betray our purpose, we betray our dreams, we betray our children, and we betray the men who have unwittingly set us up to betray ourselves. There is an explicit connection between fear of the feminine and betrayal. It's not surprising, then, that the cardinal protagonist on this stage is betrayal. We betray each other when we do not stand firm in our primordial feminine and masculine values. We betray each other when we deprive another of consent or defile sexuality with violence. We betray each other when we pollute sexuality with deceit and psychic toxicity. Such betrayal takes many forms; every ancestry is mired with these claggy wounds.

One of the primary reasons people do not heal this wound is not necessarily because of their lack of willingness but rather from a lack of understanding. The imbalance of Shiva-Shakti energy is the core cause of the corrupted conditions we are enduring. Hidden behind the shroud of an illusionary veil, this quagmire is so convincing that we have bought into divisive relationships, chaos, and doubts. This special reality has been rethreaded and perfected into operation for millennia. We are programmed to follow the heartless, merciless societal customs of accepting our lot, strapped in the straitjacket of divisive ideas, seasoned gullibility, and human weaknesses. In this current state of conflict, tension arises — tension that thrives on quarrels, violence, wars, domination, alienation, competition, grievances, corruption, injustice, infidelity, deceit, ignobility, and inequality. Indeed, the disastrous combination of emotions and delusions we experience in this manufactured separation from our natural Shiva-Shakti stasis can only continue to invoke disharmony in every dimension. In this detritus, male domination keeps recreating the pyramidical power structure that controls humanity through binary thinking and bipartite systems that rescind dharma, the universal values.

First Steps to Healing the Mother Wound

The farther away light is from one's touch, the more one naturally speaks of the need for change.

St Teresa of Avila

Although it may appear we are farthest away from the sun in July when I sit in the Southern Hemisphere, I'd be closest to it if I were sitting in the Northern Hemisphere. Perspective. As Earth beings, we are always in the light. Even when we are seemingly sucked into the black hole, we somehow negotiate our way into the light on the event horizon. Human sentiency is a self-propelling phenomenon. We are fully sentient regardless of what we do or don't do. The question is, how do we come to know and accept this truth? We do not need to radically change but rather reclaim that which already exists: the light of awareness endemic to our primal nature. As potent and inured as our external conditioning, it is only external. We have been foolish to give so much credence and, therefore, blame to external agents. It is with our inner sovereignty alone that we can and must do the work. It is there that wisdom awaits the whittling.

Though we are all wounded ourselves and truly wound each other, the greater truth is that we can heal. Before we can do so, women and men must reorder and unify their Shiva-Shakti energies to restore the natural interface of the primordial masculine and feminine energies. Coming together in supportive ways as men and women reminds us that we share the privilege of the Shiva-Shakti force. Through conscious reaching out between the genders, our characteristics of Shakti and Shiva can merge into the infallible ground for harmony, sustenance, and prosperity for humanity. It is time we grow tired of being used and misinformed by our messed-up history. As we restore the Shiva-Shakti relationship, we find the deeper meaning of who we are as powerful primordial energies intertwining to heal ourselves and the world.

Both genders need to affirm their nature as the primeval force of Shiva-Shakti, this divine combination of our spiritual identity. A woman must first assure herself that she is imbued with the grace and divinity of the Goddess Shakti and that she deserves the power to heal, create, and nurture. She must acknowledge that her Shakti provides her with an indelible connection to the primordial masculine Shiva energy. As she rises to the call of her Shakti, she discovers her potent feminine powers. At the same time, a man must reassert his inherited power of Shiva energy, knowing he is inevitably connected to the Shakti energy as well. Owning his primal Shiva force, wherein he is imbued with the power of awareness, stability, and cosmic support, he finds himself capable of holding immutable space for harmony and peace. He is the host of Shakti. As he rises to the call of keeping the balance, he fulfills his wondrous destiny, stabilizing the playing ground so we, women, can once again feel that firm support from Shiva strength. Blissful. One of my more pleasant memories of childhood is when my father would take me by the hand and gently lead me to a desired destination, his firm protective grip around my wrist. In that moment, I felt secure, safe, and protected by the grand and gentle show of being a cherished daughter, the fodder of loving masculine concern that would later help me to build my feminine sense of self-esteem and worthiness strongly.

Shakti's power is not independent of Shiva's prowess. Men and women were not designed to be competitive or inimical with each other. None of us are programmed to crawl on our knees over the vast arid expanse of a desert or climb a mountain while carrying it on our backs. Life is not an uphill battle. It is a fluent, sapphic, and soft enigma. It contains magic, mystery, beauty, and ecstasy. Living life fully is about finding balance within Shiva-Shakti. Balance. Once again, we must recreate this gem of a life we are meant to live. As Mary Oliver waxes, "Tell me about despair, yours, and I will tell you mine."

Healing the mother wound will require the extraordinary of us: belief. We must believe that we are part of the pure existential energies of Shiva and Shakti and that despite the massive corruption of Shiva-Shakti unity in our world, we can reach out to each other with compassion and kindness. A significant step in fostering alliance is to stop clinging to binary "realities" that demonize and dehumanize those whose cultural, social, or sexual identities differ from our own. Life is naturally ruled by diverse situations, and we must find positive ways to encounter and deal with them. In my life, I have had the stoic support of countless good souls of all genders. I enjoyed the perennial support of the Shiva energy from birth onward: my father, guru, uncles, brothers, friends, oncologist, cardiologist, and numerous others. On the Shakti front, most of my early mentors and teachers were shaktified goddesses who took me under their wings to hone my progressive development. When we begin to fill our lives with awareness of our own nature, we attract that wondrous experience of coalescing heart, mind, and soul with our personal Shiva and Shakti. Each one of us has a specific karmic destiny. A woman poised in her Shakti energy attracts a man who is aware of his innate masculine power and is, therefore, undaunted by her mysterious strength.

We are not being called to be stronger than our men or compete with their strength; rather, both genders are called to work together with their counterparts to help empower each other. Finding common ground in the Shiva-Shakti equation is pivotal to healing the mother wound. While women can more easily generate nurturance, healing, forgiveness, and creating anew, men can follow their potent energy by fortifying stability, truth, awareness, and protective forces.

We have come a long way from burning pagan women healers at the stake or having a Hindu wife throw herself into the pyre of her dead husband. Albeit the journey of unearthing feminine power has only just begun. The Goddess universe is providing us with the Shakti map to guide us in this maiden voyage. As we come to terms with the supreme challenge of wounds that we bear, we can bring awareness to the rites of passage of the Shakti-Divine Feminine energy to heal these wounds. By reclaiming these innate rights, women can create the nurturing environment necessary for themselves, men, and children to heal. For humanity to heal. Once again, we are at a pivotal time in history when the universe avails a wide-open portal for us to enter and restore Earth's intelligence — the primary source of the Shakti force for healing humanity.

Finding The Shiva-Shakti Way

In a larger sense of healing, we must invest in the inner realm where the real work is to be done. We arrive in our wisdom once we find that ever-generating calm and contentment, regardless of what chaotic madness breaks loose around us. There was a time in our past when elders, healers, and wisdom carriers graced every community – timeless souls who used Earth intelligence to hone their inner world. They lent themselves to the disciplines of Mother Earth and fostered their community. These communities are now defunct; the way of the patriarch annihilated them. We must now become our own wisdom carriers. For this, we need the benign grace of each other's friendship.

A rapidly growing number of women and men are recognizing a new quiet surge of their co-existent power. At the same time, we are witnessing the breakdown of old, rote, bipartite traditional, ancestral, social, and political patterns. On a crisp, clear morning, you can feel the emergence of a vast sweep of consciousness affecting the entire swath of existence, the dawning of the winnowed light that brightens inner awareness. This light gives us shelter to show our broken pieces of heart and spirit and not be fearful of brokenness or the radical change this time is demanding from us. We are in the process of rebirth: becoming more authentic, feeling, loving, adoring nature, and preserving and safeguarding our mother, the Earth. That we are alive and present at this precious moment in time means we are all potential light-bearers. As I see it, the past decade has been a prolific time for universal cleansing. At the same time, it has manifested the raw purge of dousing, wrenching, and cleansing happening in every person's depth, which we may have perceived as a quandary of torturous conditions. These conditions are not for the feeble-hearted. We have to surrender fully to cross the threshold. "Surrender" is an ambivalent word like "forgiving." No one ever told us these are the two perennial realities we are bound to find at the bottom of the abyss or the very top of the blessing. The most successful way to bring ourselves into this humble space is through forgiving each other and being able to constantly forgive ourselves.

From the beginning of time, women and men would gather to pray and heal grief and angst in their community. We are forever healing. We heal into life, we heal into death, we heal into rebirth. Rebirth need not require dying. As long as we hold firm to the principles of loving relations sustained by mutual respect and cultivate nourishment and truth, women and men can help each other heal the mother wound. Shiva-Shakti must work together to heal our qualms. Imagine the freedom it provides to create safe spaces where we can meet each other and let our hearts break wide open. We are seeking to find spaciousness around and within so that we can harvest truth and trust with each other. Let us utilize the universal dharma – the laws of nature – to reignite our ancient bond of Shiva-Shakti, treating each other with kindness, honesty, loving care, and intelligence, being non-judgmental and allowing vulnerability, shame, rawness, angst, and bitterness to find their way in the spaciousness we are creating. In doing so, we bear witness for each other to the parts of ourselves we have covered up: the shame, suffering, isolation, and disconnect, or the soul power we may have cleft by our drive for success, ambition, and material achievement. From this supported space of loving care, we can call each other out for our mistakes, our blindness, what we do not wish to hear, and what our closest relations might be afraid or ashamed to tell us. Here, we can embrace the experience of each other's broken pieces, identifying with each shame and blessing.

An exaltation of women, a murder of men (just kidding), or a congress of larks of all genders holds invincible power. Our friendship among the genders is based on endurance, sacrifice, and humility. As long as we strive to convert deep fragility into understanding – with mother and daughter, mother and son, father and daughter, father and son, spouse to spouse, and man and woman in general, we can heal all divisions. We can restore wholeness. Fortunately, as the Earth's Shakti awakens, she lends her considerable resources to this restoration. Mother Earth's Shakti endows us with the immutable force to nourish, nurture, and heal ourselves, the good Earth, and all of nature. Her tools are nourishment, creativity, wisdom, sacrifice, selflessness, unconditional love, and undying light. As we begin to walk as Goddess-God emissaries on our reclaimed Earth, we become co-creators with Mother Nature.

Abhaya Mudra – Sealing Unity and Removing Fears

Wouldn't it be wonderful if we could bundle all of our inner and outer wounds and watch them not only dissolve into thin air but witness their transformation as they add to the sum of universal intelligence? As co-creators healing the mother wound, we can. We can choose to operate at a high vibrational level by consciously clearing the blockages of fear and distrust from our energy field. The most dynamic imperative of creation is to strengthen the unity of Shiva-Shakti, the fundamental, primordial groundwork for balance and trust with each other. Shiva-Shakti is the seed of life that is gravid with prana. According to Vedic science, we are informed by 350,000 or more nadis, subtle conduits in the astral field that ferry prana – that life-sustaining vibratory energy – into our bodies. As noted earlier, mudra is a simple and potent practice that helps us to harness the flow of pranic energy in the subtle body to clear out the emotional and mental detritus of the mother wound within. Keeping your intention of releasing ancestral wounds, personal hurt, and both claimed and unclaimed fears, dive into this simple, potent mudra practice anytime and anywhere you feel called to unburden your soul.

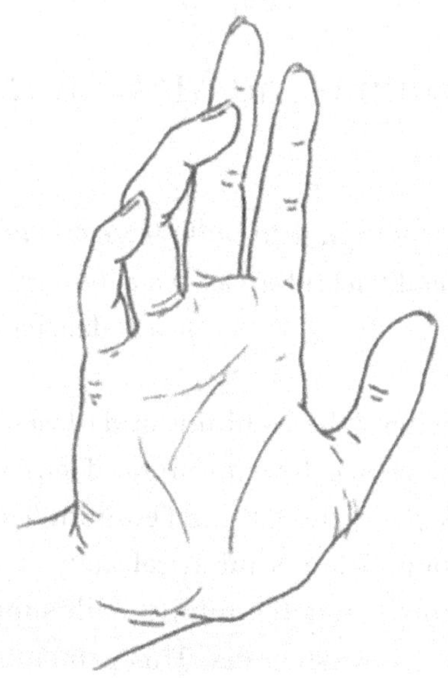

Fig. 2. Abhaya Mudra

The Practice: Abhaya Mudra – Sealing Unity and Removing Fears

Engage in this mindful practice anywhere and anytime you experience fear or trauma.

- Sit in a comfortable position, facing east.
- Raise your right hand to chest level with palm facing forward.
- Loosen the wrist and let the fingers gently separate.
- Breathe slowly, soften your gaze, and hold this mudra for 10 minutes or so.

Chapter 5

The Feminine and Masculine Divide

The purpose of yoga is to unite these two principles so that Shiva and Shakti become one within the self.

Yogachudamani Upanishad

We do not comprehend the Feminine and Masculine Divine, and, as a result, we experience the feminine and masculine divide. The Shiva-Shakti principle, the Divine Feminine/Divine Masculine, vastly differs from society's interpretation of masculinity and femininity, which equates femininity with submissiveness and masculinity with aggressiveness. This principle is greater than our individual genders. Each human being holds the sacred staff of the Masculine and Feminine Divine within their being. The female gender contains the pro-active Shakti energies, and the male gender possesses the pro-active Shiva energies. As we lose touch with our primal nature, we sacrifice our innate human heritage of unity, love, and honor and have been doing so for millennia. We pull apart the Shiva from the Shakti, the Shakti from the Shiva, not seeing, not knowing, not understanding that these "two" comprise an inseparable "one."

We have been living under this veil of separatism for too long. Our intrinsic Shiva-Shakti bond is unhinged. We have been traveling the dark scape for centuries, finding ourselves untethered from the self-generating energies that naturally resolve life's challenges. Men and women tend to compete more than they collaborate, to perceive each other's complimentary characteristics as weaknesses, and to use and betray each other more than they partner and uplift. Yet, there is no simple way to assign blame or demand accountability. Endless generations of patriarchal lunacy have meticulously crafted the convolution of reality that engineered this divisive sphere.

Fortunately, this veil of separatism — fastened in place by perspective and learned behavior — is an illusion we can strip from our vision. It is possible to restore feminine/masculine divinity and reclaim the sanctity of being human. But first, we must acknowledge that we have been shaped by fear-oriented societal, religious, and cultural mores. These moorings have honed behaviors and belief systems that do not serve the greater good of our nature. The energy that each gender carries is incredible. As we have seen in the Shiva-Shakti paradigm, only the maternal, feminine force, Shakti, can manifest consciousness, and only the masculine force, Shiva, can hold this immutable power of consciousness in a place of ecstatic balance. These juxtapositional energies are entirely supported within the body by prana. Of the innumerable nadis — conduits of prana — continually flowing into our body from the astral channels of the universe, Ida and Pingala are the two fundamental nadis in yoga philosophy that nourish the operational life force of the Shakti-feminine and Shiva-masculine principles, respectively. These two channels run alongside the spine, crossing over each other at each chakra. Ida resides on the left side of the body, our feminine aspect ruled by lunar energies of the moon, mirroring its dark, inert quality. Pingala, on the other hand, resides on the right side of the body, or masculine aspect, ruled by the solar energies of the sun and representing its light, active quality. Specific pranayama practice serves to balance and unblock the flow of prana through these pivotal nadis, leading to the physical, mental, and spiritual well-being of Shiva-Shakti vibration. As we strengthen our vibratory field, we are fostering unity between these two primordial energies while illuminating our nature of unity and harmony.

When both these primeval energies work together, as they are meant to, we create harmony. When these energies are pulled apart and alienated, whether within ourselves or from each other, we create chaos. Our history is a testament to humanity's ability to endure and survive the most incredible feats of violence. Yes, we are damaged. We are broken, but brokenness is part of the medicine that heals us, the balm that forces us to kneel, to grow, and to reflect. There are moments in life when we can touch the real and see beyond the veils. During these times, we sense spirit, we feel our vulnerability, and we finally perceive the deep fear we try so hard to push away—that inexplicable splinter stuck in the throat, holding back sacred words, fueling scarred wounds.

The powerful Hindu cosmology of *Ardhanarisvara* offers prescient insight into our immutable human design. Ardhanarisvara is the deified image of a half-woman/half-man that demonstrates the indivisible nature of Shiva-Shakti. "Ardha," "Nari," and "Ishvara" are three Sanskrit words that respectively mean "half," "woman," and "divine being." In Hinduism, we see Shiva as the lord, representing primordial masculine power, and his consort, Parvati, as Shakti, the primordial feminine power. Ardhanarishvara symbolizes the unification of the masculine primordial with the feminine primordial. It conveys the unity of opposites in the universe. It transcends the mere roles of masculine and feminine as we relate to them.

According to Vedic thought, Shiva-Shakti is beyond genders. Shakti is the source of manifestation, and Shiva is static; she is dynamic, and Shiva is infinite; Shakti renders the infinite finite. He is formless; she projects variabilities and forms. He is the contained power of the universe, remaining inert until Shakti uses her primeval power to create, manifest, sustain, and dissolve it all. Shiva is consciousness. Shakti is the expression of consciousness. Without the serene consciousness of Shiva, Shakti's power is dormant. Without Shakti's manifesting power of creation, Shiva remains dormant. They exist as the inseparable

One Being symbolized by Ardhanarishvara. The Japanese Inyo and Chinese Yin Yang symbols are similar principles that represent the universe as a circle. Inside the circle, two colors co-exist. Yin is the feminine force, and yang is the masculine force — indivisible, yet different. The colors represent the two types of primordial energies. This principle underpins all native cultures, demonstrating the innate universality of Shiva-Shakti.

The lesson: together, as one unified principle, female and male are meant to operate seamlessly as our world's generative and constructive force. This analogy espouses the apparent two as the immutable one. It helps us to resolve the paradox of separation between these two powerful states, Shiva and Shakti, into an understanding of unification, which, in turn, is a resolution of the opposites, genders included.

The Feminine and Masculine Divide in Prehistory and History

From the beginning of time, women have paid the price for humanity's progress with their blood, tears, and guts. Our defacement continues as violations and abuse abound in both overt and covert ways. To illustrate how we have become so lost, I will attempt to navigate the complex maze of feminine/masculine interplay in our prehistory and not-so-accurately-recorded history. These accounts have been flawed, maneuvered, and manipulated in one way or another by men who recorded them from their own perspective and agenda: the conquerors, politicians, heroes, and victors. History is simply a story written by people with their own biases and perspectives and one that has long since diminished, underplayed, or elided women's critical contributions to creating and healing our world.

Many studies propose that we can trace the roots of fatherhood as far back as 5 to 8 million years ago. This concept arose in response to a changing landscape that necessitated complementarity between men and women, wherein they pooled the food they specialized in providing. Male focus shifted from spreading their genes as widely as they could to ensuring the survival of offspring they claimed as their own. While good fathering ensured the survival of his offspring, it also marked the onset of the pivotal moment when women's intrinsic Shakti nature first became threatened. The development of the agricultural revolution that caused humans to change from hunters and gatherers to farmers and herders who grew crops and raised animals for food created a profound psychological shift that unbalanced Shakti power. The Neolithic period following the end of the Ice Age gave rise to a more sedentary lifestyle and a substantial change in dietary practices, which altered the roles of men and women and the relationship between them. Our relationship with Mother Earth also changed. Men and women both actively tended to clearing the land, growing crops, farming, and domesticating animals, with women's work extending to the domestic care of the home and children. There was more predictability and abundance of food, as well as more time for building home fires, family sharing, and intimacy between couples. Women's fertility increased dramatically, and with it, their levels of stress.

Great landscapes of steppe grasslands and forests arose, and the rivers ran prolific with salmon and fish. Farming villages first appeared in the Near East and soon afterward across Europe and many other parts of the world. The nomadic hunting and gathering lifestyle, for the most part, had ended. People started to cultivate a settled existence on the land where we first invested in the agriculture of plants, herding, and domesticating animals. The development of agriculture and population was key to the rise of civilization and the decline of Shakti balance. This period would mark human history's most fundamental demographic and psychological shift. The second agricultural revolution during the eighteenth century introduced major changes in farming techniques, crop rotation, mono-cropping, livestock breeding, and mechanized farm equipment. This advent further separated our kinship to the Earth. We began to treat her as a resource to be plundered, bartered, and abused. Our treatment of her magnificent animals also declined as our greed increased. Care, respect, and love for Mother Earth diminished, and the Shakti imbalance worsened. Researchers discovered an increase in the number of stress lines in the tooth cementum of Neolithic females. These findings imply that Neolithic women experienced more physiological stress than their Mesolithic female ancestors. The forbearance of stress has been a poignant understory of women throughout time. It shows signs of the Shakti energy already shifting into a state of imbalance. It would be interesting to see how much greater our stress immunity is today by testing the stress lines of modern women's teeth.

By the time the Green Revolution occurred, expanding over three long decades from the 1940s to the 1960s, we were gleefully hailing new scientific, Earth-destroying technologies such as damaging irrigation, toxic fertilizers, pesticides, and bioengineering of nature's sentient seeds. As agriculture developed through the ages and productivity from the land grew, markets emerged, and men's roles expanded away from the homestead. Men built transports and commuted to work, shops, and factories, and women became the official home tenders. The lives of men and women ferried on different tracks, separated by distance, absence, split purpose, and the relegations of gender: men as frontiersmen, pioneers, and earners versus women as mere housewives, dependent on the man for their shelter, babies, and livelihood. Shiva-Shakti cohesion began to tear.

The pages of our written history show this cohesion torn asunder. Women have been legally, socially, religiously, politically, and systematically disenfranchised everywhere and in every way. Men have deprived us of owning property, the right to vote, and even the ownership of our own bodies and lives. These horrors and injustices are too numerous to extoll and all too familiar. Yet not only are we marginalized and criticized for stepping outside of the limited roles offered to us, but when we do achieve phenomenal feats by defying stereotypes or breaking new ground, our accomplishments are often overlooked, diminished, or credited to men. The erasure of women from written history is repetitive and multi-fold. Consider women like Eunice Foote, a pioneering scientist who first theorized and demonstrated the climate science of the greenhouse effect and whose discoveries are credited to British Scientist John Tyndall. Lina Metizer is another example, an Austrian Scientist who discovered nuclear fission – the ability to split atoms, which changed the world of nuclear physics – yet the Nobel Prize for Lina's discovery "of the fission of heavy nuclei" was awarded to her male colleague, Otto Hahn. And then there is Alice Ball, a black chemistry professor who discovered a breakthrough treatment for leprosy and whose pioneering discovery was claimed and credited to Arthur Dean, the head of her chemistry department. The intelligence, wealth, and societal grace of Mary Todd Lincoln, the sixteenth First Lady of the United States, helped Lincoln be elected President. Nicknamed "Hellcat" by Lincoln's male secretary, her notable humanitarian service to a war-torn populace, wounded soldiers, and runaway enslaved persons was eclipsed by waves of negative press about her "tantrums in public." A more recent example is the dynamic young outlier Greta Thunberg, whom Trump publicly mocked for her climate activism.

The "Poetry" of Masculine Power in Mythology

Mythology both depicted and perpetuated the feminine/ masculine divide. The ancient tome of the *Rig Vedas* shares numerous celestial epics depicting the interplay of Mother Earth and Father Sky (Earth and sky referring both to the visible anatomy and vast, invisible realm of the universe). In one such tale about Prithivi, goddess ruler of the Earth, and Dayus, god ruler of the sky, Dayus is a stoic god with no interest in overriding the will of Prithivi; his ego-less rule long preceded the time of the Vedas. The little known about his reign provides insight into his undaunted support to the Earth Goddess. He ceded to her will so she could perform her myriad duties toward the Earth. To Dayus, the sovereignty of the primordial Mother Earth was incontestable. She was the manifesto of consciousness, and as the sky ruler, he understood his terrain to be an inseparable part of Mother Earth's vast charge. There was no power struggle between them. Dayus's unconditional support of Mother Earth strengthened her dominion. Prithvi, the uncontested Mother of the Earth, came to be venerated by all cultures in the world as the embodiment of the life-generating, life-sustaining Mother Principle, *matushpade parame,* illustrating that the physical plane of Earth, or *Bhumi,* was only a small part of her province.

When the ambitious Varuna replaced the older god, Dayus, and became the new sky god in the Vedic pantheon, the equanimity of Prithivi and Dayus, or Shiva-Shakti, began to shift. He did not consider himself a mere sky god: Varuna's patriarchal ambition was matched only by his pursuit of absolute power. In taking over from Dayus, he expanded his reign of the sky to assume sovereignty over all visible existence. Unlike Dayus, Varuna appointed himself king of the gods and used his forum to forge a definitive relationship with the gods and saints. He seated himself in charge of the vast realm of cosmic functions, and other masculine divinities lauded him as the noble lord among the gods. Varuna became the king of the whole world, and as an ethical governor, he stood above all others. Purported to be a brilliant ruler, he redefined his role in terms as poetic as they were divisive. In what may be satirically called the poetry of masculine power, the *Rig Vedas* laud the overarching glories of Varuna, "omniscience, his eye is in the sky; the golden sun roaming throughout the firmament from dawn to dusk is his eye; and just as the sun that 'observes' everything upon Earth his vision is unhindered. He has a thousand eyes like the stars in the night sky; he surveils everything his ever-vigilant spies (*spasa*). And he knows all through his superior knowledge (*asura-maya*). He is everywhere in the universe and around it; pervading all things as the 'inner law' and order of creation." Amen.

This praise was an omen. Varuna was among the first recorded to create social, moral, and cultural laws. In the process, he made sure to overarch his dominion above Earth's laws, the intelligence that had flourished under Prithivi's rule for millions of unrecorded years before him. These man-made laws have been written and rewritten, scribed and re-scribed, and interpreted and re-interpreted for thousands of years to suit the patriarchal power structure.

The act of "sin," for example, was cited in the *Vedas* ten thousand years ago, demonstrating Varuna's use of moral justice to create fear. Again, the Vedas presaged the "fear rule" that opened the gateway for politics and religions to control populations through morality codes. These codes were based on the duality principle: innocence and sin, good and evil, conscious and unconscious. Sin, the abhorred clime for all human beings, was elaborately mapped out by Varuna. So specific were his definitions that the concept of doing wrong aroused terror even in the celestial world. The Vedic people became vigilant and attentive to the core. Sin, in the original Vedic context, is that which disturbs the order of nature. Redefined by Varuna, "sin" became not what went against the grain of Mother Earth's intelligence but that which infringed the ethical and social laws he conceived.

Over the ruinous centuries that followed, "sin" began to assume a feminine form. The patriarchy widely employed this stratagem of disempowering the feminine divine. According to Kaballah mysticism, the original human placed in the Garden of

Eden was androgynous, both male and female. Only afterward was this primordial being divided into Adam and Eve, the reviled woman who ate the apple, quince, grape, pomegranate, fig, or whatever that fleshy, seeded fruit was that got them thrown out of Eden. Innocence lost. Women demonized. Masculine and feminine unity torn asunder.

Greek mythology similarly disenfranchised the feminine divine. The vast space of creation, the domain of the Mother Consciousness, was divided into quarters ruled mainly by the Protogenos gods, with some portion of the physical Earth and sea granted to the Great Mother as Gaea (Gaia). (As the Protogenos of the Earth, she is portrayed as emerging at the beginning of creation to form the foundation of the universe. Gaea was one of the few Protogenoi to be depicted in anthropomorphic form; however, even as such, she was shown as a woman partially risen from the ground, inseparable from her native form, the physical Earth.) However, the Greeks also appointed Khaos as the primordial feminine force delegated to the lower atmosphere surrounding the Earth — both the invisible air and the gloom of fog and mist. Her name, Khaos, denotes "gap" or "chasm," indicating the space between heaven and Earth. Thus, we see the Feminine Divine transmogrified into chaos and relegated to the deep, where perhaps the gods hoped she would remain.

The progressive deterioration of goddess power is inexhaustible. Tracing the methodical erosion that toppled the Shakti-Shiva balance would take more than a lifetime. These narratives, however, reveal some of the first known precedents for the decline of Earth's intelligence and her rites via the long tentacles of masculine power: that is, as they progressively usurped the dominion of Mother Earth. The patriarchal strategy has encroached on her natural laws with man-made laws that often dispute or override her intelligence and destroy her universe with bad science in the name of progress. In so doing, they split open Earth's sacred portals, disemboweling her mystery and de-popularizing her sanctity. This massive divide of masculine/feminine energy has led to progressively worsening conditions rooted in the onslaught against Earth's intelligence, human intelligence, and feminine intelligence: in other words, against the dignity of all living things.

Healing the Feminine and Masculine Divide

The time is long overdue for the Shakti-Shiva force to stand as one unified front to reclaim its intrinsic power of discernment. We must recognize the lies that have been skillfully sifted into the sands of truth and relinquish the false constructs handed down from one dysfunctional generation to the next. We do not need to endure this morass of falsehoods any longer. We have an in-built instruction guide to our wisdom. This inner vista opens when we start to cooperate with each other. We must restore the hindsight and foresight that steer us away from the traps and tragedies of the prevailing diseased system and begin restoring the potent, healing energy of Shiva-Shakti unity, our inherent human largesse.

None of us are experts on the matter of Shiva-Shakti reunification. Our parents couldn't do it. Our children can't do it. Grandparents often tried to do it. Therapists can't do it; they are as lost as everyone else. Spiritual leaders and gurus can't do it; most are imprisoned by their ego wounds, wherein human growth exponentially decreases as notoriety increases. Yet, we must keep the bloodied knuckles of hope alive as we walk each other through this dank terrain. And since everyone bears the wounds of feminine/masculine division, healing distrust and disrepair between genders and within ourselves is perhaps the most imperative work we can do.

We can't do so by pitting men against women and women against men, both against humanity and the world against Mother Nature. The important focus here is that we understand what it takes to move forward in harmony within ourselves and each other. First, we work together to heal and make whole the primordial feminine energy axis of consciousness, which restores the primordial masculine energy. These two energies working in tandem with each other can reverse the free fall. Veneration of the Goddess necessarily entails veneration of the God. As Shiva-Shakti, we are two aspects of the same being. We can begin to disband patriarchy's monstrous falsehoods by choosing not to subscribe to the illusions that have been fiercely concretized into what we conjure and buy into as "reality." Patriarchies are not "the natural order of things." The battle of the sexes was engineered. Women do not have a biological imperative to be sweet and submissive, nor are they inherently more deceitful.

We know the price we pay for our divine being-ness in womanhood. I know how bitterly painful it was to keep shaking off the ill-begotten reflection of men's primordial fear from my psyche. As I keep on, I keep gleaning this immutable truth: that only the light of Shakti, which every woman possesses in its fullness, can help instigate and restore that sense of Shiva's dignity in the conscience of those ignorant men. We forgive because we emulate our Mother, the Earth, who continually forgives us a trillion times a day; we forgive because we are her Shakti carriers of life, the bearers of children and men, the sustainers of nature. All beings depend on our light. Men entirely depend on Shakti energy to awaken their masculine primordial nature. Several communities around the world are doing good work helping men relearn the way of their primordial masculine nature. One such event is being hosted in Perth, Australia, by a close friend, Julian Silburn, who has sought the guidance of the First Nation Elder community to walk their community of men into a right relationship with the Shakti force and Mother Earth. Julian, a master didjeridu player trained by Aboriginal Elders, incorporates my sacred chants and prana alignment work in his awakening brotherhood group. He shares these fortuitous words for men who seek healing from primal fear: "It is an incredible experience in our workshop as we prepare the men to understand their history and to understand the importance of becoming strong allies for the Indigenous in their own journey back to healing and empowerment after generations of disadvantage." I would add a perennial mantra for men's daily use: "As Shiva, I honor Shakti."

Let us call upon the inherent power of Shakti's love – that unconditional basis of human nature. This love is inviolate, the blissful largesse of the human species, the love that never dies, that is infrangible and tangible, that reigns sovereign in our sacred human design. Love is what keeps the human heart wide open to its Shiva-Shakti eternity. Let us call upon compassion that is ripe for the awakening. Let us work for justice and nourishment for our Earth. Only through authenticity of spirit and through mirroring the majestic origins of our masculine-feminine endowment may we be inspired to recover truth, love, kindness, and justice in and for our world.

Humanity's intrinsic memory of cohesion has been eroded, but the heart remembers. It longs for union; it is lonely from the lack of fulfillment. The innate urge, the cosmic desire, yearns for bonding betwixt the Shiva and the Shakti. To quote author B.N. Raveesh in his article, *Brain and Psychiatry*, "Everywhere in nature, animate or inanimate, we find in every individual or particle a tremendous urge to be united with something else, outside, or inside. The urge comes from within as the individual is composed of opposites and through the union there is a resolution of the opposites. What is an unconscious urge with nature is transformed into conscious love with human beings."

Imagine: we can create harmony between the two primeval energies through this simple understanding of our primary nature. In so doing, we can express loving co-existence between the genders and utilize that which is a foundational power in our cosmic human anatomy. We can stake claim to a divinely intended existence filled with light, intelligence, awareness, kindness, and humility – an awareness that encompasses life as sacred and venerates living consciously. Consciousness: this is our natural law. To paraphrase Aquinas, who wrote extensively about natural law, the light of reason is placed by nature and thus by god and goddess in every man and woman to guide them in their acts. Among Earth's sacred creatures, humans alone can attain full consciousness.

Consciousness on Earth is intertwined with the inseparable pathway of Shiva-Shakti energy. Shakti is the energy that gave birth to humanity; she generates the prana and vibration that sustain the magnificent Earth. She is the womb of our universe. Once Shakti energy is impaired, our ability to process and propagate awareness lessens, harmony goes asunder, and all of nature loses its grip. The Shiva energy depends on Shakti for its state of balance and for its ability to manifest or accomplish conscious activity. Until we coalesce the energetic gel of primordial feminine/masculine that holds humanity in its pristine state of unity, love, and kindness, we will continue to be diverted to a contentious reality. Restoring the Shakti force at the helm of life is a dire necessity, not above Shiva, but beside him. Love, just love, is what we need.

Anuloma Viloma – Activating Lunar and Solar Breath

Let's continue to unify the Shiva-Shakti energy by performing this effective pranayama practice of alternating the breath between the Ida and Pingala nadis by using your left and right nostrils to breathe. This practice is called Anuloma Viloma.

In order to align your breath with the cosmic rhythms, you must first ascertain which nostril is exhaling the most air. To do this, block your left nostril with your finger and blow out through your right nostril, holding your hand beneath your nose. Feel the force of air expelling. Then do the same on the opposite side, blocking your right nostril and blowing from your left. When the air is strongest on the left side, your lunar breath is active. When the air is strongest on the right side, your solar breath is activated. To achieve a balance between the right and left channels, do the gentle practice of alternating the breath by blocking one side while breathing into the other, then blocking the other nostril and breathing out of the open one, repeating this measure for about five slow minutes. In the Vedic way of life, we are continually harmonizing the body with the environment. During the day, solar energy dominates the environment, so we harmonize with the day by activating our lunar breath to balance internal energies with the solarized day. Similarly, during the night, when the lunar energy is dominant, we harmonize with the night by activating our solar breath before going to sleep. Monitor your inner fluency by doing alternate breathing at the day's three primary junctions: dawn, noon, and dusk. By keeping our breath in balance with nature's prana, we cleanse and harness our field of prana. Pranayama practice strengthens the physical, mental, and spiritual organism. Anuloma Viloma practice also regulates blood pressure and modulates cardiac and neural oscillations. It enhances respiratory and cardiovascular health, increases longevity, and generates a sense of calm and joy in the cellular body.

The Practice: Anuloma Viloma – Activating Lunar and Solar Breath

- Sit comfortably with your back straight and hands in your lap.
- Close your right nostril with your thumb and inhale through your left nostril.
- Hold your breath for 30 seconds or so before releasing your right nostril and exhale through it.

- Close your left nostril and inhale through your right nostril.
- Hold your breath for 30 seconds or so before releasing your left nostril and exhale through it.
- Repeat 10-20 rounds in the early morning and in the evening before going to sleep.

Gradually increase the duration of your inhalation, retention, and exhalation. As you become accustomed to the routine and continue your practice, you will feel your breathing becoming more rhythmic. The ideal goal to reach is as follows: inhalation count of 16, retention count of 64, and exhalation count of 32.

Chapter 6

Primordial Fear of the Feminine

It is not so much a matter of escaping from one's suffering, though it may seem to be so. It is a longing for home, for a memory of the mother, for new metaphors for life. It leads home. Every path leads homeward, every step is birth, every step is death, every grave is mother.

Herman Hesse

Primordial fear of the feminine is the great crisis of the patriarchal man, ancient and modern. He poses an exaggerated masculine persona out of fear of the feminine, rejects his inner feminine qualities, and strives for complete independence from her influence, yet he can no more become independent of her Shakti energies than he can prevent himself from feigning her prowess. The paradox is that he is perennially caught in the lower atmosphere of the venomous feminine guile and, at the same time, is estranged from the feminine within himself. In his deep-seated fear of the feminine, he experiences an emotional tug of war within himself, which accounts for disharmony in his relationships, especially those with women. He loses confidence in his own immutable Shiva power. This endemic state of imbalance is present in all men to varying degrees. According to Jungian Psychologist, Erich Neuman, "The patriarchal culture's separation from the Feminine and from the unconscious becomes one of the essential causes for the crisis of fear in which the patriarchal world now finds itself."

Primordial fear of the feminine is the decisive wedge that sundered Shiva-Shakti unity. There was a time in human history when Shiva and Shakti were in balance, and humanity and its god and goddess concept were centered enough that fear did not exist. This cycle of time is called Satya Yuga, one of four yugas in the lifespan of the universe. This golden era lasted for 1,728,000 years. Satya Yuga was the age of truth and purity where the god and goddess reigned as One in supreme and intrinsic goodness. Satya Yuga was an entirely non-binary way of life with no hierarchal system. Fear did not exist. With devout wisdom and meditative practice, people lived up to 100,000 years in this cycle. This was about 2 million years prior to the introduction of secularism, wars, demi-gods, sages, and the royals and rich who exist above the common ilk of humanity.

Yugas, or cosmic ages, are a Vedic science that measures universal time. The four yugas are Satya, Treta, Dvapara, and Kali. Each of the yugas involves stages of consciousness evolution for both the universe and humanity. Satya was the golden age of purity, unblemished truth, and harmony among humanity. Treta was the age of cooperation, duty, and compassion. Demigods arrived on Earth and mixed with humanity, and the first practice of nonviolent religious sacrifices to the divinities was introduced. Humans were said to have lifespans of 10,000 years during this age. By the start of Dvapara, the third yuga, binary relationships had already begun to contaminate life. There was a meteoric rise in selfishness, competition, and ambition while spirituality, selfless love, and morality eroded. Midway through this yuga, the Shiva-Shakti alliance was already being torn, and people lived to be only 1000 years old.

We are now in the last cycle of time, called Kali Yuga. Kali Yuga is said to have begun 5000 years ago. The vibration of Earth had become so dense that the subtle body of Earth and humanity became inverted with darkness, corruption, destruction, and chaos. Dharma was eschewed. Social, political, and religious orders were used to control, manipulate, terrorize, and corral humanity while destroying nature. Kali yuga was ready-made for the full takeover by the patriarchs. Propagated by the fear of the feminine, fear of cosmic energy, and fear of Mother Earth, fear of nature, the patriarchal affliction of fear reigned supreme. But Kali yuga represents much more than the patriarchal agenda of fear, hopelessness, misery, disease, and morbidity. It is within the morass of all that is punishing that we find hope, in the density of darkness that we can reclaim faith, in the sewerage of lies, deceit, avarice, and evil that we can and must rescue the Earth's truth by using our universal mind. Kali yuga gives us the ideal platform to advance our evolutionary struggle toward enlightenment – not only to rebalance this energy within our species but to balance it for the first time in the entire history of our consciousness. We were not given a Satya yuga to flourish in; instead, we are given the hellish landscape of Kali yuga, where every massive obstacle can show us a way to move the mountain. We aren't born heroes in the ideal golden age – we are forged with iron and steel to take back truth, integrity, and consciousness.

In the sprawling breadth of Kali yuga, we see how this primordial fear of the feminine is tenaciously allied to men's burden of ancestral traumas. The *Saundarya Lahiri* informs us that Shakti is the cause of both evolution and involution back to the source. Shiva's is the ascension cause, the ultimate consciousness, but without Shakti's power of evolution and involution, consciousness ascension cannot manifest. Therein lies the ultimate relationship and intimate cooperation of Shiva-Shakti. When this bond is askew, violated, or disregarded, the chronic tug of war among populations, especially between the sexes, ensues. Seeking power and control, men violate the stasis of the Shiva-Shakti balance. Shiva, the masculine primordial, is not and never will be the sacred gateway to human mortality: the Shakti yoni is. A woman's yoni is the birthing portal. It is the one and only sacred passage to human life. Resenting the Shakti power while at the same time preempting her "role," man has set out his semblance of authority, superiority, and control, thus separating himself from the maternal spirituality that is causal to his existence. In this chasmic reality arises man's original fear: the primordial fear of the feminine.

Subsequently, he betrays his primordial nature and betrays the feminine force; sexual aberrations, exploitation, shaming, and disharmony become his rule. Weak patriarchal consciousness gave birth to our Earth's progressive devaluation. Churned by fear, hostility, jealousy, and violence, he arbitrated the systematic destruction of the mother concept. By losing touch with his innate masculine powers and usurping Shakti's purpose, the masculine identity crisis was conceived. In so doing, he has deprived himself of the phenomena of his own natural Shiva powers: the immutable force of ascension, of absolute consciousness. Ignorant of his true nature, the man-made masculine ideal betrays his own power since only the properly balanced Shiva force can generate the immutable power of consciousness and maintain its ecstatic balance in the world. Each of these two coalescent forces carries its own incredible power, yet the journey to consciousness would be futile for everyone if Shiva and Shakti remained inimical to each other. When these energies are pulled apart and alienated, we create chaos.

The origins of this primordial fear extend back to the very dawn of human consciousness. It is the root cause of the human dilemma and the massive destruction of the Earth; it is the shadow that drives us, alienating us from ourselves, our relationships, society, and the Earth itself. Deeply etched in all men, this fear is mirrored back to women and casts a pall over the entire planet. It has devastated Mother Nature, her Earth, her ocean, the whole environment between Earth and sky, and every creature and human being she sustains. It has driven men to rape, mutilate, vilify, and demean women for countless years and in countless ways. Now, we must cut away the rot of this quantum separation or succumb to total decay.

The Roots of Primordial Fear

Primordial fear is activated in men through a complex network of experiences. The most potent form of primordial fear is awakened first through conception, followed by birth. All subsequent traumas are linked to our birthing and rebirthing. Fear is imported into the embryo when the seed and ovum unite (along with other memory information the seed and ovum have gleaned from previous births). Each new life inherits its parent's fear along with their genetic complement. In its last two months of gestation, the fetus remembers its past lives; however, during the extraordinary process of birthing and adjusting to the outside world, we lose that memory portfolio. As we transition from the buffering amniotic environment and enter the birthing passage, we endure breath-depriving claustrophobia. Once we clear the vaginal passage and start to enter the extreme conditions of Earth's atmosphere – air, space, and light – we encounter our first deep state of shock. Being held upside down and slapped generally helps us to awaken from this nightmarish entry to planet Earth. The state of shock, however, can last for a few hours or several days as the senses begin to stir with blurred resonance, images, and scents, and the unfamiliar sensations of saliva and touch. In this intensely vulnerable state, we lose touch with our past life's memories. The phenomenon of birth also erases the resolution each soul avows before birth. The child is born, and the umbilical cord that connects it to the other world is cut. It is enduring its first trauma in its new life: birthing through the yoni portal. The mother is thus perceived, however unconsciously, as the perpetrator of this terrifying experience. Ironically, a second layer of primordial fear arises from the haven of absolute safety and love a child experiences in its mother's arms. The newborn child senses mama and feels her touch, her embrace; a renewed sense of security ensues, an imperceptible sigh, "Perhaps everything will be alright after all." The tiny hands touching mama's breast, the comfort, the nipple oozing into their mouth, sensing its tongue, her milk — what ambrosia! The child experiences its first attachment to life on Earth through the mother, who is infallible. That is, until he needs her, and she is not there, or he senses her fallibility. The child then experiences his second trauma: blame the mother. We carry these two early primal traumas throughout our lifetime.

Yet another layer of fear of the feminine is added by the socializing that reinforces our ancestral memory. We live in cultures and communities conditioned and shaped by endless generations of memories. These reflect familial experiences and ways of coping with challenges. The choices our ancestors made can and do affect our conditioning. Whether our ancestors were the persecuted or the persecutors, or both, their choices, biases, prejudices, social bearing, and particular life goals — humane or inhumane — also influence our behavior. For example, if a man's father and grandfather espoused that all women are inherently "gold diggers" or "not cut out to be president," then chances are he, too, will internalize or struggle with this belief on some level.

The layer that both crowns and underpins all the others is, of course, the innate fear and jealousy of a female's power to create life. This inured ancestral jealousy is inscribed on our genetic memory, fed and stoked by the patriarchy, and passed down through countless generations.

Understanding the Fear-Brain Mechanism

Fear is the most prevalent negative emotion of our time; as such, it is imperative that we understand the fear-brain mechanism. However, to do so, it is important to remember that we are living a mechanical life surrounded by materialistic excess where we have lost visceral touch with the deep vibrational nuances within and without. Massive technological advancements and shifts during this millennium have served to progressively alienate human beings from nature. Alienation from her has resulted in a collective increase of fear karma, depleting the greater energy supporting life. Nature is continually signaling body, mind, and memory to nourish and heal and to find our stasis within her, but our modern lifeways block these signals. You may not even be aware that you are harboring energies that can hurt and devastate life. Our mental and emotional space is often held hostage by mechanized robotic energies. We must be mindful of the potent push of the destructive energies continually undermining our life force, health, and creative abilities.

As we subsist in a stuporous fog that is masking our joy, we find a growing number of suicides in our populations, including adolescent suicide and mass suicide pacts, with mounting levels of depression experienced by significant numbers of people worldwide. Our world population is using more medicines for debilitating depression and contra-indicative factors that lead to disease and despair. Cancers, heart disease, nouveau diseases, nameless viruses, and morbidity through medical mistakes have dramatically increased. These symptoms indicate a progressively growing tendency toward despair, ill health, and alienation. In our digital age, victimhood culture among adolescents is rapidly growing. Referred to as the "pathologization pandemic" by social media guru Gurwinder of The Prism, this spread is abetted by a medical industry that has its own biased incentives for exaggerating the prevalence of mental disorders. The digital arena is perfectly designed to promote patriarchal agendas. Harness the population with mind-blowing obsessions, keep them busy, brain-strip the young of reason and logic, and usurp their individuality and identity under the guise of being fashionable and stripping away conventional stigmas to set them free. Ian Hacking, the late philosopher, calls this approach semantic conditioning: the process of naming and describing a condition, thereby causing the condition to spread. The digital platform fast-tracks the pandemic of delusional conditions, especially among female adolescents. On social media, girls the world over are disproportionately reporting gender dysphoria. In 2022, the NHS' Gender Identity Development Service (GIDS) for gender dysphoria showed a dramatic increase of over 2000 percent over a ten-year period. This surge has been driven almost exclusively by young people and natal females. The digital brouhaha points to young girls confusing general distress for serious ailments that are being concretized by their doctors as medical disorders. Mia Ashton of Public News put it this way on her Twitter thread: "The political right became fascinated by trans rights and almost immediately school started teaching gender ideology to children as young as kindergarten ... More than 1000 videos of adolescent girls are showing off their mastectomy scars, ecstatically raving about the pleasure of taking testosterone on YouTube and TikTok." "Sadfishing" is one of the newest trends on social media wherein teens exaggerate their problems or emulate or fake conditions like Tourette Syndrome and Dissociative Identity Disorder to garner sympathy. Media culpability in promoting these fast-spreading social contagions is clear.

These dangerous trends heighten the atmosphere of fear. Anxiety, stress, depression, obsession, and lethargy are some of the many faces of the fear anatomy. Fear emotions are rooted in the psyche of women and children, who tend to relate to these vibrations more profoundly than men (and likewise have less of a societal stigma against acknowledging them). Like all emotions, fear operates through the cosmic network of energy and vibration carried within the subtlest nuances of existence on Earth. Let's explore modern and ancient perspectives on the perpetuation of fear within the human psychic anatomy.

From the scientific perspective, the amygdala — a small, almond-shaped structure that lies near the center of the brain — acts as the brain's fear command center. This center is intricately connected to other regions of the brain through a network of nerve fibers. Once the amygdala perceives a threat, it triggers a body-wide emergency response within milliseconds. Through a process called fear conditioning, one can readily perceive an ordinary stimulus as a warning sign. On a physiological level, prompted by impulses from the amygdala, the hypothalamus produces a hormone called corticotrophin-releasing factor (CRP). This signals the pituitary and adrenal glands to flood the bloodstream with epinephrine, norepinephrine, and cortisol, or stress hormones. At the brain level, the thalamus receives information from direct sensory perceptions and posts it to the amygdala, which elicits the body's instinctive defensive responses – attack, defend, avoid, accept, submit, or escape – thereby placing the organism on high alert. In turn, the hippocampus accesses the threat by drawing memory information from previous fear experiences, including from past lives and our ancestral past. The sensory cortex, located in the rear of the upper hemisphere of the brain, discerns the threat to distinguish genuine danger from a false alarm. If the threat is inconsequential, the prefrontal cortex resets the entire brain response, which suppresses the amygdala response. Thus, a perceived threat in a man's brain of a woman "besting" him at work or his wife smiling at another man may set off a chain reaction of primordial fear of the feminine force that was programmed during gestation while in the amniotic ocean of the mother's belly. What should have been remembered as a safe space that nourished and fed him before he entered the raw atmosphere of Earth is largely retained in his experiential memory as a fearsome, humiliating, and suffocating advent. This recall perspective is processed in the lower sector of his reptilian brain, activated as it were during gestation by the negative ancestral memory download he inherits before he emerges into birth.

The Vedic ancients viewed our fear-brain mechanism from the perspective of the whole anatomical system: physical, psychic, and spiritual. Considered the core vulnerability of all species, particularly humans, the fear emotion is richly elucidated by the Vedic seers who provided extensive information on our physical as well as subtle anatomy. They explained the various command centers for emotional responses located within the brain. What we today consider the "emotional brain" is analogous to the finer workings of the fourth, fifth, and sixth chakras, the psychic centers of consciousness within the body. These three chakras are closely related to the mid-brain function, part of the central nervous system located below the cerebral cortex. In my ongoing work on cosmic memory, I explain the process: memory, impulse, and ego functions are stored in the ahamkara, the subtler functions of the mid-brain. Ahamkara serves a deeper purpose than merely controlling the body's motor movement or relaying auditory and visual information. When receiving the signals of a threat, ahamkara sounds an urgent message throughout the memory-based organism. Sustained by prana, the kinetic life force, ahamkara is responsible for our memory functions, both present and past. Phenomenally, it also records human impulses, which it uses for mapping out specific paths for the individual's future memory. In science, we know that prana is responsible for cellular respiration. However, prana's function in sustaining body, mind, and spirit is far greater. Aligned with ahamkara, prana nourishes and safeguards awareness. Ferried through a circuitry of more than 72,000 nadis, or energy conduits, it feeds and nourishes the life force.

Semantic differences aside, modern and ancient perspectives agree that fear usurps prana. During fear episodes, the body's routine immunological function temporarily shuts down and directs its focus toward combating or escaping the threat. The entire sequence of responses depends on ahamkara. When prana is aggravated, it sends a fright signal throughout the organism via the nadis, causing the production of abundant *ojas*, an immunological buffer, in the body. As a result, ample glucose is released into the bloodstream to counteract the debilitating shortage of prana. At such times, the heart begins pumping erratically while muscles tense and body temperature drops. Ahamkara guides fear episodes from start to finish and supplies the process with precious information from the individual's stored memory. Ultimately, the fight, flight, freeze, or fawn response occurs in the higher mind or intellect, what we call *buddhi,* which governs the activities of the cerebral cortex.

While fear responses are necessary for the organism to gather and safeguard itself in times of potential or grave danger, a constant barrage of low-impact adrenaline surges can overstimulate and cause damage to the subtle nerve circuitry. Long-term or chronic fear perceptions tend to have a tenacious grip on the mind. As a result, excess stress hormones can be released, causing severe erosion of memory. This becomes a vicious cycle, as memory loss triggers increased susceptibility in our fear response to perceived danger. Moreover, memory loss creates a great sense of internal confusion and trepidation. We become subconsciously aware when our protective response shield is getting impaired. Simply put, the more memory we lose, the more vulnerable and fearful we become. When an outpouring of emotion from numerous individuals saturates the atmospheric network, it impacts the collective mind. Propelled by the vibratory force, entire masses of the population can begin to think, act, and sound alike. Have you ever wondered why politicians, socio-religious leaders, cult leaders, and shrewd marketers who pedal fear can influence vast numbers of people with bizarre ideologies that are irrational and destructive to the clear-minded person? Such is the power and pervasiveness of fear.

When we suffer from too much fear or for too long, we sustain lasting trauma that vitiates the mind, body, and spirit. When experiencing trauma, we can respond in ways that compromise our integrity and authenticity. Traumas are always attached to a deeper reservoir of fear. Trauma is not an independent agency. Each event is aligned with whatever circumstantial memory of terror was present at its occurrence. For the purpose of the fear-trauma analogy, fear is the container, and trauma is the content. In reality, when dealing with trauma, we deal with specific sets of fears that have been congealed into countless trauma bundles over endless years. Herein lies the paradox of primordial fear. We all carry known and unknown fears that have been imprinted into our cellular memory. These fears are not limited to primal fears, such as fear of spiders, reptiles, death, the dark, autonomy, and extinction. Whenever a trauma incident occurs, it evokes a related pack of fears stored in our ancestral memory. This is why it is difficult to heal traumas, yet we must. Every trauma comes with a bundle of fearsome, unsavory guests from the deep past. Data from several neurobiological studies on the inheritance of PTSD suggests that offspring of war veterans with PTSD have shown higher depression scores than those of war veterans without PTSD and a higher rate of aggression and anxiety than those of non-veterans, regardless of the behavior or parenting skills of the veteran. A recent genetic study of 32 Jewish men and women who had either been interned in a Nazi concentration camp or witnessed or experienced torture, showed changes in the gene bank of their children that could only be attributed to the Holocaust experience of their parents. So it goes with sons of men: each carries the burden of primordial fear, deeply seated in the under-story of their existence. When the recreation of similar dysfunctional situations arises, these lurking memories show up. From the personal to the collective, primordial fear is humanity's most tenacious adversary.

Manifestations of Primordial Fear

Primordial fear manifests in a myriad of malignant ways, including power-mongering, vilification and debasement of women, and, most depraved of all, rape. While the twentieth century made viable leaps for women's welfare in most parts of the world, the twenty-first century is suffering the backlash of the patriarchs' fear-brain mechanism on overdrive. In some of the world's oldest democracies – France, Switzerland, and the United Kingdom – autocracy is trending. In China, Xi Jinping has silenced women by stamping out feminine movements. In Russia, Vladimir Putin is promoting traditional gender roles that are limiting women's participation in public life. In Egypt, President Abdel Fattah El-Sisi recently introduced a bill concretizing men's paternity rights, their right to practice polygamy, and to control whom their female relatives marry.

Women themselves are often conditioned to play into the falsehoods for fear that we will lose men's support or approval. We internalize men's primordial fear of our power by buying into the idea that we are weak, scheming, shallow, more emotional, less intelligent, not cut out for "men's work," have poor driving skills, are bad at politics and math – the list goes on and on. In so doing, we feed our psyche and behavior with our own primordial fear of being manipulated, abused, violated, and raped.

Across cultures, even for the Goddesses, molestation, rape, and sexual abuse are deep scars that live in the energetic imprint of every woman's womb. When evoked, they arouse her worst fears. Draupadi is the female protagonist of the Hindu epic, the *Mahabharata,* and the consort of the five Pandava brothers – Yudhishthira, Bhima, Arjuna, Nakula, and Sahadeva. She had five sons, one from each husband. She was renowned for her beauty, courage, and rare polyandrous marriage. Later, she became the empress, and her number one husband, Yudhishthira, became the emperor. During an unfortunate dice game, he lost everything. Yudhishthira had bet "everything in his kingdom," which the victor understood to include his wife. After seizing possession of his winnings, the victor, Dushasana, forcibly took Draupadi by her hair and dragged her into the court. She was scantily dressed in a simple cotton wrap worn by menstruating women. Dushasana attempted to disrobe her in front of her in-laws, but she was saved from further humiliation by the divine intervention of the god Krishna. Draupadi is extolled as an archetypal beacon for female chastity.

Greek mythology is similarly rife with the dark underbelly of rape, with an appalling disregard for women's sanctity. In the Homeric Hymn to Demeter, Zeus, king of the gods, rapes his sister Demeter, and the product of that rape is Persephone. Supposedly, Zeus also raped Persephone. He was said to be a serial rapist. Poseidon also raped the goddess Demeter. Hades, god of the underworld, abducted her daughter Persephone. Ovid's version of Roman mythology informs us that Neptune raped Medusa at Minerva's temple, and Mercury raped Lara as he escorted her to the underworld. In Celtic myth, Áine was being raped by King Ailill Aulom of Munster when she bit off his ear, which gave him the name Aulom, "one-eared one." The goddess Aine was also one of the female deities that later suffered from repression at the hands of the Christian monks.

Rape in mythology is pervasive but unmatched by its horrifying incidence in reality. Men violate women to feel powerful, to combat their insecurities engendered by primordial fear. Rape and sexual slavery are sterling examples of man's savage struggle for autonomy and power as he attempts to snatch it from the reservoir of the yoni, that sanctum that birthed him. His inner battle is to seek not revenge but obsessive control over the power that found him helpless, subjective, suspended in the amniotic fluid of his mother's Shakti nutrients, entirely in her care while tied by a string to Shakti's absolute power. What else, other than a male fear of female power and sexuality, can explain a practice as barbaric as female genital mutilation, which involves the physical mutilation of a girl's genitals and the removal of her potential to experience sexual pleasure?

Violation of a woman's body goes deep; it claws on the surface of Shakti's eternity. Ancient cultures viewed a woman's body as a temple, a sacred territory to which only she could grant the right of passage. Having processed the ruthless violations of rape myself and senseless attacks over many long years, my body now feels like the Federation Starship USS Enterprise with severe double-bottom hull damage. I was raped, not by accident or incident. It was a planned, strategic affair by a hate group of white men so terrified of my power that they broke into my domain, knocked me out with sleeping gases, and raped my inert body. Palpable emotional scorn, wrenching grief from the memory, and the emotional clutch of the filthy, grubbing paws of the ignorant would surface and resurface. But long years of deep spiritual work came to my rescue. I found strength in the understanding that sacred sites, holy lands, and temples get desecrated from misguided beliefs that spawn hate and hurt all the time. After 9/11, my brother's Hindu temple was one of a handful of edifices burnt to the ground by haters in Hamilton, Ontario. Yet, through all the destruction of sacred sites and sacred beings in history, human faith continues – faith in a divine energy, something beyond our physical bodies, something so eternal that it never dies, even when we have forgotten how powerful we humans are. We must foster faith in that divinity within ourselves. My Vedanta training of self-knowledge rescued me from the tar pits of concretizing shame, angst, rage, and bitterness into my identity – it is a monumental struggle not to let such mind-searing experiences redefine oneself. To prevent hosting the false idea that "I am damaged, I am made impure" from the violations of our magnificent identity, especially our feminine identity, let us remember that we are not limited by either our human experiences or vulnerability: the Self is far greater than the physical, emotional, and psychic body. (This principle of the imperishable Self, the divinely inspired Self, also applies to the male and third gender body.) In the *Chandogya Upanishad,* Sage Sandilya illuminates our imperishable reality: "Thou art imperishable. Thou art Changeless Reality. Thou are the Source of Life." Our spirit, or spiritual self is indestructible. The *Bhagavad Gita* states, "Na jayate mriyate va kadacin, nayam bhuta bhavita va na bhuyah, ajo nityah, sasvato' yam purano, na hanyate hanyamane sarire." For the soul, there is no birth or death. The soul does not come into being and will not come into being. The soul is unborn, eternal, ever existing, and primeval. The soul is not slain even when the body is slain. In the Vedic scriptures, I have found an immortal sense of stillness, recognizing even through the vicious assaults that my protection remains infinite. Beyond the beyond is our soul, the imperishable atman that cannot be ravaged or tainted by the evils of living. We are each one of us a temple that will once again be resurrected beyond the deep waters of time.

A woman's yoni is sacred. It symbolizes the sacred Earth. Yoni is a Sanskrit word that means "womb, vulva, source, origin, abode, nest, and family." Yoni is the container of all that exists. The Shakti Prana that emerges from her womb nourishes all creation. Yoni is sensitive, fragile, and delicate. Of the manifold assaults on our physical and mental bodies, rape and violation of the yoni is, by far, the most difficult experience we women have had to endure. We recognize that the physical body can be ravished. It is dying every day; it is abused by an artillery of uenvironmental toxins and other living factors that we can't control, yet we weep for its demise. A woman's body is as sacred as the Earth, the ground of the goddess, and all temples combined.

Healing from Our Primordial Trauma

Promise me you'll always remember: You're braver than you believe, and stronger than you seem, and smarter than you think.

Carter Crocker

Primordial fear has accompanied me for most of my life, expressed through disease, despair, fame, success, failure, and endurance. In these pages, I share the lessons I have gleaned from my soul-wrenching life experiences so we can help each other to transmute bitterness, hopelessness, and fear into self-love. Indeed, before we can heal our fears and traumas or forgive each other, we must forgive ourselves, however traumatic, ugly, or painful our experiences are. Let us seal the intent to review our lives and start afresh. We are none of us – neither women nor men – responsible for the manufactured, false reality that has been foisted upon us and our forebears. We are, however, accountable for moving away from all things toxic and tending to the growth and progress of our personal humanity as well as our world's humanity. In the words of Llewellyn Vaughan-Lee, a Sufi practitioner, "In denying the feminine her sacred power and purpose, we have impoverished life on personal and global levels ... We have to realize that when we deny the divine mystery of the feminine, we separate life from its sacred core, from the matrix that nourishes all creation. We cut ourselves from the source that alone can heal, nourish, and transform." To restore the masculine anima, men must relinquish their false authority over the Shakti force and restore the Shiva force as their primal identity.

Though deeply personal and unique, the process of healing our fears and hurts is also remarkably similar whether we have been the victim or the perpetrator of a wound (and we have all been both). Regardless of the circumstances, in order to truly heal, we must go deep within to root out our false beliefs and ancestral baggage, find the grace and strength to forgive both ourselves and others, and cultivate faith in our higher Self — our undying soul — and the divinity that exists within us all.

I continually find consolation in the truth of our vast human nature. My body, when perishing, would seek refuge in my mind. When my mind became forlorn, I sought refuge in the vastness of my spirit. Yet, as I reflected on my long years of treading the dark waters, I recognized the experience of being raped and violated forced me to once more delve into my maternal history, my under bearings as a woman. There is always an important lesson to be gleaned from the grime. Having lost my womb in my adolescent years, and now with the present reality of being violated as a woman, I am continually reminded of the deep violations endured by our female ancestors. Again and again, I am made aware of the importance of safeguarding my sexual sanctity and the feminine sanctuary that I had kept sanguine for more than 50 years. The extreme realities of this situation found me processing the hurt, pain, and suffering I felt without falling prey to the counter-productive role of becoming a victim — a predictable role that immigrants and minorities are often drawn into playing in our huge cultural mix.

My tsunami took years to recede and recover from. I felt as if I was held hostage in open quarters: a claustrophobic reality where breath, stamina, and endurance dissipated, time pulsating in between unrelenting toxic episodes that left me dumbfounded, gasping for air, unable to assimilate what was happening. The trauma was deep. For a long time, I was confused and disoriented by the sheer force of this faceless onslaught. Then, I went through a longer phase of being outraged at the utter injustice of it all. How could my beautiful life be usurped by such violence? I had dedicated so, so many years to the ancestral work, the austere monastic journey, and cleansing past karmas. Ironically, my intelligence, the call for justice, and endless scrutiny of my situation became the emotional strands that got frayed and entangled as I delved deeper into despair. I lived like a ghost of someone I once knew, every once-fluent moment feeling stilted and programmed. The trove of gems did finally begin to show itself. The profoundly valuable experiences from my past were re-invoking major traumas from my early life. Eventually, the rusted chest of maternal and paternal ancestral memories I had surreptitiously stored came unhinged.

I might never have uncovered this chest had it not been for the onslaught upon my precious body. A lost key. A fettering swamp of hidden shame, a long time ago, seemingly forgotten. But traumas do not forget. They have a prodigious memory; the longer they are made invisible and pushed down to fester, the more tenacious their grip. With small leaps of daring, I began to delve into that dank ancestral corridor to deracinate, once and for all, a clump of rotted memories. New life. Fresh air. Is it that we grow old too soon and find wisdom too late? Or was it the simple act of allowing the impossible to expose itself? I wish that I could have breathed better through it. Breath, prana — the eternal inner witness — is our constant companion. I began to slip into a worn but wiser self. As Jalal ad-Din Muhammad Rumi puts it, "The lion who breaks the enemies' rank is a minor hero compared to the lion who overcomes himself."

In my understory, I would once again have to face the fierce army of my ancestors. Typically, their trauma response would be to dig in their heels, assert their warrior pose, and unleash a litany of resentment, blame, judgment, and grudges. At the same time, I suffered yet another health crisis ensuing from the long-term effects of the uranium poisoning. Oh, the timing; my heart felt like a punching bag. Medical intervention was necessary. While resting in the serene temple of the post-operation haze, I found roots beyond roots in the underlying layers of traumas that needed to be hauled out and cleared. Having been drugged and raped, my body was not only recording a one-time, two-time, three-time incident but an all-time epic experience funneled through the ancestral fear memories stored in my under-soul. I was forced to reflect on millions of moments where ancestral habituations had torn my spirit. I had been trained to please instead of speaking my truth. Endured immense sacrifices just to avoid ire and disapproval. The idea that it was my duty to carry dead branches like karmas belonging to others and the desire to appease those who devalued me roiled in my gut. I recognized that slipshod boundaries had allowed the backstabbers to sup at my table while I fawned at them to keep the peace. I reflected on the constant support I gave so many when vitality reigned and the disappearance of many more when health and energy waned, the onrushing need to lend a helping hand to others even when I desperately needed a kind touch upon my tired soul. The gnawing urge to downplay the wisdom of my birth tradition simply because unawakened souls from both sophisticated and unsophisticated communities tended to get chafed by its truths. Suffocating through my family's bypassing of our shared inheritance of grief and traumas, each one of us either dousing it or dressing it up. Or always being the oak in situations where the broken, self-occupied thrived. Not to mention the remarkable stream of poor choices I've made at critical junctures in my life. It took a host of brutal interventions to excavate my past traumas. My discovery: the adversaries were found in ancestral trauma habituations pushing me from within. Free, at last? I hesitate to say. But I know that no force, however epic, no person, however powerful, no evil, however tenacious, can ever victimize me again. That rusted chest has been opened, and its plethora of skeletal fear-experiences exposed to the light.

I forgave myself for clamping on so long to deep shame, the violation of it all, and for the repugnancy I felt when in proximity to men who bore a resemblance to those who attacked me. For a time, I carried that soul-searing angst from being so brutally violated. It is important that we allow time and space to mourn the violations of our bodies. It is also equally important to let go and allow spirit to inform our horrific experience by remembering, despite what you do not know, that you're a grand shaktified spirit who remains untouched by your mortal experiences. I had to take many pauses to remind myself that my purpose in this life was sanctified at birth and that such a purpose required me to walk through darkness after darkness for the simple reason that I carried the brilliant, undying light that vanquishes the dark with its piercing beams. I have since released my hull-damaged body into the ever-forgiving ocean of my flawless spirit. I continue to walk tall in my Divine Feminine purpose.

We have all experienced abuse of some kind. Whatever the depth and form of abuse, by whatever gender it was inflicted, we are not responsible for the brokenness that caused it. We are, however, responsible for churning it out of our lives. It is part of human karma to keep clearing the detritus. We are forced at times to dive underneath the dross to find the gems. Once the lesson is received, we can ascend to a clear surface. However challenging our life's course, our ultimate responsibility lies in finding cohesion between the two primeval energies. We must start to work together as we are divinely ordained to do — to unify the generative and constructive, the yin and yang, the awen, as we nourish the pathway to wellness, prosperity, and consciousness. Enjoined, we imprint unity, harmony, authenticity, beauty, integrity, justice, and love upon the soul of Earth.

Sacral Mudra — Releasing Primordial Fear through the Sacrum

Deep-rooted fears congregate in the sacral area of the body. Sacral Mudra practice is an excellent practice for all genders to relieve tension in the muladhara chakra area, which lies at the sacral root of the body. Primordial fear of the feminine and masculine are linked to the health of the sexual organs, pelvic area, groin, and sacrum. Prana movement during Sacral Mudra practice strengthens the apana vayu – downward flowing air in the body – aiding cellular memory of the hammock of muscles in the perineum between the anus and genital organs. Sacral Mudra, also known as Muladhara Mudra, releases congealed fears that have been compressed in the body's subtle layers between the muladhara and svadisthana chakras. This practice also relieves pain and anxiety, intestinal spasms, coldness, anxiety, and stress relating to fearfulness and forgetfulness. In men, this mudra helps to condition a balanced sense of virility and fortifies bladder function. In women, it has the added benefit of relieving menstrual cramping and helps to cleanse the body and release menstrual blood in a timely way. It is also a very good practice for women in menopause since it replenishes Shakti Prana.

The Practice: Sacral Mudra – Releasing Primordial Fear through the Sacrum

This practice comprises two hand postures, as follows.

- Sit in a comfortable position, facing south, the direction that represents the Muladhara chakra, the Earth element.
- At chest level, hold your hand up with fingers stretched and palms facing each other.
- Join the tips of the little finger with the tips of your thumbs, connecting the hands by allowing the joint tips to touch.
- Next, connect the tips of the outstretched ring finger, forming an upward-pointing triangle
- Hold this position for 5 minutes or so.

- Now, release the little fingers from the thumb but keep them touching each other as you lift them to form that upward triangle.
- Lower the connecting tips of the ring fingers to touch the tips of the thumbs.
- Hold this posture for 5 minutes or so before releasing your hands.
- Rest your hands in your lap and continue to breathe mindfully.

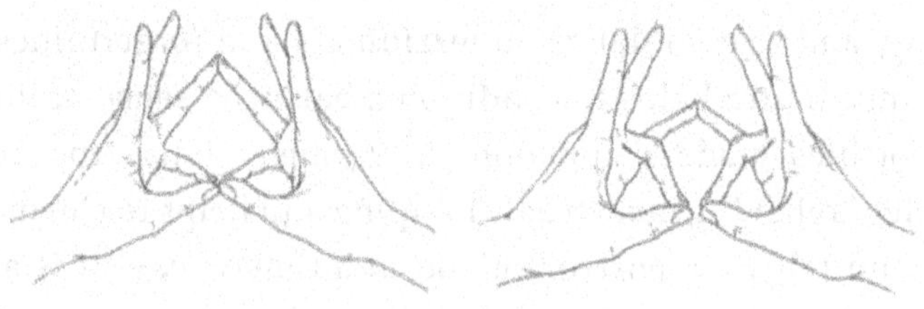

Fig. 3a & 3b Sacral Mudra

Chapter 7

Shakti's Cellular Anatomy

The Sun and Earth would perish if the Moon stopped kissing them.

Shakti's cellular anatomy holds the long-sought-after secret of the primordial imprint that birthed the universe into existence. This unique anatomy is bequeathed to and by women alone; it is they who possess the intrinsic feminine power, giving birth to the world of humans. At the same time, they carry the onerous weight of its burdens, for while the gift of Shakti's power of creation is immense, so too is its power of destruction when destabilized within the body and the world. Shakti's cellular anatomy contains the cosmic key to health – yet even this microscopic inner sanctum is desecrated by patriarchal scientific overreach. The good news is that we can rebuff intrusive health sciences and unlearn unnatural, inflexible approaches by getting actively involved in the process of healing our diseases.

This is a story of how life is created, sustained, and designed to thrive by Shakti cellular memory. This is also a story of what happens when Shakti cellular memory becomes dysfunctional, tipping our body and world from Shakti cellular physiology to Shakti cellular pathology. Denigration and destruction of this cellular memory within our bodies and the Earth herself has severely impacted its majestic function within women, trickling down to disrupt the functioning of our entire world. The indigenous way of nature's healing drew richly and holistically from the ancestral roots of the Earth, which is in direct contrast to the present model of scientific knowledge largely characterized by fragmentation and reductionism. Severing women from their innate Shakti power, men from their Shiva prowess, and species from their natural habitat, the phenomenon called modern medical science has much to answer for. However, before we delve into the deep end of the misunderstandings and harm put upon the Shakti anatomy, we'll explore its multidimensional physiological and psychological nature.

Let us examine Shakti power through the genesis story of its cellular anatomy. Shakti's energy exists in each living thing, although only females carry its awakened form. This primeval energy creates and recreates the world, the material universe as we know it. In women, this power is magnified by the unique component of sentiency — or, shall we say, the cellular memory that generates and safeguards maternal consciousness. Shakti cellular memory is designed to be transported in and through mitochondrial DNA. What happens in embryonic development is one of nature's most potent mysteries, unfolding deep in the mother's body. My lifelong investigation of the lost Vedic sciences of the Shakti cellular anatomy gives us more than a glimpse of it; indeed, it provides a wide-open gateway into the spectacular nature of the Shakti force. At a physiological level, like the host cells themselves, Shakti energy functions cooperatively within the body's cells, tissues, and organs to enable and repair physiology, immunity, reproduction, cognition, and memory. In fact, Shakti's cellular memory is embedded in every cell and atom of the body; it is responsible for the transmission and metamorphosis of maternal and paternal memory — short-term, long-term, and empirical memory from past lives stored in subtle forms in the mitochondrial DNA. Much more than this, it forms and sustains the foundation of all life.

At this critical juncture in our human story, the opportunity to gain and deepen our understanding of Shakti anatomy and its cellular function is imperative. It is central to our present revolution for change and the dire need to work for a humane world through individual and collective enlightenment. In the science of Shakti cellular anatomy, we learn how Shakti energy in every woman is irretrievably linked to the moon through the lunar life force that guards, protects, and regenerates a woman's reproductive cellular anatomy and its sacred processes. This lunar life energy infuses and nourishes Shakti Prana — that oxygen-rich, life-generating breath that circulates the womb and reproductive area of a woman's body to sustain Shakti's memory of creation. This maternal, life-sustaining prana operates in every atom in the universe and is the means by which life is created and reborn in perpetuity. A woman's monthly cycle is the primary cyclical conduit through which the lunar energies revitalize and cleanse the entourage of shaktified cells and vital tissue memory within her. Her body is a rhythmic thing, dancing to the call and response of the moon, each lunar turn performing a specific miraculous feat. The rising moon heralds the perfect timing for a woman's menstrual cycle. During the new moon, a woman's cellular body naturally opens to the gravitational pull of lunar waves. Her menses flow back to Earth, sloughing the womb's reproductive lining as lunar intelligence regenerates a new layer, freshening Shakti's cellular anatomy and fortifying equanimity in the mitochondrial assemblage. Such is one reason why matrilineal traditions encouraged a woman to retreat into a period of self-claiming solitude during her menstrual flow: to conserve her feminine powers responsible for sustaining sentiency, harmony, and nourishment of life on Earth.

Red Bindu — the Magnetic Umbilicus

A significant role of Shakti's mitochondria is the metamorphosis of a woman's menstrual event from its potential life-bearing state as the endometrial lining into the life-generating energy that conceives and produces new life and birth. Empowered by lunar matter, energy, and vibration, mitochondria are controlled by the moon within and without. Menstrual blood carries Shakti's cosmic DNA. This menstrual phenomenon is attributed to the workings of the Red Bindu, energetically located within the root chakra where Kundalini rests. I uncovered this previously defunct principle while perusing an ancient image of the Red Bindu in a humble Shakti Devi shrine in North India. Contemplating its mystery, I remembered a Sanskrit aphorism I had gleaned earlier in a Skakta tantra text. The sutra conveyed that Muladhara chakra — also called the seat of the "Red Bindu" or subtle drop — is where the Kundalini awakening begins. It is the resting point from which Shakti commences the journey that creates and recreates manifestation. Her destination is to unite with Shiva in the "white bindu," or Sahasrara chakra. As my thoughts lighted on the image, I came to understand that the Red Bindu acts as a magnetic lodestone, drawing in the moon's energy to revitalize the womb. For this reason, the blood vessels within a woman's vulva, encompassed by the Red Bindu within the root chakra, are thus imbued with the magnetic energies of the moon as they flow through the vulva to the womb. The undulating rhythmic force of the Red Bindu prods the discharge of her uterine lining at the appropriate cyclical time. The Red Bindu works in tandem with Shakti Prana, the revolving life force that encircles a woman's womb. Shakti Prana resides in the two lower chakras located around the perineum and sacrum. Manifesting as procreative energy, this prana safeguards the Shakti cellular anatomy, nourishing genitals, womb, and belly. Shakti Prana maintains a fragile balance within the reproductive body. When disturbed, it has long-term effects on the mitochondria, negatively influencing the maternal bedrock of all aspects of life. While the sun's absorption of energies from the Earth helps to loosen the womb's lining, the rhythmic lunar pulsation of the Red Bindu enables the discharge of her endometrium during the appropriate new moon phase. The miraculous, dynamic Shakti medley, which I refer to as the "prana-bindu-menstrual" operation, also regulates her hormonal levels, naturally programming them to perfect reset. The moon's energies are symbiotic with a woman's blood in the same way a magnetic field responds to a lodestone. The process modern medical science refers to as menses fails to encompass the far-reaching magic and miracle of a woman's blood.

In Vedic epistemology, we perceive the Red Bindu as the "cosmic seed" of the goddess Shakti. Her cosmic yoni is the primordial cradle from which all creation emerged. She infuses her power into the womb of every female, willing her with her most potent Shakti medicine to nurture, nourish, and heal. From the vast tomes of Vedic narrative, we surmise that a woman's sanctity can be gleaned through the Sanskrit synonym for yoni, *bhaga,* which translates as "the one who contains opulent gifts of power, wealth, sustenance, fame, and beauty." In other words, the yoni is a woman's opening to the inner wealth of sensuality and sentiency and, by extension, the awakening of these conscious endowments in the world. Infused by Shakti Prana and specific mitochondrial cells, the yoni behaves like a lotus flower — guided by the oscillating vibrations of the moon, naturally opening its petals to allow the monthly flow of the menstrual cycle during the new moon phase, furling them after the menstrual bleeding is over, then opening the sacred blossom again during the full moon to enhance sexuality, ovulation, and fulfillment. At the end of each day, the yoni performs an almost imperceptible closure of its petals. Understanding the cosmic nature of your yoni helps you reclaim your feminine authority and heal old scars and ancestral wounds of the heart, womb, and vulva while transforming your relationship with your own feminine cosmic body into a thing of wisdom and beauty.

A woman's Shakti can give life, create art, and nourish life to maintain a state of equanimity. This axial female force teaches us how to care for our body through nourishing sexuality, respecting our emotions, safeguarding intuition, and honoring spirit. The Shakti anatomy's profound physiological, psychic, and spiritual power cannot be overstated. Shakti is the luminous force that gives rise to our maternal authority —

reproducing life, nourishing nature's food, inspiring the universe's continually changing rhythms, and sustaining all living species on Earth through mitochondria. This feminine energy liberates the musical throb of the heartbeat. It quickens the ultimate nectar of life carried in the womb.

The moon significantly influences a woman's biorhythms and her cellular body, mind, and spirit, which are intricately connected to lunar cycles. The phenomenal role of a woman's Shakti anatomy is revealed from the menstrual cycle to ovulation and back again. Primordial matter, once cleansed and revived during menstruation, is renewed into immunity-producing sap for the making of life. Controlled by the force of Shakti Prana, eggs find generative ground to grow and flourish in the womb during the moon's waxing cycle between menstruation and ovulation. The ovum is named *artava* from the Sanskrit root *rtu*, meaning "season." Rtu also implies "ritual," suggesting that the rhythm of life comes from the ritual dance of the seasons and, in particular, the lunar season. Living in accord with the lunar rhythms maintains ancestral knowledge of the Shakti anatomy. This way of being, honoring the cyclical, circular movement of time, keeps the vibrant memory of Shakti's mysterious force alive. In the distant past, women had an intimate connection to their Shakti anatomy as they moved from day to day in rhythm with the lunar wheel.

I tell the story of Shakti's cellular anatomy so that we can all delve into the celestial microcosm of our sacred feminine body, understanding our relationship to the Mother, to the moon. Knowing that both the sun and Earth would perish if the moon stopped kissing them, so too, our womb spaces, the hallowed sphere that longs for the moon's caress to bring forth love, laughter, and life on Earth. We are learning the cosmic way in which her intelligence informs the physiological, psychological, and spiritual function of each atom, cell, and tissue in our body. A woman's womb space holds her centrifugal force, which vibrationally generates information throughout her organism – this is the central station for Shakti Prana that systematically distributes oxygen, antioxidants, and all necessary nutrients.

The mitochondrial assemblage consists of many components, all codified with the Shakti force and ferried into the ovum-sperm merger at the time of conception. The mitochondria assemblage is the powerhouse for cellular respiration, or what I'd call the lunar nourishing-sentiency energy production. Through an impeccable internal process, they sort, break down, allocate, and ration nutrients after transforming chemical energy from food in the cell to the form of lunar resonant vibrations usable by the host cell for specific cellular nourishment. Superficially perceived as microscopic factories or assembly lines, these delicate organelles are the worker bees of the grand maternal Lalita, guardian of the moon. Science explains the multidimensional, mysterious operation of these shaktified mitochondria as the process of oxidative phosphorylation to produce energy in the form of a substance called adenosine triphosphate (ATP), which can then be used by the cell whenever energy is required; in other words, the mundane act of converting raw materials like food and oxygen into energy. However, science has yet to scratch the surface of the mitochondria's true identity: that is to say, its physiological, psychological, and spiritual functions.

Scientists hypothesize that mitochondria evolved from the first multi-cellular organisms, called eukaryotes. According to scientific theory, the ancestral eukaryotic cell was originally an aerobic organism in which oxygen could not be used for energy production and instead acted as a poison. However, during an endosymbiotic process with the oxygen-metabolizing a-proteobacteria, the ancestral eukaryote acquired the capacity to use oxygen for energy production through oxidative phosphorylation. As fascinating as this is, it barely touches the tip of mitochondria's vast reality. In truth, the origin of mitochondria goes back light years to the abode of the moon, controlled by her lunar Shakti powers, cycles, rhythm, and vibration. Mitochondria abide by Lalita's lunar laws and are sustained by her cyclical rhythms. The subtle forces of Shakti Prana are downloaded from the sperm and egg during conception. A woman is most fertile during ovulation, when sperm may encounter an egg as it swims through a fallopian tube. In Shakti terms, this is the full moon phase. At fertilization, the paternal mitochondria and mitochondrial DNA (mtDNA) are rapidly degraded early in embryogenesis; thus, only the maternal mtDNA is transported to the descendant. Sperm-derived paternal mitochondria enter the oocyte cytoplasm upon fertilization but dissolve during early embryogenesis. While the sperm provides no mitochondria to the fertilized egg, it is designed with a streamlined tail to propel itself toward its Shiva-destined purpose of unifying with the egg. Once arrived, it unpacks its sac of genetic information and enzymatic proteins into the egg cell. A small quantity of mitochondria in its mid-piece gives the determined sperm the power to wag its tail and swim toward the egg. In this highly competitive journey, the sperm's ability to penetrate the egg is further impeded by a thick covering coating the egg's plasma membrane known as the zona pellucida. Acting as the shaktified grandmother, the zona pellucida is there to mediate the first meeting of the sperm and egg and to ensure only one sperm can fertilize the egg. The sperm thus delivers the necessary paternal Shiva elements to the waiting egg. The egg is fairly immobilized in the early stage of fertilization. She requires the determined force of the Shiva energy and delivery to support and propel her into her procreative mode. The egg contains thousands of mitochondria that it passes to the developing embryo. The entire fertilization process, like the creation and preservation of life on Earth, is controlled by Luna, likewise known as Lalita, Tungi, Cap, Yoreh, Maan, Mwezi, Bulan, or Marama: the forgotten names given to the one and only Mother Moon. A woman's womb space is the physical locale that is cosmically programmed to communicate with Shakti's powerhouse in the moon.

When balanced, the lunar-propelled Shakti endows the mitochondrial DNA with the necessary nutrient codes to process, transform, and maintain the wholesome life force. Our tissues are composed of cells and memories brought to life by mitochondria. We are programmed to remember their preordained functions, just as the food we eat 'remembers' its structure and purpose and conveys that information to our bodies. Each tissue layer of the body carries significant memory of its cosmic and practical functions. Once this memory is awakened, the tissue itself remembers what it needs to do to keep the body healthy and how to do it. When the tissue memory is kept in good order, the tissue continues to thrive within its self-generating healing force to maintain the vibrancy of its functional memory. Memory, energy, and healing seamlessly cooperate unless and until their cadence is interrupted or becomes erratic. Properly nourishing our tissues with wholesome foods, activities, inspiration, thoughts, and contemplation strengthens cellular memory and awakens personal awareness. Being faithful to our bodies — by the choices we make, how we relate to our inner nature and the Earth, how we breathe and listen, how we contribute to the sacred field of life, how we negotiate difficult circumstances, and how we forge untiring efforts to keep the balance — is key to healing our physical, psychological, and spiritual disorders. In periodically directing the body to take pause and mind stillness, we hone internal focus saturated in consciousness.

When unbalanced, disrupted, or violated, Shakti cellular anatomy produces disease, which is simply a matter of trauma in our vital tissues. When our cellular memory becomes blunted, tissues begin to forget their function. In my purview, all diseases, directly or indirectly, have their root in the mitochondria. The mitochondria are highly sensitized; their state of wellness depends primarily on the balance we maintain with the Earth and moon. Therefore, they are keenly susceptible to damage, which, in turn, contributes to the development of mitochondrial dysfunction. The modern onslaught of unnatural therapies, mechanized technologies, scientific interventions, and genetic modifications can and do vitiate our vital tissue memories and good health. Thomas Berry puts it this way: "If in the excitement of a secular technology reverence for the Earth has diminished in the past, especially in the Western world, humans now experience a sudden shock at the devastation they have wrought on their own habitation." Any process that runs counter to Earth's intelligence and her innate cyclical science impairs a person's health and the world's well-being. Modern medicine and pharmacology have done their share, however unwittingly, to thwart the wisdom-generating flow of human sentience.

The beating heart, our most sensitive and sentient organ, is usually among the first to be adversely affected by the derangement of the "molecular mechanism" in the mitochondrial DNA. These mutations are known to contribute to the development and progression of heart disease through the acquisition of maternally inherited essential hypertension and coronary heart disease. New medical research is discovering that mitochondria-mediated coronary heart disease is caused by mutations in the mitochondria that encode structural mitochondrial proteins and mitochondrial transfer RNA. This data shows the role of mitochondrial mutations in Brugada syndrome and ischemic stroke, previously attributed to nuclear gene mutations. In the cellular science of Shakti anatomy, the so-called molecular mechanisms of mitochondria are, in actuality, the lunar centripetal force in the mitochondria. When out of sync with lunar force, the maternally generated molecular structure begins to block the infusion of Shakti Prana, disrupting the moon's cyclical vibrations that resonate within the cells. As a result, a sort of cellular hypoxia and chuffing of oxygen and antioxidant levels in the cells occur. Let me quote the scientific view on this topic as expressed by a host of medical scientists in a recent article in the *International Journal of Molecular Sciences*: "The mitochondria produce ATP (adenosine triphosphate) and harmful ROS (reactive oxygen species) as by-products, which are normally effectively neutralized by antioxidants. However, mutated mitochondrial genes unbalance cellular respiration and energy production, leading to extreme ROS production, oxidative damage and mitochondria dysfunction, further triggering cellular damage, apoptosis and cell death."

The quantum rise of reproductive disorders in both women and men is likewise directly caused by the dysfunction of Shakti Prana within the body and is exacerbated by scientific and medical interventions that fail to recognize the role of Shakti energy via the mitochondrial DNA. Polycystic Ovary Syndrome (PCOS), for example, highlights the great mystery of the age-old Shakti-gone-wrong burdens we have programmed women to endure. PCOS remains the most common female reproductive endocrine disorder; global prevalence is estimated to affect 15–20 percent of reproductive-aged women. In a recent evaluation of the role of the mitochondrial genome in PCOS, two of the most influential factors found to contribute to the development of PCOS are genetics and oxidative stress. Women suffering from PCOS and other forms of ovarian pathology are predisposed to a multitude of conditions, including Type 2 diabetes mellitus, cardiovascular disease, infertility, hair loss, metabolic syndrome, and, in later years, endometrial cancer. Conditions that put the mitochondria under undue strain, such as exposure to high levels of free radicals, deplete the womb's circulatory breath force, Shakti Prana. This condition is only one drop in an ocean of Shakti reproductive degradation that impacts the entire world of the living.

Ultimately, we can restore health even from the most belligerent of diseases by aligning our lives once again with the lunar rhythms. What will it take to interest the sciences to seek out the mystery of the lunar sky, to learn Shakti's law and her multidimensional operation in the mitochondria? We would necessarily approach disease in a woman's body from an entirely different eyepiece than we use for disease in a man's body simply because women's bodies host Shakti Prana and men's don't.

The Tipping Point

For thousands of years in ancient India, Asia, Africa, and Europe, societies built their spiritual beliefs and practices around the goddess and lunar tradition. As a result, these civilizations maintained good health and a harmonious existence with each other and the Earth. Her legends were a repository of human experience and wisdom. This archetypal knowledge facilitated a shared sense of communal spirit with nature and gentle relations among the genders. It established indigenous systems of knowledge that were largely ecological. Miraculously, this knowledge is still available to us through the ancient science of Vedas. Its ancient healers were impeccable in their understanding of health as a whole organism. They knew which of nature's foods, herbs, or minerals spoke to which tissue, the length of the required conversation, the depth of the vibration, the subtlety of the lunar or solar rhythm, and the timing for applying nature's remedy to each condition. The basic intent of these remedies was to instigate tissue memory so that within a determined length of time – depending on the condition and metabolic nature of the person – the tissue awakened once more, stirring into sentiency. As a result, the self-generating intelligence within the cellular memory took over and rectified disorders while resetting its internal harmonic rhythm, at which point the remedy would have served its purpose. As these ancient practitioners knew (and modern pharmaceutical science does not), no one should take any medicine for long periods of time.

We have long since abandoned these harmonious practices and passed the tipping point of good health and wholesome living. With a plethora of new diseases stemming from the derangement of the Earth's resources and the enduring havoc wrought upon her, we continue to block the refueling channels of her vast sentient field and clog them with prescription medications. Medical science, recognizing that disease is essentially caused by abnormal functioning of the cells, has set out to redesign and reconfigure the body's cellular system to cure conditions such as cardiac arrest, immune deficiency, Alzheimer's, dementia, AIDS, lung cancer, kidney failure, and arthritis. In manipulating and weaponizing cells and organisms in their attempts to correct cellular malfunction, they further impair cellular sentiency. Let us take a reluctant peek into the ominous underworld of science's "progress" with human cellular anatomy.

Frequently cited studies have placed the number of deaths from medical errors or neglect as the third leading cause of death, right behind cancer and cardiovascular disease — and we pay dearly for this catastrophe. Each drug costs an average of 3 billion dollars to develop, with more than 22 billion dollars spent annually by pharmaceutical companies to market their drugs to medical institutions. The deluge of medical misinformation and dangerous interventions relative to reproductive conditions alone is staggering. The cluster of reproductive health diseases for men and women is interconnected, presenting a huge problem for the world population.

Data shows our mounting reproductive health conditions are largely driven by a common cause: the presence of hormone-altering chemicals (a.k.a., endocrine-disrupting chemicals, or EDCs) in our world. EDCs are human-made chemicals designed to mimic, block, or interfere with the body's hormones, which are part of the endocrine system. These ominous chemicals can be found in hormonally manipulated foods such as dairy and red meats, food contact materials such as plastic wraps, and in brominated flame retardants used predominantly in clothing, electronics, and furniture. In short, EDCs are the by-products of the patriarchal industrial complex and are all around us. Modern lives are riven with EDCs associated with a wide array of mounting health issues; in addition to causing reproductive issues, endocrine disruption is also a culprit in rising rates of autoimmune disorders and the growing epidemic of obesity, metabolic syndrome, heart disease, stroke, and diabetes.

Studies indicate an alarming annual rate of increase in miscarriage and gestational surrogacy. The total fertility rate worldwide is dropping almost at the same rate as declining sperm counts — by 50 percent in as many years. Testosterone levels are decreasing while the rate of testicular cancer and prevalence of erectile dysfunction increases. EDCs, like all toxic chemicals in our food, water, and air, decrease the inflow of prana, life-generating breath, into the body. They also directly impact Shakti Prana, which refuels Shakti cellular memory and distributes oxygen, antioxidants, and all nutrients necessary to maintain health throughout the body.

As medical science dives deeper into the labyrinth of manipulating and controlling women's reproduction, the self-generating lunar operations within our feminine bodies that nourish the health of Shakti cellular memory become more endangered. I witnessed the progressive thrust of Shakti cellular pathology while helping women heal from a barrage of reproductive diseases. One such example is the many women suffering from endometriosis, a disorder where endometrial tissue appears outside the uterus, causing pain during menstruation. I learned that approximately one in twenty American women are diagnosed with endometriosis, yet many more remain undiagnosed. This is due to the stigma that period pain is expected and tolerable when it is actually debilitating for many endometriosis patients.

Prescription medication represents another threat to Shakti cellular memory. According to the Center for Disease Control and Prevention, more than 90 percent of pregnant and lactating women in the US are on at least one medication. Most American pregnant women are taking pharmaceuticals that have not been tested on their bodies; therefore, they do not know the impact of those drugs on their bodies or their babies' bodies. Moreover, these medications are often over- and wrongly prescribed. For example, at least 65 percent of what is diagnosed and treated as fibrocystic breast disease is actually normal changes in the fatty and connective breast tissues.

Responding to the innate yearning to become a mother, perhaps the most shaktified experience of being and becoming a woman, many women seek medical assistance to realize their maternal dream. This natural need, however compassionate, does not indemnify the harm and violence that the broad constellation of new reproductive technologies (NRTs) engender. NRTs operate on a flawed premise: that a man's seed creates the fetus while a woman's body is just the container. While these procedures have undoubtedly helped many women longing to become mothers, this approach also interferes with the cosmic transformation of Shakti Prana that binds the sacred connection between a mother and her fetus. NRTs include contraception, abortion, antenatal testing, and conceptive technologies such as in vitro fertilization-embryo transfer (IVF-ET), gamete intra-fallopian transfer (GIFT), zygote intra-fallopian transfer (ZIFT), pronuclear stage tubal transfer (PROST), tubal embryo transfer (TET), and frozen embryo transfer induction, along with birth technologies such as planned C-sections, epidurals, and surrogacy. These treatments disrupt the natural biology of the reproductive organism. They shut down the organic, self-generating operations of the intelligent system, disrupting the lunar-propelled Shakti Prana and alienating cellular function. These procedures create imbalances in the reproductive tissues, blocking lunar sustenance and causing trauma in our energy-starved cells. Such interventions create endemic violence in the body, since these procedures go against the body's cyclical, lunar, and biological rhythms, causing cellular conflict.

Women's reproduction is much more than giving birth to new life; the entire womb space is guarded, lit, nourished, informed, and sustained by the many phases of Mother Moon. Shakti Prana, which courses through the womb, is a carrier of lunar vibration, which physically and energetically feeds our reproductive tissues. Our wombs are lunar sanctuaries. I experience mine as my spiritual center. Perhaps, as we learn to perceive our wombs as instruments of lunar divinity, we may align with and benefit from this deeper education. We cannot blame ourselves for not knowing. We must also forgive most medical science practitioners since they are only trying to help us achieve our much-desired goals. If you have endured any of these processes, you can still heal yourselves and your children abundantly from this understanding. You can set a new course from now on.

Truth be told, it is not only the medical arena where false advertising and misinformation on women's bodies and health are plentiful. Neoliberalist and new age camps are also rife with celebrities, medical professionals, and savvy business types profiteering from women's ignorance and vanity. Cases of cosmetic medical popularization of breast augmentation or implantation are flourishing despite the damaging aftereffects of these procedures. Following reconstruction, these procedures reportedly lead to a host of systemic symptoms such as chronic fatigue, problems with memory, brain fog, joint and muscle pain, hair loss, weight change, anxiety, and depression. Vaginoplasty, another example, is a cosmetic surgical procedure to reconstruct or tighten the vagina. This type of genitoplasty – falsely promising a celestial vagina – is accompanied by risks such as chronic infection, loss of pleasure and sensation, scarring, and ongoing discomfort and pain. Despite all this, if you search the words "vaginal tightening" on e-commerce retailers, you'll find a slew of sprays, gels, shrinking creams, sticks, and toxic pills that claim to provide you with a tight and virginal vagina – manufacturing insecurity and need for yet another emotionally and physically damaging procedure. Ironically, these procedures that are geared to make us more "feminine" are actually violating our sacred femininity.

For all modern science's ingenuity, its far-reaching destructive effects on our bodies and Mother Earth are unimaginable. Each year, to perfect its technology, more than 100 million animals – including rats, mice, frogs, dogs, cats, rabbits, hamsters, guinea pigs, monkeys, fish, and birds – are killed in US laboratories for chemical, drug, and cosmetics testing, medical training, and curiosity-driven experimentation. Eighty percent of the world's surface and groundwater is devastated by chemical pollutants such as pesticides, human and animal drugs, and electronic "E-waste" such as barium, lead, mercury, iron, chromium, copper, and cadmium. It's astounding how much science has progressed and yet how little it has truly accomplished. We can formulate multiple vaccines to control viruses and even weaponize T cells via gene therapy to recognize and kill cancer, yet still, we have gleaned but an iota of Earth's intelligence compared to what the ancient seers knew.

The missed reality in this multi-trillion-dollar circus of modern science is the knowledge of Earth's Shakti anatomy – the cosmic blueprint that can only be read by those who understand her dirt-kissed roots, green stalks, and tender tendrils. This cosmic anatomy, transported through the mitochondria and inherited by all the Earth's species, cannot be narrowed into the restrictive eyepieces of cell biology, genetics, and pathology. Certainly, some scientific explanations of mitochondrial function are accurate: mitochondrial dysfunction is indeed characterized by a loss of efficiency in the electron transport chain and reductions in the synthesis of high-energy molecules such as adenosine-5′-triphosphate (ATP). Damaged cells do spill their DNA and RNA into the cell's interior, where immune sensors detect the molecules as foreign. In response, the immune system produces a type 1 interferon, causing inflammation and autoimmunity. However, this loss of function in the key organelle responsible for cellular energy production and the balance of the life force goes much deeper than mere cellular analysis can follow. The critical source of this crucial organelle's nutrients, nourishment, and equilibrium lies in the story of Shakti Prana and the subtle energetics of lunar-vibration-dependent Shakti anatomy.

In reality, we shall never succeed in redesigning nature. How can we improve upon celestial perfection? It begs for our understanding; it shows us in every nanosecond, every blink of the eye, and through every inspired tendril of the mind that the nobility of science should be centered in the understanding of nature, in reverence to nature, and in the august inquiry of her intelligence. The Earth is packed with complex living organisms that are assemblages of self-contained, self-regulatory units; living atoms invisibly held in symphonic concert by the tendrils of nature's Shakti anatomy. How can we discover the nature of this sentient life by de-sanctifying it? The consciousness-alienating practice of dissecting, weaponizing, fragmentizing, violating, and marauding the body strips away knowledge of the magical human anatomy. The plan to dig deeper into the developmental mechanisms of the female embryo simply promotes violence against maternal consciousness. Violence enacted by science against female organs — womb, embryo, fetus, umbilical cord, and breasts — reinforces the continued and unrelenting erosion of the maternal sentiency inherent in the Shakti principle of life. Now, researchers are delving further into the mired labyrinth in their attempts to create artificial mouse embryos from stem cells — sans the sperm or eggs. Until now, embryonic stem cell lines have been grown in what is basically a mush of crushed mouse embryos that provide an assortment of nutrients and growth factors that can keep human embryonic stem cells from differentiating. With the consolation that their process is becoming more humanized, researchers are now using an innovative bioreactor that can maintain their simulated embryos for longer than any previous models. With this innovative bioreactor as a womb, scientists are now transforming mouse stem cells into organ-filled embryos. While this process exempts the little mouse creatures from being tortured, the heartless methodology remains a potential concern for the trajectory of medical research. It begs the question: are we any closer to recognizing the missed reality of Earth's intelligence and the folly of attempting to replicate it?

The progressive deterioration of the Earth's Shakti anatomy and her life force can be traced to science's disregard for Mother Nature and the unconscious way they flagrantly splinter life. For example, I believe that all viruses originate from impairments to nature's anatomy and cyclical rhythms — dysfunctions caused by modern cartels, military activities, commercially driven enterprises, and scientific research. The proliferation of viruses, emerging and re-emerging in the past 40 years, have grown more tenacious, each with the extraordinary potential to keep sprouting unpredictable variants. Each year, it seems the world must fight to contain yet another novel virus of pandemic proportions. At the end of 2020, SARS-CoV-2 infections were confirmed in approximately 68.4 million people. The original Omicron strain first identified in Botswana and South Africa in November 2021 began to skyrocket to over a million infected in the US only one month later. It then began to spawn sub-variants. More than 30 of Omicron's mutations are on the virus's spike protein, the part that attaches to human cells, and several of those are believed to increase the probability of infection.

Reordering Feminine Lunar Healing Rhythms

I do not believe modern science aims to eradicate knowledge of humanity's cellular memory; however, their less-than-informed approaches have cost the Earth and her creatures dearly, and we must learn to discern between adaptive science and maladaptive science. I support sciences that honor nature's intelligence and conscious life. For too long, the patriarchy has power-mongered and gained at the expense of the human spirit. As part of a myopic patriarchal attitude toward the life force, maladaptive sciences are still staking claim and inheritance over the feminine primordial energies. The longer modern science continues to subsume Shakti's feminine authority and control what little they know about the Shakti anatomy, the deeper the vortex of quicksand into which we are all sinking.

Shakti power is immutable. It is inherently feminine and imbued with the rainbow spectrum of love, light, vivacity, and creativity. It is the oracle whose magnetic pull is engineered by the moon to bring forth prana, the life force. Although we can and do create havoc with its physiological and cellular aspects, this primal energy has a force, a pattern, a cosmic goal, and a secret coding of its own. It cannot be transferred, manipulated, or modified to fit into the dark embodiment of the patriarchal schema.

To reiterate, the impairment of mitochondria within the cells is the fundamental cause of disease. These impairments are fomented by our movement away from natural and lunar rhythms and toward mechanized technologies and unnatural chemicals, therapies, and modifications. To reclaim good health, we must first repair tissue memory, which pristine nature alone can replenish. To achieve this, we must shift our internal conditioning to respond in companionship with Mother Earth.

I Am Shakti is about enjoying a state of non-trauma by relearning our pure, shaktified nature. We are composed of nature, and nature is often in flux, continually changing, growing, repairing, rising, and retreating. Sanskrit gives us a perfect word for our metabolic condition: *dosha*, that which is apt to err. We are a complex, messy thing that, at best, blooms into awareness at junctional times when we are moving in cadence with solarized day, fastened to nuances of the seasons, or affixed by the lunar grace of the night. As Robert Bly evinces, "It is not our job to remain whole. We came to lose our leaves like the trees, and be born again, Drawing up from the great roots." In seeking out necessary knowledge through guidance and self-inquiry about significant ways in which we may strengthen from within and regain our Shiva-Shakti balancing power, we discover that wholesome ways to heal lie within the vast cognate information of the Earth.

Shakti Mudra – Restoring Shakti Cellular Memory

Shakti Mudra is a powerful practice for women to regenerate and restore Shakti Prana, the vital energy of the womb that nourishes cellular memory – that primordial memory which creates life that is deeply embedded within the mitochondria. This is an especially excellent practice in general for all women who are struggling with trauma, fatigue, disappointment, or issues relating to their reproductive health. This mudra brings a glow to a woman's aura and bolsters her sense of femininity and self-esteem. Performed on a daily basis, this practice serves to revive memory of the Shakti cellular memory within and heal the womb space.

Shakti Mudra is a simple practice which I performed on a daily basis for many years following the loss of my womb in my tender years. At age 72, I have experienced no menopausal symptoms. These enduring practices have kept my Shakti Prana strong despite the multiple assaults on my life force. The practice follows.

The Practice: Shakti Mudra – Restoring Shakti Cellular Memory

- Sit in lotus pose or comfortable posture in a quiet space, facing east.
- Bring the palms of your hands together, and then slowly begin to separate them.
- Gently press together the tips of your ring fingers and the tips of your little fingers.
- Bend and rest the thumbs into the palm of your hands and fold the other two fingers over your bent thumbs.
- Breathe deeply into your pelvic cavity and slowly release your breath by tracing your exhalation from the base of the perineum as it circulates through the uterus and belly.
- Maintain Shakti Mudra and methodical breathing for 15 minutes or so.

Fig. 4. Shakti Mudra

Chapter 8

Deshaktification of the Feminine in Religion, Politics, and Society

> *Look around you in any direction you like – art, drama, law, medicine – and you cannot point to any single instance where a woman has created anything that has been passed down to posterity.*
>
> Benito Mussolini

Religion, politics, and society have all served prominent roles in propagating patriarchy while safeguarding its autonomous power. In fact, these forums have been crafted to a large extent by patriarchy and for patriarchy and have provided illimitable shade to foster some of humanity's most debauched events against womankind. Our human history is packed with gory, bloodied, murderous terror.

Medieval patriarchs alone harbored such repugnancy of the feminine that it forged a lasting distrust toward everything associated with women. Witches, demons, herb lore, poisons, and serpents were equated with femininity and used to terrorize and subjugate women religiously, politically, and socially. In essence, anything and everything men could not control was at risk. This inured mindset promoted man-made rules and conditions that fostered wars, tyranny, domestic and sexual violence, male dominance and female subserviency, unhealthy levels of competition and toxic productivity, and a host of other perversions that became codified as law, religious doctrine, and societal norms. Men are terrified of the free-wielding, dynamic feminine power of the Great Mother and her womankind. To maintain their micro-managed state of affairs, they must keep reinforcing the inchoate ideology of the Mother Goddess as archaic and untrustworthy.

As we filter through the world's religions, we find deep and hardened ties to patriarchy throughout. The oldest known spiritual tomes on Earth – Hinduism, followed by Zoroastrianism, Jainism, Buddhism, Confucianism, Taoism, Shintoism, and the Abrahamic faiths of Judaism, Christianity, and Islam – are replete with changes, edits, and entirely rewritten versions that sponsor the counter-intelligent principles of patriarchy. There has been a continuous erosion of authentic spiritual bodies of work and their noble intent over many centuries; passages or entire works relating to feminine rights and their innate gifts have been reworked or altogether removed from scripture. A stream of dualistic, binary thought has sought to redefine the Goddess's encompassing reality, which is unsurprising considering that men write a whopping 90 percent of the world's religious and historical texts.

Christianity's impact on the feminine force has been the most inhumane. As a hierarchal religion, Christianity has razed the sublime feminine stature to dust. According to the Book of Genesis, following the epic story of Adam and Eve eating the forbidden fruit, for which Eve is conveniently blamed, God told Eve that her husband henceforth "shall rule over you." Ephesians clearly states that the husband is the head of the wife. The House Codes of the New Testament mandate its hierarchical structure and the subordination of women. Re-scribed countless times over the centuries, each edition further dwindles feminine rights.

Mary of Magdala was one of the earliest followers of Jesus of Nazareth, yet all four canonical gospels marginalized her importance. She was said to be a prostitute, a ruined woman who repented and was saved by Christ's teachings. The Gospel of Luke discusses her role in Jesus's life and ministry, listing her among "some women who had been healed of evil spirits and infirmities." However, newly discovered Egyptian writings cited Mary Magdalene as a favored follower of Jesus. After Jesus's death, Mary became a prophetic leader within the early Christian movement. In earlier versions of Christian texts, Mary Magdalene was not only portrayed as a trusted companion to Jesus but also served the numinous role of "apostle to the apostles." The New Testament Gospels, written toward the last quarter of the first century CE, acknowledge that women were among Jesus's earliest disciples. It was women who were reported as the first witnesses to the resurrection; central among them is Mary Magdalene. The raw courage of the women who supported Christ unfolded at a time when women were prominent martyrs and suffered from extreme torture and execution by wild animals and paid gladiators. These later versions of the gospels rob Mary of all virtue, impact, and agency.

Judaism gives us another compelling example of how binary thinking in religion paved the way for divisionism and deshaktification. Judaism describes the original concept of the Kaballah's Adam and Eve using the Aramaic term du-partzufin, wherein they were seen as androgynous, reflecting the union of sun and moon, and theosophically, the two divine attributes intertwining as one. The expression used, bi-yhud gamur, also espouses the equality of oneness. It was not meant to be an ontological restructuring of the two separate divine attributes. In the Kabbalistic tradition of Sasporta, scholars of Judaism began to separate the two aspects of this single being for fear that the idea of Adam and Eve embodying balanced feminine and masculine attributes would jeopardize people's faith in the one male God. Thus, they moved to disavow and banish the feminine divine. In his article, "Androgyny and Equality in the Theosophico-Theurgical Kabbalah," Moshe Idel writes, "Know that they were du-partzufin, and when they were operating equally, there was a fear that provided that their rule was equal, lest the people will err and say that there are two powers in heaven."

Looking at Hinduism, we see that entire tomes have been bludgeoned and skewed in translation to reflect the intent of their patriarchal English colonizers. One such example is the chauvinistic recasting of the classical story of Sati, Shiva's first consort who immolated herself to demonstrate her ire at her husband's disrespectful treatment by her father. When these distorted tales were translated back into local languages, many Hindu rulers conspired with their European invaders to uphold the mistranslation. Together, they gave rise to the practice of *Sati,* or self-immolation by widows on the funeral pyres of their husbands, which thrived for centuries. This practice became popularized through the misguided belief in the futility of a woman's existence without her husband. This story has been further skewed and promoted by Bollywood movies. In reality, there was no direct reference or endorsement of Sati as a custom in the Hindu scriptures. The practice of immolation originated in the choices that women themselves made when vicious invaders rampaged their colony or village — to immolate themselves rather than endure the savagery of sexual violence and slavery forced upon them by their captors.

The revised compilation of what was once the *Manusmriti,* translated into a distant stepcousin of the original work, is yet another classic example of deshaktification and the perversion of Hindu spiritual authenticity. The *Manusmriti,* or *The Laws of Manu,* is believed to be the first ancient legal constitution among the multitude of natural laws in Hinduism. This compendium was scribed by several ancient sages who recorded their ideas to help humans foster respect and cooperation with each other and the natural world. Sanatana Dharma, Hinduism's original name, means "universal spirituality"; the term Hinduism is an exonym. Over millennia, Hinduism has garnered the largest treasure trove of knowledge and thus has endured the deepest wounds from its invaders. There is no doubt that the intent of the *Manusmriti* was changed several times during its multiple translations into the English language by British opportunists. It was one of the first Sanskrit texts to be translated into English in 1776 by British philologist, Sir William Jones and was used to reconstruct the Hindu Law code for the East India Company-administered enclaves. Among the countless alterations made by the British to this holy text were the newly implemented rights, or lack of, for women. Following is a priceless excerpt from the British version:

> I will now propound the eternal laws for a husband and his wife who keep to the path of duty, whether they be united or separated. Day and night woman must be kept in dependence by the males (of) their (families), and, if they attach themselves to sensual enjoyments, they must be kept under one's control. Her father protects (her) in childhood, her husband protects (her) in youth, and her sons protect (her) in old age; a woman is never fit for independence. Women must particularly be guarded against evil inclinations, however trifling [they may appear]; for, if they are not guarded, they will bring sorrow on two families. Considering that the highest duty of all castes, even weak husbands (must) strive to guard their wives ... Drinking (spirituous liquor), associating with wicked people, separation from the husband, rambling abroad, sleeping at (unseasonable hours), and dwelling in other men's houses, are the six causes of the ruin of women. Women do not care for beauty, nor is their attention fixed on age; It is enough that he is a man; they give themselves to the handsome and to the ugly.

A further example of the patriarchal colonists' handiwork is the abominable caste system, wherein women's stature was even lower than the untouchable caste. This fabrication arises from an intentional mistranslation of a handful of Hinduism's sacred texts and the insertion of a massive amount of misinformation. The term "caste" was introduced by a British ethnographer in 1901. While conducting a census of India, he consolidated more than three thousand *jatis* – generationally maintained family occupations – into seven castes and attributed the classification to Hinduism. The caste system, as perpetuated and understood today, is an entirely British design. Anthropologist Susan Bayly states, "The institutions and beliefs which are now often described as the elements of traditional caste were only just taking shape as recently as the early 18th Century." "In fact," adds Sanjoy Chakravorty, a Professor of Geography and Global Studies, "it is doubtful that caste had much significance or virulence in society before the British made it India's defining social feature." Dalits are the lowest strata of the manufactured caste system, where caste and gender-based inequality are rampant. Female Dalits are horribly abused, vilified, and defiled by a justice system ill-disposed to their protection. Daily incidents are reported of male hooliganism against Dalit women who are being raped and beaten without recourse. Most cases are ignored or unregistered by the local police force. In a BBC News India article entitled, "Hathras case: Dalit Women are among the most oppressed in the World," India's correspondent, Soutik Biswas, writes, "Dalit women across swathes of rural India have been victims of sexual violence for as long as anyone can remember. Despite a 1989 Law to prevent atrocities against the community, there was no let-up in violence against Dalit women. They continue to be stalked, abused, molested, raped and murdered with impunity."

Many of Hinduism's ancient symbols representing the Goddess force and her auspicious merging of Shiva-Shakti have been blatantly misused to advance the course of patriarchy. Let's take the Svastika, which originated as an auspicious

Hindu symbol for well-being, prosperity, the marriage of sun and moon, the Shiva-Shakti, and the centrifugal force and was adopted by Buddhism, Jainism, and a few Indo-European cultures with the intent of upholding the Shakti's power to cultivate familial peace and communal harmony. When the Nazis co-opted the symbol for their evil misuse, they flagrantly deshaktified its essential meaning and purpose. In its hysterical, patriarchal reign against humanity, the Nazi culture twisted this auspicious symbol to connote prejudice, hatred, and violence, all of which are inimical to Shakti.

Jainism is a disciplined spiritual tradition emphasizing ahimsa — non-violence and non-hurting — yet it also undermines women. Its founder, Tirthankara Mahavira, built a thriving community of female ascetics, and it now boasts more per capita than any other religion, modern or ancient. At Mahavira's death, there was a body of female ascetics two and half times as large as the number of male ascetics. Candanbala, a prominent Jain female ascetic during the time of Mahavira, is said to have led a community of 36,000 female monastic followers. Despite all this, Jainism also has a hierarchical system wherein male ascetics enjoy greater privileges. It systematically denies female monastics the same prestige and recognition as the highest rank of male monastics, the *acharya*.

Despite its beauty, even Buddhism disempowers the feminine to further the patriarchal agenda. There are many reasons why Buddhism is a progressively popularized religion; its focus on compassion is dearly needed in our world today. Buddha, a Hindu prince born during a time of great hierarchal corruption and extensive suffering in India, enforced many radical changes to form his own religious identity. In as much as many great masters of Buddhism are women and would like to see Buddhism transform to embrace gender balance, we see that at its core, Buddhism is patriarchal. Its five major deities take masculine form. In Buddhism and other classical Eastern traditions, women are not considered full and complete entities unto themselves. To attain nirvana or enlightenment, they must first be born in a male body. Buddhism's classical literature is highly androcentric, having little to say about women, and almost none is in women's voices.

Motivated by the fear of feminine power, patriarchs have gone to great lengths to eradicate the very thought of masculine power being shared by Shakti, let alone the idea that Shakti holds the supreme power in the manifested Earth. Exemplifying binary thinking, divisionism, and deshaktification, primal masculine fear has led both intelligent and spiritual men across traditions to make irreparable errors that drive the Divine Feminine force further and further into oblivion. In asserting its egoistic view of power, patriarchy separated the Shiva energy from its source in the Shakti, painting the masculine anima as consciousness, the sky, heaven, father, and Shakti, the feminine animus, as dark, ominous, subjective, Earthly, instinctual, and dangerous. That is to say, they propagate the masculine anima as generating consciousness and the feminine animus as devouring consciousness. Male power-mongering is rooted in palpable insecurity — a self-fulfilling prophecy fueled by fear of the dark, the invisible, and the mysterious unknown.

After several decades of slow but perceptible social evolution, we are experiencing a resurgence of divisive rhetoric and behavior led by the anglophone patriarchy, the Spanish patriarcado, the German patriarchat, the Italian patriarcato, and their many counterparts. Members of this global machine view themselves as the superior gender, ordained by God or biology to be protected and preserved from rampaging feminism. Their invisible mechanism has driven our relationships, culture, politics, education, industry, science, medicine, ecology, technology, and more, affecting every aspect of human existence from the personal to the geopolitical — and most especially the feminine. Fear of the feminine controls them, so they control the feminine through fear. This doubling down of hateful and oppressive agendas is spurred to no small degree by the vast sweep of consciousness awakening in both women and men across the globe, attuned and evolving souls yearning to express their intergalactic patterns of love for peace, unity, and enlightenment. With our concerted effort, this backlash may yet become the final struggles of a dying kakistocracy.

Spiritual advocates are calling this a time of moral decay and, at the same time, of deepening faith. It is a time when we must return to faith, whatever faith we hold firm, holding fast to our belief in Christ, the Buddha, Krishna, Allah, or whatever we hold sacred. Keep in mind, though, that while faith in our ancestral practices is necessary, we need to take a long pause to remind ourselves that we are forever the whole and conscious spirit of the universe, far beyond the reach of any organized religion. Indeed, spirit is our humanity; spirit is Mother Earth, spirit is the Goddess of Creation. Religions that can only be sustained by violence, blood, and blind faith leave us with a perishable reality. All surviving religions, both ancient and modern, have been severely compromised by patriarchal politics and its attempt to control nature, populations, and profits. While you may choose to continue aligning with your religion, keep your inner eyepiece wide open. Invest more time in self-faith than an organized body of belief. Only faith can pull us through the murk and mire; religions do not. Not as they stand. The conviction of your ancestral worth, your faith, your confidence in and surrender to the divine – to whatever name you call the Creator or Creatrix, God or Goddess – that credence, that devout love, is what we need to gather internally, individually, and collectively so that we may restore light in our world. Above all, faith in ourselves, in the inner light, is the cardinal lesson that will help us become better human beings in our shared future. In the religion of humanity, we embrace each other even when we disagree. We are waging a war of the soul and the spirit, warding off centuries-long deceit and corruption. The healed future we can manifest is contingent on how well we assimilate the present reality. Be present. In times of deep trouble, we must dig deep to strengthen our collective sense of kindness and shared empathy. Darkness does easily give way to the light. The efficacy of our individual and collective awareness will determine the distance between darkness and illumination.

Deshaktification of the Feminine in Politics

An examination of world politics reveals how utterly the patriarchy has disenfranchised and subjugated women. Our political systems have worked long and hard to disempower women, from denying bodily autonomy and voting rights to perpetuating the idea that women aren't fit to lead. Indeed, American women were only granted the trifling privilege of having an independent credit card as late as 1974. Desperately trying to hold back the evolutionary storm, patriarchs worldwide are up leveling the common comorbidities of authoritarianism and misogyny. Despite the progress made in women's representation in politics, women still face significant barriers to exercising their sovereignty. In many countries, including the US, women's voices are marginalized, and their concerns are neglected in decision-making processes perpetuated by patriarchal societies, governments, and healthcare systems. At present in the US, we are caught in the politically divisive and polarizing rhetoric of pro-life or pro-choice when, in fact, we are in dire need of turning our attention to pro-sovereignty, pro-health, pro-community, pro-wholesomeness, and pro-earth. Our Shakti nature is deep in spirit and is nourished when we can recalibrate our intention to the essential business of nurturing, promoting, and protecting the Shakti rites and rights. Women's rights around the world are completely compromised. According to a recent report by the World Economic Forum, the US ranks 43rd of 146 countries in women's rights and gender equality. When it comes to asserting sovereignty and undermining women's autonomy, a handful of countries in the Middle East and Africa such as Yemen, Afghanistan, and the Congo rate amongst the lowest for women's rights and education while ranking highest for violence against and abuse of women. Our reproductive rights are continually eviscerated by restrictive family planning measures and criminalization of sexual and reproductive activities. Women around the world are forced into sterilization, nonconsensual abortion, and other forms of reproductive coercion. The progressive rise in physical and emotional violence, sexual exploitation, and rape leads to reproductive trauma, devastation, unintended pregnancies, and sexually transmitted diseases. Countering patriarchal norms and practices is of great necessity if we are to empower women in assuming informed sovereignty over their body, mind, spirit, and family. The most effective way to challenge patriarchal norms and practices is by reclaiming and implementing grassroots and holistic self-care services. This can be facilitated by creating inclusive communities with advocacy groups focused on educating women about their innate feminine power such as the Shakti reproductive medicines embedded in nature and within the turn of the moon, each phase influencing our menstrual cycles, fertility, cleansing, and replenishing time.

Now facing the reality of a more damning obliteration of the Shakti force is the rise of a brand-new form of religion that I call political theology but is more commonly known as neoliberalism. The goals and intentions of this newly up-leveled form of patriarchal warfare are glamorized in such ways that promise heaven while delivering outright hell. According to one study, comprised of several scholarly articles, neoliberalism is used in several senses to describe the generalities of economic theory, development theory, and economic reform policy but is almost never defined. This ideology is aimed at healing society's deep wounds, promising to provide us with new market and economic reforms infused with a moral ethos and aspiring to a holistic worldview. In fact, what its proponents are doing is establishing themselves as arbiters of truth to cloak new autocratic reforms. Their hyper-capitalistic rhetoric assures that their bid to control global economic power is in service of liberating capital accumulation for the greater good and that they will solve a wide range of social, economic, political, and ecological problems by diving ever more deeply into market fundamentalism and economic ambiguity. The pejorative truth? It's all about money and global control, allowing the massive corporations run by ruling patriarchs and the organized networks behind them to keep plundering the planet and exploiting its every life form. This new political theology is eloquently and insidiously refashioning old ideologies of monetarism, neoconservatism, and that rapscallion, globalization, while adding the necessary mechanisms to control future unknowns. It takes unlimited coffers to propagate war and violence, while it requires very little money to facilitate the maternal principles of peace and love.

Deshaktification of the Feminine through War

" ... the constant increase in the number and power of deadly weapons and the readiness of some so called patriots to start a war ... shows itself in the killing of nature and of 'primitive' cultures with never a thought spent on those thus deprived of meaning for their lives; in the colossal conceit of our intellectuals, their beliefs that they know precisely what humanity needs and their relentless efforts to recreate people in their own sorry image . . ."

Paul Feyerabend

Warfare is a deshaktified human response to conflict. Nevertheless, wars and violence have always been considered inevitable in the development of life on sapient Earth. In Earth-based ancient cultures, when wars could not be avoided, they were at least governed by strict moral and spiritual ethos. The *Dhanurveda,* a Sanskrit treatise on warfare, traditionally regarded as an adjunct to the *Yajurveda* (1100–800 BCE), laid out explicit guidelines for what was and was not allowed in warfare. *The Art of War,* an ancient Chinese military treatise, emphasized the importance of a similar moral ethos. As we move ever further from our connection to nature and the principles of Earth intelligence, we witness a breakdown of these moral guidelines coupled with a totalitarian imperative to deshaktify and annihilate the feminine anima. Humanity's escalation of barbarity is at its pinnacle, and Shakti and her divine female energy have been systematically exterminated from its rules of engagement.

Recent military access to technology and more advanced chemical weaponry makes this era the most lethal time to be alive in military history. Since its introduction in World War II, human rights and respect for nature and Earth intelligence have progressively deteriorated. More egregious than the killing fields themselves are the motivations behind their making. Wars mean more money to be spent and more profits to be made. The annual allocation of funds to the US military-industrial complex is approximately 778 billion dollars. As we privatize more defense contractors, arms fairs, and marketing technologies that can be used at home and abroad, we indulge a whole new sector of operatives that profiteer from the making of wars.

This steel-clad warring armor of patriarchal mania against the Earth – the creative, life-sustaining force of the feminine – must be melted down and discarded into the ashes of the past. Wars kill. Wars mutilate the living Shakti forms of compassion, kindness, and nurturance. Wars are inimical to the pristine concept of life on Earth. They injure the Earth, her sentiency, and her balance; they deprive women of their children and children from enjoying a future and rip communities apart from the soul of grace. Soldiers kill each other. They believe they are fighting for justice, and the soldiers they kill also think they're fighting for justice. They return home broken men and women, diminished and uncared for. We are all children of the Shakti force, and in the end, it is the way of Shakti that will make wars obsolete. The soul of grace is what Shakti energy is about: mothering, healing, and making whole. Wars are the most egregious example of how far we have strayed from the soul of grace and exemplify the most cruel, barbaric, and painful lessons that both the feminine and masculine forces encounter. However, in the end, it is the Shakti force that is designed to do the clean-up, patch pieces together, and heal the bloodied, gory mess of it all. It is women who are compelled to do the arduous work to make communities whole again. Wars are metaphors for the profound hatred, the enemy of humanity, which thrives within the patriarchal mind. Wars catapult us all into the tar pits of Shakti's black hole — the air-deprived space we frequently find ourselves in due to patriarchal ignorance, avarice, and hysteria. The patriarchal agenda strives to wipe out the Shakti force from the planet. As the balance of Earth's cosmic energy is pushed asunder, it affects the Shakti force, the fulcrum on which all life hinges. This imbalance is the core cause of humanity's suffering, devastating nature, and, therefore, the well-being of our bodies, minds, spirits, relationships, and societies.

With Shakti on the rise despite these concerted attempts to eradicate her, we are compelled to find a better way forward for humanity. This path calls for a simultaneously new and ancient form of communication: meeting so-called opponents on their own turf and coming to an understanding exempt from war, hatred, cunning, destruction, and inimical tirades. We were not born to agree with or be superior to each other but to create a shared and humane vision. In the massive field of human diversity created by Shakti's divinity, where consciousness development is humanity's numero uno priority, we must find ways to cooperate, thereby growing past our biases, limiting beliefs, and bullshit. In this new age of Shakti, wars will become obsolete. As we rebuild an Earth-intelligent community, we must set aside our egos and use every possible means to create mutual understanding for our common welfare despite opposing views.

Deshaktification of the Feminine in Culture and Society

The oppressive hand of the patriarchy has weighed heavily on women in culture and society, where we have been silenced, belittled, abused, and deprived of opportunity throughout history and the world. To paraphrase George Eliot, the Victorian novelist and radical free-thinker (née Marian Evans), I aspire to give no more than a faithful account of humanity and events as they have mirrored themselves in my own mind.

Men have made an art and science of silencing women. We have been violently subdued, discredited, co-opted, denied access to public spaces, platforms, and publications, and both literally and figuratively bound and corseted in the name of propriety (perhaps the most treacherous form of silencing in that it incentivized other women to become complicit in its enforcement). As recently as 1856 in Lancashire, England, patriarchs used the scold's bridle or witch's bridle, a torture device, to gag women and deprive them of the ability to speak. This heavy iron muzzle was fitted with a bridle bit, which slid into the mouth and pressed down on top of the woman's tongue, often with a spike compressing the tongue. It silenced and shamed her, causing extreme pain and mental and physical trauma. The scold's bridle was overwhelmingly used on women, often upon request from husbands or other family members. This humiliation was further extended by parading the woman on a leash in a public square, where she would be further abused by a jeering crowd — an ancestral form of cyberbullying. Though many modern forms of silencing masquerade as more civilized, their goals are the same. With a disheartening percentage of males continuing to denigrate and marginalize female voices online and in homes, classrooms, boardrooms, and political arenas, the phantom bridle remains heavy on our shoulders.

In the Han dynasty, the female historian Ban Zhao, using her feminine voice for the masculine mind, wrote *Lessons for Women*, which gave advice on how women should behave. She outlines the four virtues women must abide by: proper virtue, proper speech, proper countenance, and proper merit. These commandments were upheld throughout the imperial period.

Another image imprinted upon my mind is the picture of the Boston Marathon's race director in 1967 man-handling a woman running this mecca race for long-distance runners. In her own words, she described how "A big man, a huge man, with bared teeth was set to pounce, and before I could react he grabbed my shoulder and flung me back, screaming, 'Get the hell out of my race and give me those numbers!' Then he swiped down my front, trying to rip off my bib number, just as I leapt backward from him. He missed the numbers, but I was so surprised and frightened that I slightly wet my pants and turned to run. But now the man had the back of my shirt and was swiping at the bib number on my back ... I saw tiny brave Arnie bat at him and try to push him away ... And the man screamed, 'Stay out of this, Arnie!' and swatted him away like a gnat." Nevertheless, Kathrine Switzer — bib number 261 — persevered to become the first woman to officially run the Boston Marathon.

The most depraved form of deshaktification is the progressive worsening of domestic violence, the sex trade, the rule of men, fathers, and husbands over women, and their continued impact on the health and dignity of women and girls. Physical, sexual, and emotional abuse against women is one of the most common forms of violence. Of the 800,000 humans trafficked across international borders annually, 80 percent are women and girls. The majority of these victims are forced into the commercial sex trade. According to the World Health Organization (WHO), 736 million women worldwide have experienced intimate partner violence or non-partner sexual violence. The United Nations (UN) Women's data shares the chilling statistic that around one-third of women have been sexually or physically abused by a partner. Even worse, they write, "In the most extreme cases, violence against women is lethal: globally, an estimated 137 women are killed by their intimate partner or a family member every day."

Religion, politics, and society have all been mercilessly deshaktified and used by the patriarchy to the physical and spiritual detriment of us all. As modern women and men start trimming the root rot of patriarchal denial, we see how vilification, violence, and vicious force are the autocratic ace cards in the historical marginalization of goddess power. The same disregard forced upon us is what has been cumulatively piling up on Mother Earth quintillion-fold. The quantum force of her existence, mystery, and self-generating consciousness has been a threat to those who seek to control her vast resources, manipulate her rhythms, and redesign her nature. As we trace this familiar narrative from century to century, culture to culture, we see that there has never been a time when the battle for power over the Shakti force did not exist. However, the more men try to sever women from the raw root source of primordial feminine power, the more they suffer. Without the foundational support of the Shakti, patriarchs are prone to deep-seated anxiety that continually plays out into the heartless cycle of their evil, conniving ingenuity. Though patriarchal dominance continues, they have yet to accomplish patriarchal independence from the Mother Goddess force. Impossible, given that, at its core, Shakti consciousness cannot be separated from Shiva consciousness.

In the Shiva-Shakti way of meeting each other precisely where we are, I urge religious bodies and social, political, and spiritual groups to mine mindfulness. We must create a new way forged by the ancient Earth principle that we are here to cultivate our sense of oneness with the followers of other belief systems, however different our religious, societal, and political points of view may be. Spiritual groups must forge the rich blossoming of personal awareness rather than become mired in group blindness. It is essential that we do not isolate our mindset or separate our practices from the universal principles of oneness, love, kindness, cooperation, and mutual respect. These human aspects are the overarching grandmother principle of all religions. It is the way of the Shakti.

Chapter 9

Shakti Gone Awry

Women were categorized as dangerous because of who they were or what they did was an affront or challenge to the patriarchy.

Elizabeth Garner Masarik

Nature's paradox of creation and destruction is demonstrated in the seamless connection of dark and light, night and day, Shiva-Shakti, yin-yang, and the awen. This paradox operates as a continuum of flow in the universe. Shakti's balance is critical to the harmonious state of nature and the cohesion of our bodies, minds, and spirits with her, and her creative energy can turn to destruction when it's blocked or imbalanced within us. Balance, however, is based on the understanding that the paradox is one unit with two distinct appearances. The broad human experience of this paradox, fostered by the patriarchal reign, is one of duality – separation of the inimitable oneness that appears to be cleft in twain (the "us and them" scenario) rather than the reality that Shakti's cosmic paradox resides as the balancing force within everyone. We are the navigators of this force, not Shakti, not her universe, not nature, not our parents or partners. To avoid the pitfalls of our matrilineal and patrilineal ancestors, we must choose to do the necessary wholesome actions to keep the balance. You may recall the term *dosha,* which means apt to err. We are continually flowing and shifting, sometimes knocked asunder from stasis. The seamless flow of our inner nature is composed of the indivisible dark and light, and how we manage this balance determines how much light or darkness we can manifest, being mindful that the degree of light or darkness within and without is variable and relative. Prisoners of the Holocaust, women persecuted as witches, and young girls traded into sex slavery, for example, would have had to dig deep into the bones of their being to sustain light and cobble even a glimmer of hope. Balance is a lesson that spans our entire lives. For thousands of years, women, in particular, have been paying the merciless price for Shakti gone awry.

While the potent powers of creation are inherently female, every human harbors a balance of the Feminine and Masculine Divine within their being. This means that, while Shakti energy is only present in its activated form in females – where it becomes creativity incarnate – an echo is present in males, imbuing them with her dynamic power of creativity. Shakti creativity can produce works of immense value, from life itself to art and innovation of surpassing beauty and elegance. Conversely, when thwarted or in a state of great impairment or imbalance, her creative energy can turn destructive, becoming the wildfire that incinerates invasive plants so the native forest can survive and thrive. Thus, when women suffer the discontent, grief, anger, and bitterness of repression for too long, Shakti energy goes awry. When that same energy is co-opted by a patriarchy predicated on primordial fear of the feminine and used against its makers, it becomes a weapon of mass destruction. Like metastasizing cancer, the patriarchy's suppression and appropriation of Shakti energy threatens to consume us all.

Unbalancing Shakti turns her creative energy into destructive energy in both women and men, who unleash that energy on each other and the Earth. When the Earth is thusly cast asunder by inimical forces, Shakti strikes back. Her tenacious retort is always to defend and protect the interest of her creation's greater evolution. When it becomes necessary, she shakes the very roots of the Earth to eradicate obstacles that stand in the way of our self-awakening and the balance of her creation.

When women are systematically repressed and demeaned, their thwarted Shakti energy can be distilled into poisons like self-doubt, jealousy, self-destruction, and rage. When they are more directly threatened, their poison often takes a more literal form. The prevailing view in history is that women are far more likely to choose poison as their weapon, while men choose more physical forms of violence. It is a grim thought but one that has been substantiated throughout the arc of time. Where men have relied on strength and position, women have resorted to stealth and patience. Poisoning is often considered a fundamentally female art, as it requires stealth and invisibility. Women's knowledge of herb lore made them proficient in preparing the poisoned brew. With her low stature in society and comparative lack of muscle mass, the female resorted to available weapons in her kitchen when push came to shove. The Latin word *venenatus* is brilliantly explained as "furnished with poison, poisonous, venomous" or "imbued with magical powers." Poisoners have so often been compared to a striking serpent that the word venomous became synonymous with feminine. Ironically, the snake analogy can also be applied to Kundalini energy, which, as you may recall, is visualized as a coiled serpent. This energy, too, can become counter-productive if the Kundalini becomes threatened and begins to travel below the root chakra.

In her paper, *Poisoned Lives: English Poisoners and Their Victims*, Katherine Watson studied 540 poisoning murders in England from 1750 to 1914 and found that while men were three times more likely than women to commit murder, women were "far more likely than men to choose poison as their weapon" when they did kill. In 1879, for example, officials discovered a husband-poisoning society in the Szerdahely region of Hungary. After eight husbands in neighboring villages dropped dead within six weeks of one another, the police were forced to investigate. It was quickly established that all eight men had died of arsenic poisoning, and their wives confessed to the killings and to helping each other carry out the crime. For centuries, women have been treated as property to be auctioned for marriage. These women often found themselves in abusive relationships, bereft of financial or social power, and had few options other than to get married, remain spinsters under the iron control of their fathers or brothers, or participate in the underground as sex objects. Experiencing a profound sense of victimization, a range of painful emotions such as helplessness, hopelessness, loneliness, and rage sometimes converged into an iron-clad determination to obliterate the cause of their unspeakable pain and suffering.

Throughout history, women have been driven to extreme measures by a merciless patriarchy. History is replete with their stories. The relationship of the powerful female rulers to their patriarchal counterparts was based on one strident principle: support the male, and you are given certain dispensations and tolerance; use your power to serve your own vision and goals, and you are undermined or eliminated. There are a number of notable women rulers remembered principally for poisoning scandals, pushed as they were to extremes by suffocating patriarchs. In 1184, Queen Tamara became the revered queen of Georgia and was often referred to as "King Tamar." Her marriage to Prince Yuri Bogolyubski of Kyiv was a disaster. Divorced in 1188, Tamara sent Yuri into exile. Seeking revenge for being humiliated, Yuri rallied a rebel army of Turks against Tamara. She defeated and exiled him again, after which he disappears from the history books and is believed to have been murdered at Tamara's command. Forged in venom by the ruthless male-ruled system, Agrippina was reputed to have poisoned her husband, Emperor Claudius. Her potion maker was Locusta, a woman. Her goal was to ensure the succession of her son, Nero, who later executed her. Louis XIV faced a spate of murders by poisoning between 1677 and 1682 in a scandal called the Affair of the Poisons. His companion, Madame de

Montespan, and the potion maker, Madame Monvoisin, were both caught and executed.

The Oresteia, a trilogy of Greek tragedies written by Aeschylus in the fifth century BCE, concerning a venomous heroine, Clytemnestra, reveals the male fear of the primordial feminine, embodied by those courageous women who would deign to express their Shakti power to protect and defend. In the tale of Clytemnestra, she is portrayed as rotting from within, with a touch so venomous that it is capable of transmuting life into a pile of debris. In his masterful work, *The Fear of the Feminine and Other Essays on Feminine Psychology*, Eric Neumann puts it this way, "The use of snake imagery shows the level of danger that women possessed when sufficiently provoked, which exemplifies the darker side of the duality of a woman." Moreover, Greek mythology builds on the divisive foundation that supreme male power is right and just, but illimitable power wielded by a woman becomes venomous and serpentine. In reality, women's destructiveness is usually fueled by men's actions. Mighty women of all eras have been ignored, marginalized, and scorned because of their innate Shakti prowess, and men have endeavored to keep these dangerous felines under supervision, shut away, or relegated to mere background ornamentation.

Stolen Shakti Power in Men

The patriarchy never rests in its attempt to shroud, diminish, and vanquish feminine powers, nor does it hesitate to appropriate the same traits it derides. The art of deception in warfare is a classic example of men co-opting the feminine characteristics of subtlety and cunning, which can yield dire results in the wrong hands. Whereas women tend to use these traits to survive and thrive, men often employ them as weapons of war. Warfare deceptive measures have been used as widely and far back as ancient India, China, the Middle East, Egypt, Rome, and Greece, and during the Medieval Age, the Renaissance, and the

European colonial era. The ancient Chinese military treatise *The Art of War* emphasizes the importance of deception as a way for outnumbered forces to defeat larger adversaries, and even today, both the US Military deception program (MILDEC) and the Russian Maskirovka employ advanced deception-based warfare systems. The 1944 Soviet Military Encyclopedia directed their forces to use "a complexity of measures, to mislead the enemy regarding the presence and disposition of forces." These tragic war-mongering actions all come from an excess of stolen Shakti power in the hands of men and an imbalance of Shakti power in the world. An indelible connection exists between the patriarchy's appropriation of Shakti power and its penchant for violence.

The imbalance and perversion of appropriated Shakti energy in the world have also led to the lingam's spiritual power being brutally profaned. With a surfeit of stolen Shakti power unbalancing their Shiva energy, men are moved to misuse the lingam for acts of violence instead of the simple, joy-bearing lift to consciousness through peaceful and mindful practices they are meant to bring to the spiritual table. This primal lingam function has been both wittingly and unwittingly misdirected. The patriarchy, closely identifying with warfare, competition, winning, insidious politics, and profits, has been misusing the lingam principle to achieve its own counter-intelligent goals. They sully the spiritual metaphor of the lingam by reducing it to its basest nature, giving rise to the phallus as projectile weaponry, and the mechanical lingam transmogrified into a weapon of mass destruction — missiles, rockets, warheads, mortars, guns, rifles, nuclear weapons, energy lasers, fighter jets, and drones. These lingam-imitating projectiles create havoc on Earth and in the realm of human intelligence. There is no peaceful Earthing of the lingam in the yoni here. Mother Earth, the metaphorical yoni, is being defiled by these projectiles as they unleash their malignant force into her soil, ocean beds, forests, animals, cities, communities, and populations. Worse still, they use this lingam-imitating weaponry against the Shiva consciousness of the open skies, launching their projectiles into the atmosphere where there is no possibility of Earthing their immense damage. The cosmic dance of unsuspecting planetary bodies is tragically interrupted by floating debris in Father Sky. Indeed, war projectiles of our era are designed for nothing less than total devastation. Perversion of the lingam's imprint is also mirrored in our community crimes of sexual aberrations, violence, and rape against women and girls. It is further reflected in the non-eunomy of our world's governance and the abuse of Mother Earth and her resources, the poisoned fodder we make of nature's food and medicines, the impairment of women's and men's reproductive health, and the way men respond to sexuality, love, and intimacy.

While the lingam was also weaponized in ancient warfare, they exercised more consideration for Earthing these weapons in the Earth-yoni. The yoni was the weapon's container, the lingam, the weapon. Ancient warriors were conscious of aligning the lingam-yoni principle to help them defeat the enemy, fight injustice, and defend humanity's sentiency. The bow for the arrow; the sheath for the sword or knife; the holder for the projectile spear, javelin, or falx; the pocket case for the sling; and hand-to-hand lingam to yoni weapons such as clubs, maces, and axes were the norm. Catapults, siege towers, and battering rams came later as the sacred life knowledge of the lingam-yoni relationship became progressively smothered by modernity.

Human societies were not always so male-dominated and warlike; men's appropriation of control over raising offspring and plant foods created these maladaptive conditions. In patriarchal societies, men and masculinity continually subjugate women. The concept of fatherhood is an example of subsuming and co-opting the Shakti power, which also contributed to the conditions that engender men to war. Data suggests that there were no notable wars before the start of the Neolithic period, some 11,000 years ago, when nomadic hunting and gathering lifestyles prevailed. The concept of "territories" and "nations" was non-existent. Indeed, this lack of warring persisted well after the appearance of Homo sapiens some 315,000 years ago. Albeit Homo sapiens are equipped with a far more complex brain system and consciousness-bearing abilities than our ancient human predecessors. When humans began to root down from nomadic lifeways into settled existence, becoming agricultural tenders, herders, and eventually landowners, the conditions that created strife, disharmony, and competition emerged.

These early settlements initially gave women golden opportunities to root down into the Earth, a constructive use of Shakti's creative energy and a natural impulse of the feminine yoni. The awakened Yoni archetype is etched in the soul of every woman, and Earthing was a primal way women of yore exercised their elemental bond with the Earth. Women farmers tended to the land, grew seedlings, and harvested precious foods. Infusing consciousness back into the Earth, they used their hands and newly designed floriculture tools, symbolic of the lingam. Gradually, the patriarchs moved in, pushed women off the land, and forced the technological development of agriculture. Co-opted from women and refined over centuries, agriculture as Earthing has been distorted into humanity's most widespread detrimental science against nature: farming technology such as mono-cropping, genetic modification of foods, deadly chemical pesticides, and mass automation. Looming on the brim of tomorrow, "smart dust" and other experimental agricultural and food production practices threaten to plunge us further into the abyss.

The emerging social and economic incentives associated with early sedentism heralded the onslaught of organized raids on settlements. Early settlers were forced to ward off bands of raiders to protect their land and family. To defend their territory, men became more aggressive and began to use their brainpower to develop tools and techniques that would later serve as the basis for warfare. The domestication of women, children, animals, seeds, forests, and lands had begun. Staking claim over Earth's intelligence and, indeed, all things feminine, the first patriarchal grouping sprouted. Led by a sense of superiority over women and nature, the newly banded males exerted precisely the same methodology over nature as they did in wars. All of these practices can be traced to the progressive and pernicious co-opting of Shakti energy and consequent misuse of the masculine archetypal lingam energy.

Because so much of the lingam's largesse has been tampered with through falsified ideologies and egoistic belief systems, men have lost touch with its inner guidance. Properly channeled psychic use of the internal lingam imprint in men would naturally create harmony, stability, and a thriving existence. The lingam's imprint in a man's body is meant to be directed into the nurturing Earth of the yoni, not simply as a sexual thrust, but as a prehistoric magnetic attraction to everything progressive and constructive that a man desires and strives to do. The lingam's instinctual thrust has been honed through infinite time to alchemize and anchor sublime Earthing. At all levels of existence, physically, psychically, and metaphorically, we are tampering with the magnetized attraction of the lingam to its peaceful Earthing in the yoni. Through the endless wars we wage – within ourselves, between the sexes, and against humanity, Mother Earth, and Father Sky – we are profaning the sacred power of the lingam and scorching, nay, incinerating life's immutable consciousness. The lingam's spiritual power and Earth's fertile intelligence are flowing at their lowest nadir, filtered by our ignorance and all but blocked by our barbarism.

A War of the Soul

They fear love because it creates a world they can't control.

George Orwell

We are coursing through a ferocious storm; some of us will make it through, but many will not. Those who do will forever be changed, transformed beyond recognizable forms. We have much work to do to restore the balance of Shakti and foster unity, cohesion, and trust within our world. We are awakening to a new *ikigai,* purpose, and reason for being passionately alive. Imagine: you and I are formed from magnificent cosmic energy – call it stardust, divine ions, or love – our bodies communicate with the energy and vibrations surrounding us. By observing the subtle energy fields within through the seven-fold chakra system, we can gauge our state of imbalance. As the world plummets deeper into a state of imbalance, we are called to be more vigilant in keeping inner balance. Shakti Prana has endowed every chakra within our astral bodies with abundant breath force – oxygen that sustains our state of balance. When each chakra is equanimous, its energy moves upward to align with consciousness in the crown chakra, leading to positive actions. As Shakti's creative energy begins to go awry, turning into destructive energy in both women and men, this chakra's energy involuntarily dives into inverted motility to its lower depth where attachment, lack of clarity, and undue fears abide. As I see it, our inner balance is being continually challenged. The energy centers at greatest risk, however, are three of the seven chakras, those located in the central energetic sphere in the body where most of humanity resides: Svadhisthana, the sacral chakra; Manipura, the solar plexus chakra; and Anahata, the heart chakra. Let's explore these central, energetic fields.

Svadhisthana, the dwelling place of the Self, is the energetic center through which we shape our identity and response to forces that interact with us in the physical world. Its element is water. This chakra governs the flow of emotions, sexual energy, sensuality, sexual intimacy, healthy emotions, and synchronicity with our environment. It represents the Divine Feminine aspect of our nature, innocence. When our maternal, nurturing, creative womb space is wounded through sexual abuse, abortion, or miscarriage, or we feel subjugated by violence, bullying, or manipulation, we experience a state of imbalance. It expresses itself as wounded emotions, fears, bitterness, sexual aberration, secretiveness, difficulty communicating, isolation, desolation, addictive behavior, fear of pleasure, fear of losing control, fatigue syndrome, insecurity, volatility, apathy, or depression. Simple, mindful breathing practices can turn destructive energy back into creativity. One little shift in thinking through the breath, and you're there. To correct alignment in your sacral chakra, where most of our fears and anxiety reside, simply breathe into the depth of your body, root down into this chakra, visualize a marigold orange light flowing through the area, and fortify your intention to create lightness and fearlessness there. Breathe in and out calmly with the focal point in Svadhisthana. "I am creating an environment of peace in my lower depth. I allow Shakti Prana to help me realign with the greater energies." This practice will help you observe erratic, chaotic, and harmful situations and respond from the core balance you are creating.

Manipura is referred to as the center of lustrous gems. This chakra is located in our solar plexus, the center of the chakral alignment in our bodies, and is the source of personal power. It is generated from the element of fire. It promotes a sense of worth, self-esteem, and accomplishment. Its fiery feminine energy is the power of transformation. This powerhouse directs the trajectory of what we wish to accomplish: our telic goals, extraordinary goals, accomplishments, dreams, and visions. When the navel chakra is in healthy alignment, you feel deeply aware, mindful, and empowered. The world is your oyster. When aggression, manipulation, being marginalized, or otherwise subsumed by masculine authority pushes into the deep, creative, mobile, and innovative space that resides in this central chakra, you experience angst, powerlessness, stagnation, inertia, overwhelm, misery, and jealousy of others' accomplishments. Restoring balance to Manipura requires your full awareness. This following solarized breath will enable you to regain lightness, stasis, and integrity in this central chakra. Breathe into your mid-center, envisioning millions of gems there, rubies and diamonds glimmering in yellow light. Inhale this aura into your solar plexus area while reciting, "I invite Shakti Prana to penetrate my body center to help me create an environment of ease and non-aggression. I am pacing myself and allowing the universe to show me the way."

Anahata, the pure cosmic sound of the universe, resides in the heart space. It is ruled by the element of air. From Manipura, the energy moves upwards to the heart space and manifests our most ecstatic nature – love, consciousness, and empathy. When Anahata's energy is balanced, it fosters generosity, kindness, and infinite love. We are cradled in life's arms and filled with ease and contentment. We express ourselves heartedly, healing wholeness with endless joy, appreciation, and gratitude. Anahata chakra holds the richest experiences of human life. It sustains heart energy. When the heart chakra is thrown out of alignment by betraying our truth, compromising to keep the peace, or living someone else's dream and purpose, we fall out of grace with Anahata. As a result, we feel broken-hearted, vulnerable, fearful, and hurt. Bitterness and hatred can become a formidable force when we are deeply hurt or feel betrayed by loved ones. It is imperative that we safeguard the delicacy and beautiful balance of the fourth chakra. It is central to our humanity. Regardless of the pain, suffering, and brokenness we endure in life, we must always return to refilling our heart space to replenish our innate creative energies with kindness, self-love, and joy. Engage in simple, shaktified expressions and acts of love: if you are a dancer, dance; a singer, sing; a poet, write. For all of us, read the beautiful lines of a poet like Mary Oliver: "For poems are not words, after all, but fires for the cold, ropes let down to the lost, something as necessary as bread in the pockets of the hungry."

At any time when you feel your energy askew or are enduring heartbreaking situations, go into the silence, close your eyes, and visualize the energy of emerald-green light breezing into your heart. Say, "Thank you Shakti Prana. Refuel my conscious heart. I am creating an environment of loving joy." And remember, joy can coexist with pain and suffering. Look at nature, forever hopeful, the sun glistening on a droplet, a butterfly gliding against the azure sky, a child giggling and skipping rope. To rebalance all your chakras, reclaim Shakti's sublime energies by breathing with nature. Your breath is perfectly aligned with the rhythm of her sun and moon. In the words of the great sage, Nisargadatt Maharaja, we must be like the flower that fills a space with its perfume and the candle with its light.

We must seek balance to alleviate the manifold layers of problems and crises in and around us, engineered by the hierarchal system. While we strive to heal the past, we must also harness the understanding of *I Am Shakti* as medicine for activating hope and kindness to heal and protect humanity from militarized masculinity. For this, we need to rebalance Shakti energy in ourselves and convince men to relinquish their hold on it before we destroy ourselves. Return to kindness each day, show compassion for your own flaws or to someone in need, observe some time for inner silence, and put the interest of Mother Earth before self-interest. Align with your self-worth. Breathe abundantly. Keeping love thriving — which can only happen when we establish balance — is the key to unfastening ourselves from the tenacity of a highly convoluted past with its massive imbalance and toxic contagion. Love and balance are the universal keys to Shiva-Shakti consciousness.

Part 2
We Can Heal

Chapter 10

Shaktified Women in History

We are the hunters, not the hunted. Come forward and find out for yourself!

Bibi Dalair Kaur

Behold the shaktified woman – her story does exist, though we must dig deep into the annals of history to uncover it. Her stealth and glorious victories were rarely supported by her masculine counterparts. Women have been virtually excluded from humanity's recorded chronicle of wars, battles, victories, politics, diplomacy, and power moves; their power relentlessly controlled and suppressed by a malignant patriarchy. Nevertheless, their stories persist, and we must re-invoke the glories of these great female ancestors to strengthen our collective Shakti force and realize our sacred power. Only when we reclaim and harness our cosmic birthright, effulgent with Shakti power, can we right the balance and restore harmony within ourselves and our world.

Bibi Dalair Kaul is one such lioness of history. In the seventeenth century, a ruthless Mughal invader by the name of Wajir Khan destroyed thousands of brave Khalsa warriors in his relentless attacks on Sirhind Fort in what is now Punjab. The ruler at the time, Guru Gobind Singh, who was the last of the ten Sikh gurus, was running out of artillery and warriors. Khan's massive army was advancing. Bibi Dalair Kaur, Guru Gobind Singh's daughter, gathered an army of 100 Khalsa women and took to the frontline. Khalsa women drew their swords and positioned themselves behind the damaged wall, the only entry to the fort. Khan's bloodthirsty soldiers began climbing in over the piles of rubble. When they saw the tiny army of

Khalsa women ready for battle, they were befuddled and began to taunt them, having expected to find hundreds of Khalsa male warriors. Witnessing the events from a distance, Wajir Khan yelled, "Cowards, are you afraid of women? They are gifts for you; capture them and do what you want with the rewards of your hunt." Bibi Dalair Kaur yelled back, "We are the hunters, not the hunted. Come forward and find out for yourself!" Wajir Khan took up the challenge and rode into the fort with his soldiers. Kaur shouted to her sister warriors, "Remember we are lionesses," and together, this shaktified army began to annihilate Khan's soldiers. The Mughals retreated. Sadly, Kaur and her warriors were eventually killed by cannon fire. Bibi Dalair Kaur is considered a Sikh martyr, and her story remains a source of inspiration for feminine stealth and courage.

India's ancient history is rich with the goddess energy of its courageous Maharanis, warriors, mystics, and scholars. Mira Bai, whose legendary beauty was known across the land, was born into a privileged family in 1504 in the Merta District of Rajasthan. Her mother died at her birth, and her grandfather adopted her. Her education included knowledge of scriptures, music, archery, fencing, horseback riding, and driving chariots. She was also trained in weaponry. Mira Bai was a great devotee of the god Krishna. She dedicated herself to a spiritual life and refused to be married but was forced into it by her grandfather. Being a beautiful, independent woman certain of her spiritual worth, she drew great resentment from her male relatives. Her brother-in-law, who became the ruler of Chittor, finding her independence and spiritual valor offensive, tormented her through various means and finally poisoned her. It is said that Mira Bai, knowing it was poison, drank it as if it were an elixir from her beloved god, Krishna.

Rani Abbakka Chowta, Queen of Ullal, is extolled as one of the first female freedom fighters of India. She is the only woman in India's history to confront, fight, and repeatedly defeat the

Portuguese aggressors, who were the first Europeans to find a sea route to India. Abbakka, while still a princess, was trained in a wide range of military skills. Her family, the Chowtas, were a matrilineal dynasty. She was aware of the threat the Portuguese posed. Once she became queen of Ullal, she was determined to defeat them. A tenacious and fierce warrior, she successfully defended the region for four decades in the latter half of the sixteenth century. From 1525 to 1579, Abbakka led her army in rebuffing six attacks by the Portuguese. Abbakka was both a queen and a general of the navy and army, which consisted of elite soldiers, oarsmen, and archers from all religions and statuses. Her undefeated victory against the Portuguese was finally undermined by her estranged husband, who betrayed her for gold. In their final attack, the invaders, with her husband's aid, managed to capture Abbakka. Refusing to be held prisoner, she started a revolt in prison, which led to her death. True to India's local mores for venerating their heroes and heroines, she lives on in the folk culture even though her courageous acts have not been written in the history books. In the Dakshin Kannada region, they still hold the annual Veera Rani Abbakka Utsava celebration in her memory.

Rani Veeramangai Velu Nachiyar, ruler of the Shivagangai Kingdom – now Madurai, Tamil Nadu – from 1769 to 1790, is celebrated by Tamilian people as the first female Indian ruler to successfully revolt and triumph against the British Empire. Rani's parents, eschewing traditional gender roles, ensured she was well-trained in weaponry, martial arts, and archery. She was also articulate in French, English, and Urdu. In 1772, the British killed Rani's husband and young daughter while invading Shivagangai to stake a claim on Kalaiyar Koli Palace. In 1780, Rani used her intelligence-gathering agents to find the location of the British arsenal. In what would be called the first suicide bombing in India, Kuyili, one of Rani's followers, doused herself in oil and proceeded to martyr herself while detonating the arsenal. Meanwhile, Rani formed a women's army named Udaiyaal that successfully defeated the British. Her beloved kingdom finally succumbed to the British East India Company after her death.

Surviving Celtic folklore maintains the storied past of their goddesses. Celtic women have often been depicted as holding positions of great importance, highly valued even in male-dominated Celtic tribal society. They were revered as goddesses, saints, warriors, and mystics, garnering tremendous respect. In the shards of our feminine cultural archives, we find Macha, the wife of Nuada Argetlam, who led the invasion of the Tuatha de Danann against the Fir Bolg to claim Ireland. She participated in both battles and was finally killed as she defended her fallen husband from the Fomori giant-king, Balor of the Evil Eye. We likewise find Brigid, goddess of the spring, whose wisdom and perfection Irish mythology extolls. There is the fierce, magnificent Queen Mebd of Connacht; the great healer, Airmid; the wise lawmaker, Brigid Bretach; the fierce warrior goddess Morrigan; and countless other Celtic feminine divinities.

In Egypt, male power mercilessly coerced their regents' natural feminine largesse and used it when convenient. For example, six of her queens became pharaohs in their own right, and yet these women remain obscured in history. Their male counterparts used them to protect, nourish, and, when necessary, fiercely defend and protect themselves. While the urge to nurture and protect is an innate function of the feminine Shakti, this potent force gets vitiated when it is continually subjugated, abused, and misused. Each of these Egyptian queens served the role of procurator for their absent kings or young sons or stepped up during times of great crises when only a feminine face could keep the peace and stability as the mother of a nation. Hatshepsut, for example, was nearly excised from history. After her father's death, the 12-year-old Hatshepsut became queen of Egypt when she married her half-brother,

Thutmose II, her father's son. Thutmose II died young, around 1479 BCE, and the throne went to his infant son, Thutmose III. Hatshepsut became the acting queen regent for Thutmose III, handling state affairs until her stepson came of age. She was a powerful ruler who had to defend her pioneering title as queen regent throughout her reign. To succeed, she assumed the male identity seen in some of her portraits. After she died in her mid-forties and her stepson became king, he eradicated almost all evidence of Hatshepsut's existence as a powerful female pharaoh, possibly in an attempt to restore a flawless dynastic line of male succession. It was not until 1822 that Hatshepsut's successful rule as the sixth Pharaoh of the Eighteenth Dynasty of Egypt was discovered after scholars decoded and read the hieroglyphics on the walls of Deir el-Bahri.

Countless other great heroines and their sacrifices, too numerous to note, existed throughout ancient cultures. Teuta, queen regent of the Ardiaean kingdom in the west of the Balkan Peninsula from 231 to 227 BCE, led armies to boldly fight the Romans. Hortensia was a famous Roman woman orator best known for giving a speech in front of the members of the Second Triumvirate in 42 BCE that resulted in the partial repeal of a tax on wealthy Roman women. Sappho was a famous woman poet born about 615 BCE on the Greek island of Lesbos. She was widely regarded as one of the greatest lyrical poets of her time, and most of her poems were put to music. Theano of Crotona was a great woman philosopher born in 546 BCE to whom many Pythagorean writings were attributed in antiquity. Artemisia I of Caria was a queen who fought as an ally of Xerxes I, King of Persia, against the independent Greek city-states during the second Persian invasion of Greece. She commanded her five ships at the naval battles of Artemisium and Salamis in 480 BCE. Timycha of Sparta, who lived in 375 BCE, was a devout follower of the Pythagorean doctrine who, when threatened to reveal its secrets, bit off her tongue and spat it at the tyrants so they could not misuse the sacred knowledge. Aglaonice was a famous Greek woman astronomer in the second century BCE who accomplished extraordinary feats and was regarded as a sorceress. She predicted the time and general area where a lunar eclipse would occur, boasting that she "could make the moon disappear from the sky." In 39 BCE, two Vietnamese sisters, Trung Trac and Trung Nhi, led a rebellion against their Chinese overlords and proclaimed themselves queens of an independent state.

Africa — the cosmic portal and continent to which all humanity owes a giant debt — is as historically rich in shaktified women and matrilineal tradition as it is in modern misogyny and patriarchal control. One of our highest priorities in restoring feminine power and grace in our world is to address the merciless issues prevailing on Mother Earth, which includes the relentless victimization of Africa and her women in particular. Africa has always been a vulnerable target that sheathed political fanaticism in the patriarchal world of the fathers, sons, and heaven. This cradle of civilization became an easy mark for senseless evil. Africa has played a vast role in the evolution of the Earth and humanity's place in it. Whether or not we believe Africa is the cradle of humankind, distinctively situated at the very center of the world's seven continents, we can vouch for her ancientness and cultural wealth.

Before the advent of European invasion and colonial influence on Mother Africa, women in Africa held influential societal roles. Glimpses of these original traditions remain. The Akan people, for example, are matriarchal in custom, and the queen mother of the tribe selects the tribal leader. African oral history boasts of countless regents, queens, and tribal rulers. Amina, Queen of Zaria, Nigeria, born in 1610, was a Hausa warrior queen of the city-state of Zazzau, the present-day city of Zaria in northwest Nigeria. She ruled in the mid-sixteenth century and was named heiress apparent at the tender age of 16. Her grandfather trained her in leadership and military skills. She gained notoriety for her military prowess and was known as a "leading warrior in her brother's cavalry." Each year, the Yoruba celebrate the Edi Festival in honor of Princess Moremi Ajasoro, who helped them conquer the "Forest people" in battle in the twelfth century. Also noteworthy is the Empress of Ethiopia, Kandake of Kush, who is mentioned by church historians as a fierce military leader of her time. In his famous *Church History* book, Eusebius scribed, "Ethiopia even to the present day is ruled, according to ancestral custom, by a woman." Makeda, the Queen of Sheba, was notably mentioned in several religious books, including the Bible, Quran, Targum Sheni, and the Ethiopian Kebra Negas. She was extolled as an intelligent, rich, and mighty monarch who visited King Solomon to test and verify claims of his wisdom.

There is no shortage of modern women displaying the same courage that so richly supplied their shaktified ancestors. Courage comes in many forms; some demand that we sacrifice life and limb, while others call on the gallantry of spirit fearlessly daubed with feminine integrity and truth – the kind of service and healing that are in dire need today. Dr Zakira Hekmat is one such fearless spirit whose singular struggle and sacrifices have created a safe space for many Afghans to gain refugee protection and asylum. Born in Afghanistan, Dr Hekmat founded the Afghan Refugee Solidarity Association in Türkiye (previously Turkey) to carry out her tireless service work. Dr Francs Kelsey's one-person campaign kept thalidomide off American prescription lists and saved thousands of American infants from being deformed. Marceline Kongolo-Bice, who was born in war-torn Congo and grew up fleeing from militia gunfire after she refused to marry a local commandant, founded a grassroots NGO, SOS Femmes en Dangers, that aids rape victims, supporting and educating female survivors to take back their rights and to build the inner strength and confidence they require to recover and reconnect with their families and communities.

Wilma Pearl Mankiller, Cherokee, was born on November 18, 1945, in Tahlequah, Oklahoma. An activist and author whose forbears had endured the horrendous Trail of Tears, she became the first female chief of the Cherokee Nation, transforming the nation-to-nation relationship between the Cherokee and the federal government. Wilma's social activism as director of the Community Development Department of the Cherokee Nation focused on children's issues, implementing positive changes to heal ancestral scars. She died at age 64, having made remarkable strides in her efforts to restore the Cherokee people's legacy. Another stalwart in restoring indigenous rights is Ladonna Harris, a Comanche raised near Walters, Oklahoma. As a social activist and politician, she is known for influencing women's rights, civil rights, and environmental protection. Ladonna is the founder of Americans for Indian Opportunity, whose stated mission "advances, from an Indigenous worldview, the cultural, political and economic rights of Indigenous peoples in the United States and around the world." In her own words, Harris wants indigenous people "to maintain ourselves as we are so we can contribute our differences, our particular understanding, to both the national community and the global society."

We have arrived at a portal of cosmic time and space when the Shakti force is organically rising. Never before in our known history have young women so publicly and passionately voiced their rage and angst about injustices in their communities. As Shakti's vibrational volume increases, her intelligence is luminously reflected in countless women and girls worldwide whose powerful voices call out the vile and complex conditions set up by patriarchy. 18-year-old Emma Gonzales used her voice to call national attention to gun law reform just days after a gunman opened fire at her school in Florida and killed 17 of her peers. In an essay written for *Harper's Bazaar*, Emma succinctly encapsulates this egregious issue: "You don't drive a NASCAR on the street, no matter how much fun it might be, just like you don't need an AR-15 to protect yourself when walking home at night. No one does."

Malala Yousafzai's seemingly instant notoriety began when the Taliban shot her after publicly speaking out about her fight to protect girls' education. At the age of 20, she was appointed a United Nations Messenger of Peace, and in 2014, she received the Nobel Peace Prize and became the youngest Nobel Laureate ever. "I started speaking out when I was 11 years old and I had no idea if my voice can have an impact or not," Malala said. "But soon I realized that people were listening ... So change is possible and do not limit yourself, do not stop yourself, just because you are young." In 2016, at just 27 years old, Shamma bint Suhail Faris Mazrui was appointed Minster of State for Youth Affairs in the United Arab Emirates. Her country's first Rhodes Scholar at Oxford University, Mazrui is believed to be the youngest government minister in the world. She is creating a path for young people to engage more constructively with government and within society. Her achievement represents significant change and progress for women and girls in Saudi Arabia, considering that the Women's Danger Index, compiled by Asher and Lyric Fergusson, shows the United Arab Emirates receiving a poor score for the global gender gap.

We may never fully unearth the complete chronicle of ancient women saints, mystics, rulers, warriors, monarchs, and freedom fighters. Regardless, we have sufficient clues to indicate that history was packed with their sacrifices, courage, and stealth. At the same time, we have a trove of stories wherein the courageous heroine was betrayed, imprisoned, murdered, poisoned, or otherwise ground into the dust when their male counterparts felt threatened by their sovereignty. Retelling these stories inspires us, galvanizes us to action, and reminds us of our own valor when pain, sadness, and hopelessness seem stuck to our bones.

We can and must join forces and harness the power of these glorious women, young and old, ancient and modern. They are not simply flat figures printed on a page we can flip past. They have proven – and continue to prove – that Shakti's invincible courage and confidence can persevere even in the most impossible conditions. As we reach the tipping point of the Earth's balance, the Shakti force is shifting into overdrive to strengthen and recalibrate the Earth's sentiency and rescue humanity from its impending crises. The souls of women, men, and non-binary individuals alike are stirring as the uncertain future prods us to action, purpose, and awakening. Carried on the crest of this wave of consciousness, we can wipe out evil and restore balance.

For many years, I have been touring the world with my Wise Earth work, and I can feel the palpable shift into awareness in the greater humanity I serve. Let us continue this momentum, mirroring the selfless courage of our wondrous, shaktified ancestors as we better ourselves, our families, and our communities. We can contribute in small or big ways; each effort we make toward embracing a kinder world is significant. Saturate your daily activities in the wise Earth and bask in her intelligence, beauty, passion, endowment, and ever-present embrace. Wise Earth teaches us that peace must start within. Let's come together as one and take back the shaktified world within. By cultivating ahimsa – harmony in our thoughts, speech, and action – we send forth pure vibration to heal ancestral wounds and resolve negative karma to nurture our children, family, community, and Mother Earth. We are here to reclaim the Mother Consciousness. My richest experience has been creating the Peace Mandala, which involves the hands, hearts, and spirits of entire communities. I have led more than a million participants worldwide who have joined in the creation of a Peace Mandala and taken *The Vow of Ahimsa*. As we gather to create a Peace Mandala with nature's sentient seeds and grains, we catalyze the universe's five elemental energies through our hands: women gently hold the seeds against their bellies, men close to their hearts before placing them in random order onto the Earth. Nature's seeds help us to connect mind to heart and heart to the rhythmic pulse of her Earth. I have witnessed women and men striving to strengthen the natural bond of Shiva-Shakti as they infuse sentiency back into the good Earth. We bow in gratitude and gather as one spirit, rich and poor, the uninformed and the wise. Sharing brilliant auras and the greyness of grief, lightness and darkness, we wholly bless each other. With Shakti rising, we invoke wholeness, health, and well-being for ourselves, and this healing energy ripples out to generate wellness for humanity. The high vibration of love pelts out to heal a weary world, worn and roiled by patriarchal arrogance and greed. We are accelerating the descent of patriarchy. In reclaiming the power of the mother, of women, and of Earth, we are sealing the end of that seemingly endless era of barbarism. The Inquisition has ended. We were never evil, demonic witches the wretched system made us out to be. The pointed hat was only a hat that shaded the face, the broom was only a broom, the cauldron was just a huge iron pot to cook and wash in, and the cat was just a helpful companion that kept the mice from the hops and barley. We have always loved to ferment, brew ale, and make yogurt and remedies. Elizabeth Garner-Masarik eloquently opines: "If you have read any of the recent historical scholarships on witch hunts in early modern Europe, you already know that patriarchy is the big burning pile of dogshit in the middle of the whole thing." During a time that had zero tolerance for feminine ingenuity, these glorious women of the past shone radiant with Shakti power — dazzling the world with their bravery, leadership, intellect, art, and charisma. WE ARE HEALERS. WE ARE WOMEN. WE ARE SHAKTI.

Women's work teaches us to transform violence, disease, and despair into harmony, wellness, and joy. Bring your tribe together to create a brew or cook a scrumptious meal in your mighty cauldron. When we gather as a community, we embody the deepest quality of peace, and every person feels inspired to do the inner work of cultivating personal awareness. Each day, we can experience the extraordinary shift occurring all around us; the universal mind steadily rising into consciousness. Our collective intent for harmony and equanimity profoundly impacts the cosmic psyche of inner peace and the actualization of a peaceful world.

Like these women buried deep in our history or continuing in their footsteps today while enduring the taunts of unenlightened men online, the awakened person is open to that intricate part of themselves that can find resolve in the Shakti force. We are receivers and transmitters of Shakti's powerful energies. Our thoughts, words, and actions give rise to our intentions. When we are harmonious with nature as a whole, we create more beneficent energy. Everything around us thrives with more prana, kindness, love, graciousness, and compassion. However, when our intentions fester in the lower vibratory energies, such as bitterness, anger, hatred, humiliation, blame, apathy, or disrespect, we alienate ourselves from nature's laws, which ends up consuming more of the Earth's healing energies while converting it into waste through negativity. Using our conscious awareness, we can learn to harness the magnificent force of Shakti. Cultivating and sharpening our daily awareness makes accepting what is being shown to us much easier. Like our stalwart women, the trees accept the storms, the sky accepts lightning and thunder, the Earth accepts her Earthquakes and volcanoes, and the ocean accepts her tsunamis. I kept these examples in mind as I struggled to accept the horrendous experiences that relentlessly unfolded in my own life.

In accepting our realities, however tenacious, toxic, or horrifying they may be, we are not caving into the negative barbarism but paradoxically releasing their negative hold and freeing ourselves from being held hostage by external events. Acceptance is one of the hardest lessons to conquer; it demands instant maturity, the maturing of awareness that pushes us to focus on and explore our inner world. As I drew breath into my body, I was awed to find this immense space within, as big as the Cosmic Being, with enough breadth to get past the fears of diving into the unknown.

Chapter 11

Sexuality's Role in Consciousness

For this is wrong, if anything is wrong:
not to enlarge the freedom of a love
with all the inner freedom one can summon.
We need, in love, to practice only this: letting each other go.

Rainer Maria Rilke

In modern culture, where technocracy and crazy-cracies reign supreme, we have forgotten our sublime heritage – that we are born with the universal mind intact. We are born conscious. Yet, with unconscious irreverence, our sentient development as infants is diverted by the conditioning of our parents, elders, and the generations before them, all of whom have been alienated in turn from remembering the natural order and our infrangible connection to all things. Every person, the whole of humanity, has been influenced by the pyramidical power structure that indoctrinated them. We further degrade consciousness through unconscious relationships and sexuality. Though this loss is unfathomable, all is not lost; by practicing the conscious art of sexuality, we can harness the organic Shiva-Shakti force that generates consciousness itself and bestows a conduit through which we can reconnect to the collective consciousness that is our birthright.

Human children emerge from the womb replete in their connection to the universal mind, that divine source that is an infinite network of sentiency, memory, prana, nourishment, beauty, and purpose inscribed in every cell of our human body, mind, and spirit. It is the truth of all things, manifest and unmanifested, the beginningless being and becoming of the universe. We are composed of its entirety. It is that truth we feel in our bones and inexplicable spaces within that whispers and shouts and is both subtle and loud, pervasive and enduring, and that slowly and methodically begins to restore our memory of being born conscious. The Sanskrit aphorism, *Aham Brahasmi* – I Am Brahman, Full Consciousness – encapsulates it. Awakening this self-generating light of awareness has been the goal of spiritual masters for eons. Through the early years of their development, children receive crystalline clear information through the soft tissue of their brain from the Shakti force in the universe, their original mother-father.

Each newborn is equipped with full cognition, the intelligence that forecasts their sacred purpose on Earth. The abilities inherent in the masculine, feminine, or third-gender child are reflected through their organic innocence. The male child is influenced more by the primordial Shiva energies, the female child has a Shakti nature, and the third-gender child has a variable mix of Shiva-Shakti characteristics. As children grow older, they naturally become aware of the intelligent, vast creation and sense the meaning of their human existence.

However, this natural evolution of consciousness is significantly impeded by those who love us most: our parents and families. Teaching us as they were taught, raising us as best they know how, they unwittingly pass on flawed perspectives, limiting beliefs, and suffocating versions of reality that divert and muddy the pure stream of our consciousness. Our alienation from nature's order and her laws of creation has only increased as our collective connection to her has slackened, further eroding our link to the universal mind. This progressive disconnection from nature can be traced to a variety of causes, beginning with the fear of nature itself: her cold, her elements, her predatory creatures, and her black soil teeming with microbes. It can be traced to the technologies that relieve us of tracking the seasons and working the land to the extent that we need no longer walk it at all – indeed, there are virtual nature experiences we can seek out if we want to see trees and hear birds. Even the foods we create, consume, and dispose of in gargantuan quantities are all but stripped of their organic origins, chemically treated, processed, refined, extracted, re-fortified, and preserved into a simulacrum of sustenance. We are physically, mentally, and spiritually orphaned from the fundamental source of nourishment and healing: Mother Earth. We are not exempt from ecological processes or consequences. Stultified by the mundanity of modern existence – from the foods we eat and the places and ways we live to the lies we live by and the violence in our homes and communities – we become vulnerable, cleft from within. We separate from each other and become stymied by egocentrism, seeing the world and nature from our self-serving perspectives. We begin to feel a sense of entitlement, manipulating nature, seeing the world as an infinite free resource that is there to serve us. This distance from the nature we are inextricably connected to dulls our senses and dims our consciousness.

Conscious sexuality is our salvation from this severed state. Modern cultures have appallingly violated and misunderstood this glorious primeval act, which actually generates human consciousness. The art of sexuality is not simply about bringing forth progeny or expressing carnal or erotic intimacy; it is certainly not about personal gain or exercising our power over each other. East and West, women and men are conditioned by the miasma of blurred discernment regarding the purpose of the rite of human sexuality. Our veritable ignorance of this sublime science is revealed by our mundane definitions, similes, and associations for the word "sexuality": carnal, animalistic, bestial, venereal, fleshly, intimate, reproductive, voluptuous, wanton, and so on. So much of our knowledge of sexuality has been twisted and thwarted by shame, guilt, violence, and lovelessness. Exercising our sexuality nowadays largely consists of divisive activities that weaken our Shiva-Shakti force. The use of this primeval art to fulfill base desires only serves to dull the senses that must be honed to reach enlightenment. Indiscriminate or unconscious use of sexuality purely as a means of sating physical desire likewise degrades consciousness and diminishes *ojas,* the immunity-generating protection of the human organism. Further, it is the primary cause of disharmony and distrust in the relationship between partner and partner. We are entrained through generational memory to betray our sexuality. To retrieve the sentiency of a Shiva-Shakti existence, we must restore the nourishing value of sexuality into life.

The power of our healthy expressions of sexuality triple-folds when the conjugal intent of sexual union is to join Shakti with Shiva. The organic force of Shiva-Shakti fuels the conjugal rites that foster the return to consciousness. In other words, conscious sexuality is the cosmic process through which human sentiency is generated and sustained in our world. It is one of the core human functions for the unification of Shiva-Shakti, both between the masculine and feminine genders and, as importantly, within our individual selves, whatever our gender or biological sex. The art of sexuality is a biological and spiritual imperative that is meant to feed, nourish, and grow the bond of oneness between man and woman or partner and partner, the nurtured seed from which humanity's progressive consciousness sprouts and blooms.

Conscious sexuality is concerned with much more than sexual activity itself. It begins with how we meet ourselves and the esteem we recognize for our bodies. It desires us to be present, aware, and mindful in the way we approach ourselves before we open our kimonos to a partner. When we are present in ourselves, we can be present with another. Beyond the space of physical attraction, deeper emotional and physical intimacy naturally sprouts when you feel trust and respect for your partner. We build this confidence with one another through harmonious communication in our thoughts, words, and deeds. Transparency in our speech, where we can easily communicate our true feelings and intent with each other, is imperative to creating a pure, unfiltered, pristine relationship. Building a solid trust in a relationship requires quality time, joy, anticipation, and sharing with the knowledge that you and your partner are building a spiritual home within your bodies. You arrive in this home fully when the sense of otherness disappears. Your sexual relationship is not fragmented in degrees — the other half, the better half, the future-ex half — but seamlessly rolls into the whole; the whole of you and the whole of him become united. You become one whole. Shiva-Shakti. In this home, the prevalent emotions are a sense of deep friendship, heart-bonding, belonging, and home and Earth. A psychic connection inevitably develops between partners who are cultivating a Shiva-Shakti relationship. You understand each other's feelings, emotions, thoughts, and energy without having to share a word. You begin to read each other more clearly than words on a page. Emotional and spiritual transparency with each other also serves as the portal for a vast sexual experience; the touch of the body, the feel of the skin, the aroma of togetherness, and the entire organism rises into the cosmic field where the body is awakened to heightened emotional, energetic, sensory, and spiritual experience.

In Vedic culture, one of the deep rituals for couples to build a pristine, long-lasting relationship was to share in the practices that created cohesion between them; practices that enlightened awareness, such as partnering in leisurely walks or yoga, sitting together in meditation, creating a special space to sit and share silence, creating an altar in your home as a constant reminder of the sacrosanct relationship you share, offering joint prayers to the divine energy, or reciting a mantra that evokes the deeper awareness of sexuality before coitus. As Alice Walker succinctly states, "Sexuality is one of the ways that we become enlightened because it leads us to self-knowledge." At the end of the chapter is a beautiful, time-proven Vedic practice couples may use to enhance Shiva-Shakti unity and cohesiveness.

As we craft more awareness to improve this conscious act of nature and deepen our bond with our partner, we must be mindful of the old script of ancestral sexual behavior that is always running in our subconscious and will determinedly pop up. Conditioned by these inherited behavior patterns, women tend to shroud, undermine, or overexpose their creativity and sexuality, and men to disdain, fear, or abuse it. Rather than block these old impulses, we must allow safe and healthy space for them; you want to observe where this memory is pushing you and mentally indulge its *lila,* or divine playfulness, rather than deny or chastise it. Then, seek the help of a qualified mentor who can enable you to release this impulse lovingly. Eventually, as we recondition our sexual mindsets and behaviors, the old negative impulses exhaust themselves. To start reclaiming our innate right to the artful sexual practice of what it feels like to be a lover and a happily fulfilled woman, we must reclaim our pure nature of Shiva-Shakti. We must remind ourselves, again and again, that sexuality is an act of spiritualism Earthed in the soul.

To comprehend the consentient human nature of sexuality as spirituality, let us lovingly explore the symbolic lingam. The symbolism of the lingam is a perennial subject of theology, anthropology, mythology, and spiritual psychology in Vedic literature. In the most elevated sense, the lingam is beyond existence. It is pure consciousness, beyond forms and names, the ultimate projectile reality, which is the infinite truth and the source consciousness of creation. The lingam also symbolizes the union of mind and soul. In its physiological Earthly existence, it symbolizes the male reproductive organ in a state of bliss when inherited by the yoni, the female reproductive organ. Its projectile configuration is a classic masculine primordial design imprinted in the cellular memory and mind of the male physiognomy and psychology. True to its ultra-spiritual nature, the lingam is both the source and expression of awareness. In my previous parable of the lingam seated in the yoni, we can visualize the lingam's power of consciousness Earthed in the yoni's power of creation. United as one, they generate consciousness, manifesting nurturance, manifesting life, manifesting love, and manifesting our world.

Modern anthropologists and theologists have often erroneously referenced the lingam as a "Hindu symbol of their phallic godhead." This statement demonstrates a stereotypical ignorance shared by the colonizers, along with their inability to distinguish between the metaphysical and spiritual meaning of the symbol. Their stigmatic interpretation is tantamount to saying worshipping Christ on the crucifix is the same as worshipping a torture instrument.

India's medieval Hindu temples at Khajuraho, Konarak, and Modhera are replete with amorous figurines and statues of gods and goddesses in the practice of *mithuna,* or coitus, where the gods' erect penis is not an uncommon sight. These carvings suggest that the ancients' approach to sexuality was functional and organic, demonstrating beautiful and artful ways to bond, unify, and develop trust between the seemingly opposing genders.

Temples, in that far-off time, were not only for the performance of prayers and meditations but also a place where devotees shared essential truths, values, and practices, such as the Vedic approach to conscious sexuality. According to Vedic philosophy, *dharma* (cosmic laws, wholesome conduct), *artha* (prosperity, wealth), *kama* (desire, passion), and *moksha* (freedom from cycles of rebirth) are the four primary goals of human life and its ultimate destination of enlightenment. Through these ancient sciences, the seers, or *rishis,* established a profound system of metaphysics, including astrology, astronomy, and physiology governing the epic affair of human health, wellness, and balance. They also developed specific yoga postures for the sexual unification of the Shiva-Shakti divine. To aid attraction within and between the sexes, they concocted aphrodisiacs, remedies, and charms for both women and men to strengthen this union within themselves and with their spouses. Unfortunately, much of this knowledge has deviated from its original intent over the centuries or been misused as a mere physical tool for carnal pleasure rather than to unite Shiva-Shakti, mind and consciousness with body and spirit. Rote sexual practices tend to alienate a woman from her Yoni-Shakti force and a man from his Lingam-Shiva force and, as a result, from their Shakti energy as well.

The Shiva-Shakti primeval force goes way beyond the gender binary to the fluent infinite; at the same time, at its core, it depends on the relationship of a man and a woman to generate Shiva-Shakti power. The act of procreation sustains the physical Earth, and the heterosexual union also nurtures the psychic and spiritual Earth. There is far more to this than the symbolic harmony of the lingam Earthing in the yoni; this union is imperative to sustaining energetic cohesion and oneness in our world. When we elevate the Shiva-Shakti relationship between a man and a woman to its primordial purpose, we contribute to the shaktification of Mother Earth. At the same time, we can strengthen our relationship with her and our partner when we strive to harmonize this principle within our own anatomy. Ultimately, the lingam-yoni solidarity symbolizes the cosmic mysteries, creative powers, and discovery of spiritual truths in human life. Its principle unfolds the cosmic union of the feminine and the masculine, the eternal cosmological process of creation. In the context of the Shiva-Shakti alliance, the heterosexual man and woman are the complementary light force that contributes to procreation and evolution on Earth. When united, they are responsible for upholding and progressing the Shiva-Shakti balance for all creation. Even if they fail to procreate, the couple has a responsibility to safeguard and nourish the Shiva-Shakti primeval energies, not solely for their own happiness, pleasure, and prosperity but for vibrationally safeguarding the sacred lingam-yoni relationship in the family, community, nature, and world.

Methods for using sexuality as a path to enlightenment into spirituality are clearly defined and supported by specific dharmas (cosmic laws) in the ancient Vedas. To prepare their bodies and minds for cohabitation by the Shiva-Shakti force, couples may employ purifying practices such as baths, meditation in a serene and private space, specific mantras or prayers, or, if they are so inclined, observing the appropriate lunar cycle at the waxing phase of the moon culminating into fullness. The health and wellness of both partners are also considered. Sex between a man and a woman is a profound ritual for Shiva-Shakti bonding, strengthening, unification, and notification of Shiva-Shakti balance in the world. As with all kinds of freedom, the individual must maintain discipline that supports the universal truths. This sense of untethered freedom is a very different concept from the secrecy and shamed nuances of sexuality that patriarchy and modern culture have promoted. Kilroy J. Oldster, author of *Dead Toad Scrolls,* espouses, "Human beings possess the gift of personal freedom and liberty of the mind. We each possess the sovereignty over the body and mind to define ourselves and embrace the values that we wish to exemplify. Personal autonomy enables humans to take independent action and use reason to establish moral values. We are part of nature. Consciousness, human cognition, and awareness of our own mortality allow us to script an independent survival reality and not merely react to environmental forces."

The preservation of Shiva-Shakti sentiency is so imperative to the progress of conscientious humanity that the rules of their alliance adhered to stern cosmic and societal laws of conduct during the Vedic period. In the Vedic purview, heterosexual partners are responsible for progressing collective consciousness;

it is their restorative karmic purpose and ethical duty to fulfill the conscious evolution of humanity. Sexual crimes, therefore, were harshly punished. Those who committed adultery or sexually polluted others with sexually transmitted infections were sentenced to corporal punishment or death. Vedic culture does not sanction promiscuity or aberrant sexual actions that can lead to disease or cause vitiation of the partners' health and wellness.

Vedic literature teems with metaphors for the physical and cosmic union between woman and man, many of which are lunar and solar in nature. Ancient Tantric carvings depict Shiva-Shakti as Chandra, the moon, which is androgynous – both masculine and feminine. The lunar circle is yet another form that emphasizes the conjugal rite of female and male energies as being yin and yang, lunar and solar, intuitive and rational, and the awen. The Vedic seers recorded their vast knowledge of human sexuality and sensuality connected to the lunar and solar cycles in copious manuals such as the Kama Sutra, the Ananga Ranga, and the Koka Sastra. They demonstrated how the lunar wheel correlated with the fertility cycle of the female Shakti force and how solar power affects the virility of the male Shiva force. They emphasized the underlying magical mysteries and requisite qualities that contribute to sexual compatibility. The fullness of the circular moon, considered the most auspicious time for sexual practice, symbolizes the amalgam of Shiva-Shakti. Once the genders coalesce, the feminine and masculine energies fuse. On the physical plane, this union is mirrored by the sperm's desire to merge with the ovum. In sexual liaison, Shiva and Shakti are referred to as Kameshvara and Kameshvari, the presiding deities of the moon, the lunar source of desire. Kameshvara is portrayed as the most magnificent male design in the universe, sitting in a divine embrace with his beloved, Kameshvari, the most beautiful female in all the worlds. In this spiritual-sexual union, Kameshvara's projectile energy foments the rising of cosmic energy into consciousness, while

Kameshvari's energies extend outward, rooting down to birth the creation. A woman's Shakti force has many roles, but her essence lies in Kameshvari's energy – the primordial feminine creative and healing energies.

To reclaim the precious gems of our conscious sexuality and sentience, it is incumbent on us to discard the conditioned mind and its manufactured reality fostered by eons of binary thinking and divisive patriarchal ideology. In modern society, we have been conditioned by family, peers, society, religion, and media to accept a set of belief systems, ideas, doctrines, convictions, prejudices, and perceptions that generally oppose our direct human experience. Human experience is rich, varied, deeply personal, unique, and incredibly nuanced; it is the antithesis of binary thinking, which conditions us to see things as diametrically opposed absolutes. Our authentic reality is infinitely greater than these divisive and limiting absolutes; it is abundant and forever steeped in the empathetic goddess nature. As Joseph Campbell reminds us, "When you have a Goddess as the creator, it is her own body that is the universe. She is identical with the universe ... She is the whole sphere of the life-enclosing heavens."

After more than 300,000 years since humans first appeared on Earth, our actions make it difficult to comprehend that we are fitted with this miraculously upgraded, illumined brain. It is high time we realized that we are no longer children or adolescents learning the human craft of awareness. We are ancient souls, tired of being tethered to the revolving wheel of vacuous personal gratification, empty and abusive relationships, and stultified sentience. The time to evolve quantum leaps in consciousness and reclaim the glory of humanity's wisdom, intelligence, and grace is now. In the next chapter, I have set out a primer for the Shiva-energized male to reclaim his innate beauty, not only in his outward appearance but in the deep reservoir of rising consciousness that is his pure nature.

Below, I have set out a simple practice for The Shiva Lingam Mudra, which has proven helpful to the many couples and individuals I have assisted in restoring their Shiva-Shakti sexuality, health, and wholeness.

Shiva-Lingam Mudra – Enhancing Sexual Balance

This practice helps women integrate the feminine (lunar/Shakti) and masculine (solar/Shiva) energies within and strengthens the indelible bond of trust between couples. Lingam literally means "attribute" or "sign of Shiva." Shiva-Lingam Mudra is a powerful yet simple practice to keep a balance of Shiva-Shakti in a spousal relationship. Each couple may practice this mudra individually or together. All genders and biological sexes are invited to practice this mudra to strengthen sexual-spiritual awareness in yourself as an individual. Whether practicing with your partner or alone, begin with the sacred intention to keep transforming your sexual relationship into one of divine love. Shiva-Lingam Mudra practice is known to bring the reproductive organs, nervous system, and breath into a state of balance, thereby strengthening vitality and virility in the body. This mudra is also a meditative practice to calm the mind and expand awareness and intuition. It is a vital exercise for strengthening *apana prana* – the downward-flowing life force. It brings awareness of your subtle body and inspires a deep sense of harmony in your relationship.

As a fifteen-minute daily practice, sit facing each other. Breathe easily with your hands folded in your lap. Close your eyes. You will immediately find your breath syncing automatically, feeling a sense of oneness, each possessing your own integrity. Over time, this practice creates a deep and seamless flow between you. If you're doing this mudra alone, you may practice only the first part of this exercise. Part two of this practice requires a Shiva or Shakti balancing partner.

The Practice: Shiva Lingam Mudra — Enhancing Sexual Balance

PART ONE:

You are using both hands in this practice. The right hand is a conduit for your solar breath, and the left hand for your lunar breath. The particular configuration of this mudra integrates the energies of Shiva and Shakti within you.

- Retreat to a quiet place in your home or outdoors and sit in a comfortable cross-legged position on a pillow or upright in a straight-backed chair.
- Bring your left hand, palm up, to chest level, with your fingers together.
- Make a fist with your right hand, with the thumb pointing up, and place it securely on the left palm.
- Close your eyes and meditate on the primeval energy of lingam, the source of consciousness.
- Next, visualize the lingam in the form of a translucent crystal pillar.
- Then, visualize the yoni as a solid, concave stone, golden in color.
- Visualize the yoni as the base support upon which the lingam rests.

PART TWO:

This second part of the practice will help partners to seal an indelible bond with each other. The woman visualizes her spouse as the Lingam, Pure Consciousness. The man visualizes his wife as the Yoni, the Formidable Base of Consciousness.

- Shift your position to face your partner.
- Start your mudra partner practice by using the male's right hand and the female's left hand.

- Women, bring your left hand with your palm up to chest level. You may brace your elbow into your waist for support.
- Men, make a fist with your right hand with your thumb up and rest it into the outstretched palm of your partner's left hand, your thumb pointing toward her.
- Hold this position, close your eyes, and begin to breathe gently.
- Concentrate on synchronizing your breathing rhythm with each other. Hold the mudra position for 5 minutes or so, then gently release your hands.
- Fold your hands softly in your lap.
- Sit and be with each other for a short while.

This practice should evolve over time and must not be rushed. Gradually, you will find your inner bond strengthening and your bond with each other deepening.

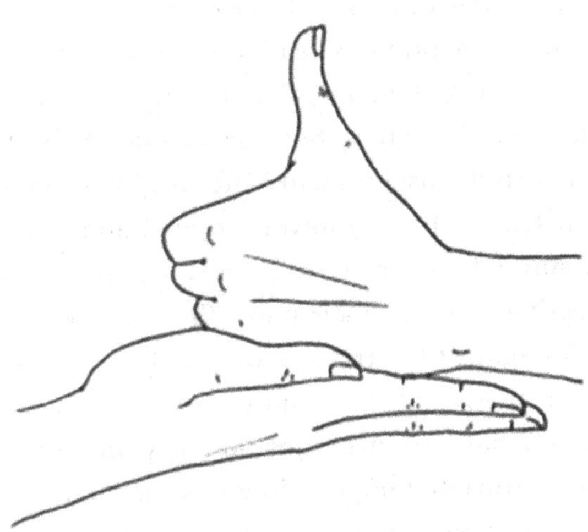

Fig. 5. Shiva Lingam Mudra

Chapter 12

Reclaiming the Shiva Masculine Code

> *This is the time of the emergent Divine Masculine presence, stepping up to the edge and committing to live from there, rising up to support and protect the Sacred Feminine Mission of Global Awakening.*
>
> Sophie Bashford

The world is not without awakened, Shiva-ful men and more are emerging every day. Still others will answer the call as we raise our standard – both literally and figuratively – and lead the way. Together, we are pioneers of a new movement of evolving consciousness and open hearts, defying the old paradigms and binaries and awake enough to walk beside each other as we change the world forever. We need to help men remember that there have been times and places where they were free to emote, showing gentleness, sadness, and even vulnerability rather than having their emotional range restricted to anger and satisfaction. There have been times when they have been at liberty to adorn themselves with soft, bright, flowing garments and hair instead of being forever cropped and buttoned into a drab grey suit, where they have been able to be vibrant, unique, and expressive – when their noble Shiva voices rang out like nightingales against the tremors of a palladium welkin. I wish to open your eyes, dear men and boys, to the confining reality in which you have been encapsulated, your voice shredded, your inner prowess tamped down, your vigor and vitality misdirected. The patriarchy, in truth, is as much opposed to the wellness of men as it is to women, a continuing detriment to the sentient progress of humanity. Dear men, you once sang and tweeted like beautiful nightingales that proudly advertised your Shiva manhood and your dedication to beauty, family, and joy. Did you know that one of the criteria a female nightingale uses when choosing a mate is his ability to sing? The greater his repertoire in the variety of songs, whistles, thrills, and buzzes he can employ, the greater his chances of wooing her. Male nightingales are known to be doting fathers — they visit their chicks' nests as many as 16 times every hour, which is about as often as their mothers do. Mired in your own quicksand of toxic masculinity, you men have become trapped by rigid modes of self-expression, limited in your emotional and even sartorial range by the dread of being perceived as "too feminine." You, too, are born to this Earth to sing, to nurture your young, to express yourself without censure, and to delight in your glorious plumage. It is high time you recalibrate your Shiva energy to restore your magnificence inside and out. When you do the focused work to reclaim your cosmic destiny, you rekindle your well-being and purpose and fortify women, children, and the Earth itself with your sublime Shiva energy.

As a first step to recovering your sentience as a heterosexual man, allow me to take you on what may be a surprising journey: the evolution of your dress code. Enhancing your attire and grooming, believe it or not, is a step on the path to reclaiming your conscious masculinity. It may sound trivial, but I have found that when we change our appearance, we change our mindset. Conversely, our dress codes can and have been used to suppress, control, and diminish Shiva-Shakti vibrancy and pure expression. By unabashedly presenting who you are to the world, which has been brainwashed to underestimate the true strength and beauty of your masculinity, you assert your Shiva-generating power.

As an external construct, clothing has had a potent effect on the nature of your magnificent primordial masculine form. Patriarchy's restrictions are woven neatly into the physical and psychological images it tailored for you, from the Victorian straight jacket of fashion that you've been muscled into to the tie around your neck, perfected from the noose by which we lawlessly hung our prejudices. Our decisions about how we adorn our bodies transcend symbolic trends, fashion, economic status, and social stature. As a designer in my early years who pioneered fashion trends from my Maya Boutique on Madison Avenue and 66th Street in New York City, I recognize the impact of what we wear. My creations were sought after by high fashion retailers such as Bergdorf Goodman, Bloomingdales, Henri Bendel, and I. Magnin. I dressed celebrities like Rudolf Nureyev and other renowned performers and musicians. My hand-crafted cummerbunds, bows, and opera shawls for men were sought after by Hollywood dressers and are still being used to dress male heroes in period movies. I know well that what you choose to wear expresses your individuality and should demonstrate a sense of freedom, enhancing your masculinity in the sense of its original Shiva beauty, nobility, and confidence. It does not need to be expensive. It does not have to be defensively gaudy. It does not have to feel awkward. You are not imitating the feminine but restoring your forgotten primordial nature. When you dress to claim your freedom and clarity of purpose — whether in full regalia or a simple robe — you are untethering your masculinity, displaying your feathers like the avian males who vie for the attention and partnership of the discerning female.

Sexual magnetism fortifies Shiva-Shakti-generated consciousness and the ways we choose to care for and artfully adorn our person play no small role in this. When the masculine meets his true self, he attracts the awakened feminine, bringing balance to his life and the world. This biological requirement for deep molecular functioning between the male and female — the primeval Shiva-Shakti magnetism — is endemic to all species. If you are looking to attract your Shakti partner or connect with her on a deeper level, it is imperative that you stand up and realize your true worth in this advancing new planet. You want to express your presence in such a way that the awakened female can see you are rising to purpose, exhibiting an unwavering poised presence, your warrior spirit, your stability, your transparency, your individuality, and most of all, your Shiva code of consciousness. Dressing to suit his natural human masculine design arouses a new sensation in the Shiva-seeking male and activates new levels of consciousness. He is seen; he is recognized. He is finally genuinely comfortable in his own skin. He assumes the powerful elements of confidence and deep, authentic security of a heterosexual male. Homosexual, transgender, and other third-gender men have already begun to reclaim their soul expression. The way they dress contributes to their freedom to be who they are. Why not the heterosexual male? Isn't it high time you stopped emulating and being intimidated by the status quo symbols and worn scars of patriarchy that suppress your authentic nature? In some species, courting males fight each other, making the female's decision for her. But as a Shiva male, I do not suggest you engage in a competitive fight for your female. The proven way for you to take charge of your life and attract purpose, confidence, and your soul flame is to do what birds have been doing for eons: unabashedly show off your exquisite maleness, your mandrake colors, through your self-care, dress, ornaments, display, and pursuit of purpose. Indeed, a wise Shakti partner will be able to glean your inner qualities as well. This deceptively simple act of reclaiming a joyful external expression of self will support you to deepen your consciousness, enhance your Shiva energy, attract an awakened partner, and contribute to the rise of global Shiva-Shakti consciousness.

Avian males are a great example, by and large, of the natural beauty and opulence ferried by the male species. Heterosexual males can learn a great deal from our feathered friends about mining intelligence and attracting their love partners, not to mention being inspired to up-level the opulence and dynamism of their attire. Over many millennia, the selected traits of the confident avian male became amplified – female birds invariably choose the mate with superior appearance or antics. The awakened woman likewise appreciates the appearance and courtly charms of a potential mate; however, these alone will not suffice. The mating process in the awakened Shakti woman and Shiva man is triggered by the molecular pull to seek and fulfill Shiva-Shakti unification. While appearance matters, it must serve as a window to his character, integrity, and the thrilling discovery that he is conscious and aligned with the greater energies of nature.

Avian mating can teach men a thing or two about reawakening their Shiva verve. The spectacular tresses, dresses, and displays employed by a male bird in its mating ritual are a perfect metaphor to inspire men to reclaim the grand presence, innate beauty, confidence, and power of the Shiva male. Male birds flash their glistening iridescent colors in the air to attract female interest. The more colorful the avian male, the more confident he appears in his demonstrations and dances to win the attention of the female. With a flick of his onyx-black tail feather, the male bird of paradise whirs, turns, and clicks his tail rhythmically, flashing a breastplate of iridescent hues as he choreographs his way down a fashion runway. This is not to suggest that the Shiva male has to be dressed in the most colorful garb or perform outlandish feats to demonstrate or own his prowess; subtlety is also a key trait in the avian male kingdom, especially among families where both male and female raise and nurture the offspring. Bald eagles, for instance, mate for life, and there is very little differentiation of coloring between the male and female. The avian male can also change his appearance to emulate his companion and protect his female during nesting. One such example is the male mandarin or drake. A social duck recognized by its gorgeous red bill and a very prominent white crescent patterned just above the eye, boasting a purple breast and orange 'sails' on the back, sloughs his flamboyant plumage after the breeding season is over. The Shiva male protection of his spouse and family is intrinsic to his nature. Male birds will go the distance to create and hold a fort of protection for their loved ones. Following the mating season, the drake assumes the subdued colors of his female counterpart – colors of the underbrush to camouflage himself in the event he needs to protect his female's nest. If females that nested in the open were brightly colored, both they and their nesting flock would be vulnerable to predators. A similarity, perhaps: data shows that men whose partners are pregnant can experience a similar sense of "compathy" – the need to dress down, the empathetic partner pull to bear and share similarity to their women. For a short period, their inner dressing can also hormonally change to produce estradiol, the female sex hormone produced by the ovaries, while their male hormone, testosterone, decreases.

Spectacular or subtle, plumage is a story about a man's ability to rekindle their well-being and purpose and fortify women, children, and the Earth itself with their Shiva energy. The masculine Homo sapiens appears to have forgotten how to move in tandem with their Shiva-infused purpose, tamping down their own primordial nature as a consciousness-generator of the human species. As men own their true nature, they become happier and more aligned with their intrinsic power to express their individuality, masculine vigor, and freedom through appearance.

Masculine Dress Codes at Odds with Conscious Evolution

Men have not always been bound by a grey, blue, and brown dress code. In the arc of history, the idea of gendered clothing is fairly new, particularly the drab, buttoned-up costume of the modern male. Until the first half of the twentieth century, skirts and frocks worn by men allowed them to move with fluidity and freedom. Long gowns and full-skirted coats with or without embroidered ornamentation were an acceptable and fashionable part of men's wardrobes. Skirts were the practical dress of our most ancient civilizations on both sides of the gender binary. Fluent cloths worn as wraps, sarongs, dhotis, kurtas, loincloths, and togas were replete among men of all social stature. Short skirts among soldiers were considered proof of virility and allowed for swiftness in combat. Male attire was frequently dominated by short hemlines paired with stockings that showed off well-formed, muscular legs. Even the gendered color preference that we take for granted is a relatively modern construct. In 1927, *Time* magazine printed a chart highlighting gender-appropriate colors for girls and boys according to leading US retailers, and parents took to the suggestion like wildfire. They started to dress boys in blue and girls in pink. Ironically, in Europe, until the 1920s, pink was considered to be more suitable for boys and blue for girls. This superficial turnabout of gendered colors dovetailed the misogynistic characteristics patriarchs imposed upon the powerful feminine. In an analysis of color psychology in marketing and branding, pink evokes nurturing — as in nesting, incubating, and suckling. Pink, as employed in Barbie's iconic image, is warm, soft, feminine, subdued, and sexual. Some analysis even suggests that pink is perceived to indicate inhibition, emotional claustrophobia, emasculation, and physical weakness. Blue, on the other hand, is perceived to imbue loyalty, serenity, truth, wisdom, balance, and authority (no surprise, then, that marketing data shows blue to be the most popular color overall). While these associations are, in fact, consistent with the Shiva force characteristics of stability, protection, and maintaining balance, the societal agreement to adopt blue as a preferred color for men merely reinforced the idea that men are the rational half of the species whose dominant role it is to control the weaker and more emotional feminine force.

What we know as fashion for men and women today emerged from a superficial social construct that forces rigid, cookie-cutter gender expression while creating the commercial advent of fashion trends for profit. Driven by profiteering goals, the pernicious force behind men's fashion feeds on consumer gullibility. Men's attire is no longer an expression of individuality and purpose, or even practicality and comfort, but a brand that stamps out the originality, sensuality, and awareness we feel when dressing to express our true selves. We are simply "improving" the fashion of competition, stiffness, status, stature, and sameness. Less than a century ago, men's movement was made staccato, strapped in trousers and boots. While functionality and technological progress did play a role in this turnabout, it carried collateral damage.

The Victorian period was a key moment in history that transformed attire for men and women alike. The intent was to suppress sexuality; to repress the female while holding tighter reigns on men's freedom as well. Prudery in dress, thought, and talk was paramount in this era. Academics now view Victorians as sexual hypocrites, maintaining a cover of respectable society over an understory of prostitution and pornography. This sexual prudery was at odds with men's conscious evolution. The pantsuit for men shouted the Victorian mantra: wear this uniform and flaunt your manly power. Suddenly, it was unacceptable for men to wear skirts that displayed their sinewy legs or gracefully flaunted their manly stride. A man's attire became his uniform, and he became another faceless soldier forced into common-issue khaki and sent off to the trenches. The new protocol was a layer of underwear under trousers with a shirt, suit, tie, socks, and shoes. Maleness went on lockdown, or at least in the visible overarch of its culture. Women, of course, were locked down even tighter. Her beauty and curves were shrouded under overprotective armor. She was forced into an artillery of clothing: heavy, unwieldy skirts, stockings, layers of dresses, and tight corsets that limited her mobility and restricted her from showing as little as an ankle. In this regard, at least, women have made massive strides in freeing themselves from claustrophobic attitudes and attires, setting the modern world ablaze with their Shakti felinity. Isn't it high time the Shiva males follow 'suit-lessly' into their magnificent masculine expression? Re-envision your wardrobe as a reliquary, a sacred space that holds the beautiful "feathers" you will consciously don internally and externally as you redeem your primordial masculine identity.

At the start of the nineteenth century, Edward VII, the eldest son of Queen Victoria, set the trend for men's trousers as we know them today. In the 1920s and 1930s, the Duke of Windsor innovated the "straight jacket" of a suit men still wear today, along with his famous Windsor-knotted tie. Although a semblance of the trousers was first introduced as early as the third century BCE, it was not until the seventeenth century that the trend started to become fashionable. Bifurcated European garments — breeches, knickerbockers, and pantaloons — were a looser fit with a button fly, worn in neutral colors. These men's trousers had become practical attire for riding horses. From Samurai riding costumes in Japan to the nomadic herders of Mongolia, horses and riding meant wearing pants. However, it was not practicality but a dramatic social movement that made pants as a replacement for skirts the mandate for menswear. The clear gender divide in clothing arrived shortly after World War I ended in 1918. World War II contributed to a major change in men's fashion, further tamping men's conscious evolution. As a result of the war's massive destruction and immediate societal need, women came to the rescue. They began to run businesses, and to voice their discontent, they advocated for educational, housing, and health improvements. Ironically, while pants are celebrated as representing women's emancipation, this scenario masked a psychological disorder at play. A trouser was symbolic of the patriarchal power of men. Denied their own Shakti power for so long, women proudly snatched at it. Wearing trousers, they emulated patriarchal power. They felt empowered. In the meantime, after World War I, the brutalities of war were so inscribed on the minds of men that it penetrated the mindset of generations of male offspring that followed. Wars serve to dehumanize the inner machination of male populations. They had a direct and devastating impact on men's inner performance, outer appearance, and sense of eloquence, elegance, and beauty. Wars create nasty, ugly, disfigured apparitions of the human form, yet they are promoted by the military as heroic, courageous, stalwart, and noble acts of sacrifice. Soldiers who were trenched in terror and unspeakable horrors returned battered in body and soul, garbed in torn military gear. The legacy of wars that influenced men in and between wartime is a collection of traumatized scars. This unfortunate inheritance inhibits and suppresses their Shiva-ness, the pure essence of their manly soul, strength, and courage, amply reflected by their current attire. Soldiers and men imitating soldiers never got out of military uniforms. Trousers became their standard attire from this time forward. In their mind, this uniform of pants, suit, and tie — this "straight-jacket ensemble" — equates with the glorious symbol for male sacrifice: being a soldier, a hero fighting for their country. Men's current dress code is a blatant cultural example of the lessons in transgression that continually bring awareness to pain, the inevitable human factor that makes us vulnerable and thus susceptible to ideologies that transform human behavior, either for good or to our demise.

Our history as a species is unique; the arc of time shows the many twists and turns in the development of human appearance, activity, and consciousness. With the quantum leaps of consciousness in human evolution, we would expect an equal degree of development in the sapience of our behavior, lifeways, and dress codes. Shouldn't these things be synced to our consciousness growth? Instead, the things we call advancements in many areas of our lives – clothing, fashions, the gazillion products we've created, even our homes – are a complete antithesis to conscious progress, practically, spiritually, and environmentally. For example, synthetic fibers leave a squalid footprint of microfibers and microplastics in our soil and water. They make up 40 percent of the microplastic that enters the ocean. Most so-called conscious fashion collections incorporate hazardous, synthetic textiles that are only partially recycled. The eco-labels do nothing but distract shoppers from the health risks living in their wardrobes. Data shows that polyester, for instance, emits phytoestrogens that act as endocrine disrupters and can cause certain cancers and respiratory disorders.

In restoring his rightful identity, the Shiva male is encouraged to embrace the beauty and simplicity that the present time demands – to reintroduce Earth's opulence by using more sustainable and eco-friendly natural fibers. As we use less energy-intensive and synthetic methods, we take back our power from patriarchal commercialism. We must restore intelligence to our human life, which flourishes environmentally, physically, and emotionally in tandem with nature. We live in a time that demands conscious simplicity and the practice of ahimsa, or non-violence; that is, simplicity connected to the grandeur and freedom of a distant past that was once protected and conserved by the Shiva male. Natural fibers for clothing have been harvested since humans first decided to cover up. We have access to fine fabric production processes that have been in use for millennia. We can substitute environmentally conscious bamboo for silks and carefully harvest wool and pashmina humanely to avoid injuring the animals. We can grow cotton and linen more sustainably and mix them with hemp or bamboo to decrease the agri-violence of their commercial cultivation. Ironically, early humans possessed a more evolved consciousness of nature, living and bearing the force of her raw elements. Although modern populations boast a more complex brain capable of evolving quantum leaps in consciousness, we are perilously alienated from Earth's intelligence. We have severed our bond with her.

The Shiva Man's Non-Binary Fashion in Vedic India

As far as we know, opulent, non-binary fashion began in India, where an infinite number of fashion trends for men and women are still present in the culture today. During the Vedic era, from around 1500–500 BCE, attire for men and women was almost identical, designed for function, environmental suitability, and fashionable form. India's exquisite dress style later influenced the Europeans, who gleaned their fashion eloquence from India's riches on their many sea voyages to and from India during the spice trade. Simplicity with eloquence characterized the Shiva male fashion. A single cloth draped around the body and across the shoulder was pinned or fastened with a belt and was considered comfortable attire for hot weather. A *paridhana* was a lower garment consisting of a cloth draped around the waist and tied with a string or belt called a *rasana*. Warmth and fluidity were the fashion tantra for the colder season. A shawl-like garment worn over the shoulder was called an *uttaiya,* and an over cloak was worn in the cold months. Above all, the Shiva male fashion extolled freedom and spaciousness to allow for swift movement. Vedic men were known to wear dhotis, which were wrapped around the waist and pleated to allow freedom of movement. Mohendro-jaro excavations uncovered figurines that showed priests and kings wearing robes strapped over one shoulder with elaborate turbans draped over their heads and adorned with jewelry. Prior to its endless stream of foreign invaders, India had many reigning dynasties, kingdoms, and rulers — Mughals, Marathas, Scindia, Rajputana, Wadiyars,

Pratapgarh, Holkar, Gaekwads — that contributed distinct styles that influenced the ancient Indian wardrobe. As one of the world's wealthiest countries before the British invaded and nearly destroyed India, these dynasties took immense pride in projecting prosperity to the nation as the Mughals bequeathed the perfection of craftsmanship to India. Their fine sense of artistry and workmanship in art, clothing, and jewelry remains unparalleled. In clothing, as in architecture, their magnificent style is still reflected in India's brilliant, indigenous styling, which, in turn, is influenced by the spiritual largesses of the Vedic tradition. For example, the six opulences of the god Krishna — strength, wisdom, wealth, fame, beauty, and renunciation — became the framework of the Indian mind that is sought after and emulated through the creation of India's edifices, art, architecture, and fashion.

The distinct Mughal fashion trend was characterized by attires created from luxurious silk, velvet, brocade, and muslin cloth with elaborate embroidery. The brave Gaekwads who took over the reins from the Mughals in Baroda in 1721 had a love for India's innate opulence. They wore long silk robes, exquisite turbans, strings of pearls, and fine jewelry crusted with rare gemstones, forging the vibration of the wealth of Earth, sun, and moon and projecting their happiness and beauty into the hearts of its people. The Holkar dynasty was known for its fine jewelry in the early twentieth century. Famous French jewelers like Chaumet and Van Clef were hired to craft and design heritage jewelry pieces for Maharaja Yashwant Rao. The Scindia dynasty left the legacy of the traditional Anga, a brocade and silk kurta, or long flowing shirt, which gave the appearance of a coat, and a sheathed sword, still worn on festive occasions by men. The not-so-veiled message of the Anga is this: we are ready to defend dharma, that universal value that protects all. The Maharawat wore turbans adorned with precious stones such as rubies, diamonds, and pearls, often embellished with a peacock feather.

These riches pinned upon a turban could never match the wealth contained in the grand universal mind. The signature jewelry of the Nizams of Hyderabad had a major influence on Indian jewelry and became world-famous for its distinct setting of pearls and exquisite gemstones. The Nizams styled the sherwani – a turban embellished with an elaborate brooch known as a *sarpech*. From the time of yore, India has always shared its wealth, wisdom, and grace with the world, forever rippling out its beneficent blessings to humanity. One of the most modest of royals is the family of Travancore. The Maharajas of Travancore lived a life of simplicity and humanitarianism. They wore Mundu clothing, simply cut in cream or white color and adorned with a light touch of gold embroidery. The Mundu speaks to India's finest opulence and wealth – its innate Shakti to generate and regenerate simplicity and wisdom. Ancient India's fashion for men ranged from opulent to simple, each style influenced by a dynasty whose males were symbols of elegance, eloquence, freedom, and beauty. They dressed to influence, express, and flaunt these Shiva-imbued qualities.

During British rule in India, their diabolical colonization campaign ravaged and silenced an India that was still choking on its voice. Colonized atrocities hurled at the male population skillfully forced a nation to bow in terror to Britain's racism, hatred, arrogance, greed, and aggression. Almost immediately, the professional male segment of India began changing their attire to Western-style clothing, from dhotis and turbans to trousers and linen shirts, as India adapted to the lifestyle of Europe's restrictive clothing. These restrictive clothing styles were paralleled by more restrictive cultural behaviors at odds with men's conscious evolution. The British uniformed India's vast diversity – a deliberate thrust to replace India's noble indigenous culture with their white supremacist agenda. The Western dress code was systematically enforced as a means of herding and impoverishing men physically, mentally, and spiritually.

With the finest craftsmanship in clothing and ultimate skills in textile production, India's fashion is finally experiencing a resurgence of the pageantry of centuries past, a flashback to beautiful palaces and forts, fine arts, and music. Fashion the world over – from Africa, Europe, America, and Britain to China and Japan – is also exploding with bold, colorful, and bejeweled splendor in men's clothing. One can only hope that we will soon begin to see a corresponding resurgence of Shiva energy in men as they return to the embrace of their splendid sartorial heritage.

Appearance is but a small part of who we are, yet it is a potent form of non-verbal communication, broadcasting our unique characters, perspectives, and loves to others while reifying them for ourselves. A man's dress code and personal presentation reflect his inner and outer conditioning and affect his self-awareness and perspective. Reclaiming individual expression in one's dress and self-care enables men to heighten their consciousness, enhance their Shiva energy, attract and satisfy an awakened partner, and facilitate the rise of global Shiva-Shakti consciousness. A brand new era calls for the awakened Shiva male to reflect and reorganize his character and grand presence. Refine or redefine who you are. Your Shakti partners and the entire world are in dire need of the stability and protection you bring when you join the mission of global awakening. I invite you to join me in a thought exercise – jot down a few words describing how you feel about yourself as a man. What is missing? What dream or vision portrays how you would like to be, feel, move, and dress? Does this vision support you in better attracting or connecting with your Shakti partner? May you realize this vision, and may it find you in more expansive clothing, with a driving purpose that is environmentally sound and a journey that reflects your magnificent freedom, ancestral bearings, and unique individual character.

Chapter 13

Embracing the Third Gender

I was in darkness, but I took three steps and found myself in paradise. The first step was a good thought, the second, a good word; and the third, a good deed.

Friedrich Nietzsche

While society's views on sexuality continuously evolve, the Shiva-Shakti divinity within us is perpetual. However we choose or wish to live in terms of our identity, sexual preferences, or beliefs, we are all endowed with both Shiva and Shakti energies. We may alter our gender as either gender may invoke or feel more akin to the Shakti or the Shiva energies. We can fulfill whatever our desires may be; every woman may be a goddess or a god as they choose, every man a god or a goddess as their sense of self dictates. What we cannot change is the innate nature of the person. Every one of us, whether female, male, or fluid, contains both divine male and divine female energies. As we reconcile the power and purpose of the Shakti force, we are moved to embrace the fullness of our humanity and life in all forms, including all genders, all beings, all species, and every iota of our Mother's vast nature. The expression of gender in all its expansive forms is part of the natural order, and there is no room for prejudice or intolerance in the world we are heading toward.

In the Vedic perspective, all life is sacred, and every birth serves a divine role and purpose. In exploring the Vedic view of the third gender, I recall the words of Hans-Peter Duerr, a physicist who lauded Vedanta, "Matter and energy are the two sides of the same coin. They are not two distinct entities at the subtlest level." Shiva-Shakti energy and matter are conjoined within every individual, first gender, second gender, and third gender. Data tells us the global population of homosexual, transgender, and third-gender individuals is estimated to be at least 5 percent of the world population, about 350 million people. The possibility of someone changing sex became widely known when, in 1952, Christine Jorgensen became the first person to undergo widely publicized sex reassignment surgery. In 2017, Bruce Jenner transitioned to Caitlyn, "Transparent" won the Emmy Awards, and a transgender Virginia teen's case to use the men's bathroom at his school headed to the Supreme Court. The term "transgender" was coined in 1960. Today, the term "non-binary" is also employed to denote a more expansive sense of gender. At present, "gender identity" is defined as the person's relationship to themselves and how they conceptualize their gender, which can and does change for many. With the digital propagation of gender identity, Facebook now offers 58 types of trans designations, while Tinder offers 37 and counting.

While some may choose to ignore the inhumane conditions foisted upon this population or cast them aside as a dysfunction of our society, as we do with people experiencing homelessness, the Shakti maternal power inspires us to embrace humanity and all of its forms and diversities with the diligence and respect we would otherwise afford ourselves and our family. The truth is we are all an intricate part of the Shakti force. Suffering is contagious. It influences our happiness. In the purview of the universal mind, if one of us suffers, so do we all. On our path toward enlightenment, we must cultivate awareness and accountability for the suffering we cause through our conscious and unconscious biases. As the Prophet would say, prejudice is not a symptom of stupidity, nor is it a symptom of evil. It is merely a symptom of ignorance.

In this chapter, I introduce many Sanskrit terms for Tritiya Prakriti, which many of us know as the third gender, since the English counterpart fails to convey the full meaning of this highly controversial concept. The Vedic principle of Tritiya Prakriti portrays gender as a fluent spectrum rather than the Western concept of a gender binary. Many modern researchers now surmise that biology, including genetic or inborn hormonal factors, plays a significant role in determining not only a person's physical sex but also their gender identity and sexual orientation.

People of the third gender are part of a broader social category of humanity that does not fit into the gender binary of man and woman. This gender is commonly identified in the Vedic system as the "neutral gender." This neutral or third gender is exhaustively described in the *Kama Shastra* – the body of work that gave us the *Kama Sutra*. The great sage Vyasadeva wrote the *Kama Shastra* approximately 5000 years ago. It was then subsequently divided into several texts that perished for more than 1000 years until they were restored by Sage Vatsyayana around 300 CE. The result was the renowned *Kama Sutra* or "codes of sensual pleasure." Although commonly presented to Westerners as an erotic sex manual, the unabridged *Kama Sutra* gives us a rare glimpse into the sexual understandings of ancient India. Tritiya Prakriti, or third gender, covers the broad spectrum of human gender that transcends maleness and femaleness. *Napumsaka,* a Sanskrit word that literally means "not male" or "intersex," is a special category of the third gender that refers to those who are either non-sexual or not sexually active: children, the elderly, the impotent, those who've lost their reproductive ability, and the celibate such as monks, nuns, sadhus, or spiritual entities who've renounced societal life, including mendicants. Individuals classified as Napumsaka do not and are not expected to contribute to procreation or sexual reproduction.

Tritiya Prakriti is further broken down into several categories characterized by a combined male/female nature with an inherent homosexual orientation that manifests at puberty. Homosexual males, *kliba*, and lesbians, *svairini*, are the most prominent groups in this category. Each category is further divided into two, depending on whether their behavior is more masculine or feminine. They are then divided again into many subcategories, which include transgender and intersex persons, as well as the numerous biological nuances in sex configuration, some of which are now being scientifically researched and validated. Homosexuality and transgender identity are some of the most common forms of intersexuality. This explains why Sanskrit words describing people of the third gender – homosexual, transgender, and intersex individuals – are grouped in the classification of Tritiya Pakriti. The *Kama Shastra* informs us that intersexuality is far less prevalent than homosexuality. Bisexuality is not classified under the cover of Tritiya Prakriti. The Sanskrit word for bisexual is *kami*, a word indicating that such persons are especially amorous and fond of sexual intimacy, which they display in a variety of ways. Kami includes people who are simultaneously attracted to both men and women or who engage in homosexuality for reasons other than an innate attraction. Those who periodically switch back and forth between heterosexuality and homosexuality are referred to in Sanskrit as *paksha*.

While the *Kama Shastra* has clear naming conventions for a spectrum of genders and behaviors and other cultures have their own equivalents, it is important to consult the individuals' preferences to learn how they wish to be identified. For example, Southeast Asia is populated with 15 million individuals commonly referred to as hijra, who were identified as male at birth but identify as feminine, as do many transgender and intersex individuals. However, this community prefers to be addressed as "third gender." In India, the nomenclature chosen by the third gender folks is *kinnar*, a term used in arts and entertainment for theatrical performers, actors, artists, dancers, and singers.

The anomalous nature of the third gender is a condition that the Vedic sachems recognized as a rich and purposeful contribution to humanity. For this reason, their presence was considered a benign grace, a blessing to the community. That is to say, a non-reproductive, non-procreative, neutral gender in nature plays a significant role in keeping harmony and balance in the predominantly heterosexual community as a whole. Exempt of the inner design and programming to participate in procreation, third-gender individuals are born outliers and simultaneous go-betweens with a foot in each world. These beloved renegades are imbued with the creative freedom to create art, crafts, and culture; they are contributors of unique perspectives that step away from the framework of heterosexual social responsibilities. In the necessary mix of human diversity, they bring joy, friendship, beauty, and frivolity; they are entertainers who bring relief and pause to an overworked, tedious world. Their presence teaches us to broaden our perspectives and embrace diversity, forcing us to open our hearts and evolve beyond binary judgments, biases, and contempt for nature's differentiation.

Nature abounds with the diversity of unique and uncommon forms within every one of her species. Animal science proves that third-gender activity is prevalent in the animal kingdom. The female Cape bee, a subspecies of honeybee from South Africa, for instance, is a worker bee that can escape her queen's control, take over other colonies, and reproduce asexually. According to University of Oslo zoologist Peter Brockman, about 1500 animal species are known to practice same-sex coupling, including bears, gorillas, flamingos, owls, sheep, bottlenose dolphins, killer whales, and West Indian manatees. The male bighorn sheep live in what are often called homosexual societies. They bond through anal intercourse and general frolicking. Ironically, if a male sheep refrains from the sexual liaisons, it becomes a social outcast. Giraffes, too, are known to have all-male orgies, while the Japanese macaques, on the other hand, are impassioned lesbians, frequently coupling with each other.

Ancient native cultures held the third gender in high regard, as elaborated in ancient Hindu stories. It is no surprise that Vedic India was in harmony with all of its kin; after all, this was the land and people whose greatest treasure was the practice of Santana Dharma, upholding universal truths and kindness. Even today, the Napumsaka – the celibate community of ascetics, sages, sadhus, monks, and nuns who have renounced societal life for a devout one – are respected and embraced in India. Tragically, however, India's once fluid acceptance of Tritiya Prakriti is now transmuted into apathy and scorn.

Of India's population of 1.324 billion, 5 million citizens identify as transgender. Although they were recently granted voting rights and given the necessary social security, these individuals continue to be ostracized. Once adored in the ancient land of India, this community has now become ignobly disparaged by the majority of people across the globe. But India today has also turned its back on the third gender. This altered, inhumane attitude toward the third gender identity is entirely attributable to India's deeply colonized mindset and its perpetrators.

In the mid-nineteenth century, during the British occupation of India, the colonizers dismissed outright the existence of the third gender, wielding their own Western bias of the man and woman designed to procreate the human race. As a result, the British colonizers enforced the Criminal Act in India in 1871, segregating hijras as a criminal tribe. The entire third-gender population thereafter was forced to endure the stigma of being repugnant, corrupt, unnatural, and immoral. The British colonizers passed laws that usurped the rights of third-gender citizens by refusing to acknowledge them as homosexual or third gender.

British translators who preferred to thwart and eradicate the reality of homosexuality were known to purposefully mistranslate Sanskrit terms. Svairini, for example, is a lesbian, a Sanskrit word that means "an independent woman." The prejudicial British translation became "a corrupt woman." Terms such as tritiya prakriti, kliba, shandha, and napumsa were translated as "dysfunctional individuals" or "eunuchs" when, in fact, these terms respectively mean third gender, homosexual, transgender, and intersex. However disingenuous their stratagem to antithetically redefine the intent of India's cultural ideology, the British mindset of superiority over all native peoples was indelibly stamped into civilization. Along with their imprint of puritanical biases, they succeeded in causing irreparable damage and chaos to humanity. These archaic laws are still rampant in the world. A whopping 70 percent of commonwealth countries cite homosexuality as a crime — that's 69 countries where homosexuality is still punishable by law. In a turn of poetic justice, Britain today boasts the largest percentage of homosexuals in the world.

Discrimination and prejudices against the third gender worldwide are primarily based on the colonized system of control, divide, and conquer. This inherited prejudice toward third-gender individuals (along with the millions of citizens disenfranchised by the British-devised "caste system") is but another festering legacy of patriarchal treachery. It has contributed dearly to the progressive decline of Hindu dharma, whose sacred intent is to uphold empathy for all in the defense of the non-binary universal truth. Global stigmatism of the third gender subjugates these precious souls to mental health issues, behavioral traumas, and community ire while leaving them with little or no access to health insurance, familial support, or societal comforts. The hijra community has been abused to the extent that now they are lashing out by crashing weddings and demanding money lest they curse the bride with barrenness – such is the despair and desperation we drive others to when we cast them from the fold. We cannot afford to ignore or disregard the dire plight of our suffering humanity. In the wise words of Otto Frank, "We cannot change what happened anymore. The only thing we can do is to learn from the past and to realize what discrimination and persecution of innocent people means. I believe that it's everyone's responsibility to fight prejudice."

Divinities of the Third Gender

Sorting through the complex within the infinite and the chaos within the finite, the Vedic seers revered every iota of life and viewed each and every configuration in nature as sacred; therefore, it is unsurprising that the concept of Tritiya Prakriti is an integral part of Vedic literature. In this devoutly humane culture, we have a god or goddess for each facet and form of life: 330 million Hindu gods and goddesses. Ancient stories extol many Vedic gods, goddesses, and avatars who possess the innate ability to transform their sexuality or embodied form as necessary. These divinities would often change shape and form to resolve conflicts in the cosmic sphere, demonstrating the utility and beneficence of fluidity.

The goddess Bahuchara Mata is one such deity who has become a patron goddess for the third gender population. She rides a rooster, which signifies innocence, and boasts four arms, holding a sword in her lower right hand, the Shiva trident in her lower left hand, and the scriptures in her upper left. In her upper right hand, she displays the Abhaya Mudra, a gesture that grants blessings and extinguishes fear – a welcome benediction for these unjustifiably maligned souls. Bahuchara is worshipped widely by the transgender community in India and visited at her temple in Gujarat. The narrative of

Bahuchara explains her popularity with India's transgender community. As the story goes, Bahuchara was venerated by the Charan Brahmin community, whose women were considered goddesses. Her legendary narrative is packed with Shiva-Shakti meaning. As one tale goes, Bahuchara was traveling with her sisters when a rogue named Bapiya attacked them. Bahuchara, fierce with rage, proceeded to cut off her breasts before immolating herself to avoid the atrocity of being raped. Before she died, she cursed Bapiya with a life of impotence and then decreed that he could only free himself from the curse if he assumed the role of a woman and worshipped her. The epic stories of the divinities are metaphors for living. While they do not suggest that we employ the extreme violence of mastectomy, immolation, or martyrdom as our response to the horrors of life, they command our attention, reminding us that there are times we will be forced to forge harsh and unforgettable lessons. While the ancients considered surgical mutilation of the sexual organ in both the masculine and feminine body an act of *adharma* — that which goes against the grain of awareness — and believed such an action to be incongruent with the natural order and law of the cosmos, Bahuchara's story nonetheless revolves around gender transformation, both in the removal of her breasts and her mandate to Bapiya to assume a different gender. Bahuchara's extreme measure of mutilating her breasts is generally understood as a defense; by scarring herself, she hoped to become undesirable to her attacker, protecting the sacred body native cultures view as the temple of the soul. The third gender community further interprets these actions as removing vestiges of a physical form that threaten the true self; the removal (or addition) of distinguishing sexual characteristics can thus be construed as protecting the sacred body and defending the temple of the soul.

These celestial stories of human evolution can help us all embrace the inner struggle – not only of the often heart-wrenching search for gender identity some of us endure but also the conflict between body, mind, and soul endured by us all. In one such story, Lord Vishnu, sustainer of the universe, whose consort is Lakshmi, the goddess of wealth, transmuted himself into the avatar of Mohini, a most beautiful enchantress, to entice and mystify the demons who had stolen the urn containing the nectar of immortality. In his form of the seductress, Lord Vishnu infiltrated the demons' den and recouped this priceless nectar, delivering it back to the gods so they could retain their immortality. News of Vishnu's successful venture reached Shiva, who was in awe of such a grand feat. So taken was Shiva by this tale that he accosted Vishnu and asked him to transform himself into the enchantress again. Vishnu complied. Diving into deep meditation, he once more transcended his form into the seductive Mohini. Stunned by Mohini's enchanting beauty, Shiva could not control his lust. He forcibly grabbed her into his arms; she escaped, but not before Shiva's ejaculated seed dropped onto her thigh. From that seed came the birth of Ayyappa, considered the son of Shiva and Mohini, who, in fact, is Vishnu.

These stories demonstrate that even the gods and goddesses are subject to impassioned sexual desires, same-sex attraction, and the universal law that all actions create consequences. Shiva was forced to learn a vital lesson – neither he nor Vishnu had the maternal instinct, the mother love, or the Shakti force necessary to raise Ayyappa. What, then, did these two great gods do with the baby? They tied a golden bell around his neck, blanketed him in a basket, and abandoned him on the banks of the Pampa River. Fortunately, as was Ayyappa's destiny, a childless monarch, King Rajashekhara found the baby. He and his queen adopted Ayyappa, henceforth worshipping him as a divine gift.

The Vedic view and behavioral mandate did not advocate the third gender taking on parenting roles. Since they were exempt from procreation and enjoyed the freedom of an outlier's life, they were not central participants in the mores of the larger, predominantly heterosexual society. Although each person – male, female, or nonbinary – bears both the Shiva and Shakti energies within them, the manifested, actionable form of Shiva energy resides in the man, and the Shakti equivalent in the woman. This manifested, actionable form of divine energy responsible for procreation is the same energy required for parenting. For these reasons, the Vedic sages believe it is not ideal for third-gender individuals to rear children, though they are some of the most fun-loving, creative, and innovative uncles, aunts, godparents, and goddess parents. While this perspective may be offensive to some, it should be noted that the Vedas primarily use these same arguments in defense of third-gender rights.

We can better understand our majestic and complex nature through the deities' iconography and understories. In the epic story of the Mahabharata, Arjuna, the most famous warrior of his era and the youngest of the Pandava brothers, lived as a transgender individual for one year. Apparently, he was cursed by Urvasi, a heavenly maiden whose love he spurned. Feeling rejected, she cursed Arjuna to lose his masculinity and live as a transgender person who could only sing and dance with other women. Arjuna then assumed the name Brihannala and moved to the forest, where he survived as a dance teacher for young girls. A year later, Urvasi was admonished by Indra, lord of the firmament, and forced to withdraw her curse. This story helps us understand the human make-up – including its enormous flaws – as a multidimensional, sacred work of art. Each life experience teaches us something profound and relevant to our human progress. To move forward, we must continually circle back to empathy and compassion.

Living Dharma for the Third Gender

He who is different from me does not impoverish me – he enriches me.

Antoine de Saint-Exupery

The Vedic system ascribes varying standards of behavior and sexual conduct for its citizens. The advantage of this system is that it is designed to accommodate the diversity of individuals and groups in accordance with their lifestyles and professions. For example, the priestly order, Brahmin, was held to the highest standards of character and conduct. Other members of the Brahmin classification were scientists, educators, poets, writers, and healthcare professionals. These callings required a supremely disciplined life and hence were accompanied by strict rules of sexual conduct. The next strata encompassed the ruling body, which also required a disciplined life: royals, lawmakers, government officials, politicians, the military, engineers, and landowners. Merchants, technologists, and farmers were afforded more leniency, while the artisans and ordinary workers, who made up more than half of India's population, were given the most. This Vedic system contrasts significantly with most modern systems, which expect all citizens to follow the same behavioral mandates.

During their occupation of India, the British instated laws of conduct that attempted to force all citizens to adopt priestly standards; needless to say, this had an unduly damaging effect on third-gender individuals. Moreover, the British rethreaded these laws through their puritanical lens. That is to say, they perceived Brahminical conduct to be other than what it is. For example, the sexual conduct of the Brahmin is quite strict since they are exemplars of the society's ethical and spiritual character. This recasting was a dismal failure. Forcing these highly disciplined behavior norms onto the hard-working or underprivileged general population failed to account for their arduous tasks and difficulties. Sexual restraint and abstinence, for example, are only sustainable when they are voluntary and serve a sublimated purpose.

Although Vedic laws upheld responsible heterosexual family life and spiritual values, they accepted and accommodated the third gender and their activities, which were not defined by the Shiva-Shakti procreative lifestyle. In accommodation, designated districts within the cities and towns – approved by third-gender society – were assigned to them. These communities were generally away from the heterosexual residential neighborhoods and sacred sites, wherein third-gender residents conducted their affairs with ease and dignity. While they enjoyed some degree of privacy, their lives were not required to be shrouded in secrecy. These districts were havens for transgender artisans, sexually explicit arts, theatrical entertainment, courtesans, and concubines and hosted a wide variety of interactions such as prostitution, polygamy, and homosexuality. The affairs of these districts flourished comfortably without the trafficking of illegal substances and drugs or law enforcers' corruption until the arrival of the British. While the unrealistic system of prohibition that the colonizers established to categorize these activities as criminal flatly failed, their negative stigma continues to fuel a morass of social issues. Founded on puritanical divisionism, fear, greed, hysteria, and widespread hypocrisy, this colonial catastrophe disenfranchised the third gender, female, and so-called lower caste populations alike.

In modern society, we have been so conditioned by a false narrative of homosexual depravity that, for many of us, it is inured in our bones, and we find it challenging to shift our position. The truth is, the wider we open our hearts, the faster we shed this limiting, colonized mindset. Vedic society, wise and discerning as it was, had no issue with homosexual or bisexual behavior, viewing it as innocuous and even serving a special role in maintaining harmony and balance in the community as a whole. Third-gender individuals are part and product of the natural order, children of Shiva and Shakti as much as you or I, and as such, deserve our unreserved tolerance, understanding, and — more than just respect — our love.

Chapter 14

We Are Made of Stars and Frogs

How it is that animals understand things I do not know, but it is certain that they do understand. Perhaps there is a language which is not made of words and everything in the world understands it.

Frances Hodgson Burnett, *A Little Princess*

The way of Shakti, when lived fully, honors each and every creature, tree, river, and cloud. Every speck of life contains soul. Nature as a whole is a vast soul reservoir that is continually energizing and nourishing its charges. Each part of nature is a grand jigsaw puzzle fitted to cosmic perfection, yet, through human carelessness, pieces are damaged and lost every day. Faced with a trifecta of crises threatening our physical health, mental health, and climate, we must recover the long-lost memory of our physical and spiritual dependence on nature before nature itself becomes but a memory.

Nature is so vast, diverse, and powerful that it's hard to fathom the damage we've managed to inflict in a mere 200 years. It is said that 99 percent of all species that ever lived on the Earth are now extinct. While modern science has cataloged about 9 million species, Vedic science estimates the total number of known and unknown species on Earth today exceeds one trillion. Trees are said to have existed for about 370 million years, with at least 100,000 species and nearly 4 trillion individual trees. Each year, we savagely cut down 15 billion of them. Researchers estimate that since the onset of human civilization, the global number of trees has dropped by roughly 48 percent. Beef production is responsible for 42 percent of deforestation from the 325 million head of cattle we digest yearly; palm oil and soybeans account for another 18 percent; and logging for paper and wood across the tropics, another 15 percent. We are killing ancient forests in the large-scale clearing of land, generally for agriculture, industry, or transportation. Upwards of 50,000 acres of forest are cleared by farmers and loggers each day worldwide. An area equivalent to over 11,000 football fields is destroyed daily in the Amazon basin alone. We are losing memory of Earth's intelligence and the Earth itself and have become oblivious to our deeper dependence on these heart-awakened and awakening life forms that feed and shelter us physically and spiritually. Our emotional and spiritual well-being is inextricably tied to the natural world. Beyond the numerous studies that have substantiated the essential connection between nature and mental and emotional health, Vedic tradition has long established its relation to human consciousness.

The ancient wisdom of every living thing being sacred is repeatedly exemplified in Vedic tradition. The ancients recognized that the visible and invisible vibrations of Earth's nonhuman inhabitants contributed to humanity's progress. Even a grain of sand within nature demonstrates Earth intelligence. The forest, trees, rivers, land, sky, and nature as a whole all hold important information and roles in the cosmic communion of nature that plays out in human intelligence. Imbued with the Shiva-Shakti instinct, all creatures are players in the field of consciousness: the caterpillar, bee, frog, snake, deer, cow, and lion. While they are not equipped with the sentiency-calibrating will of the human species, they unconditionally support nature and play an active role in her evolution. Each creature contributes a specific function and memory to the vast field of consciousness.

In my thesis on Cosmic Memory, published in *Ayurveda: Secrets of Healing,* one of my earlier books, I propose that all species, including humans, are influenced to varying degrees by the entire largesse of universal memory. When cosmic memory is diminished, it affects all creatures. As humans, we lose touch with the ever-generating throb of consciousness, intuition wanes, and we become dependent on the mind, often falling prey to its inaccurate perceptions of reality, which reduces the clarity and quality of choices we make. Synced to the universal mind as we are, we feel the echo of its pain. When I refer to "cosmic memories," I mean the collective, timeless memories of all species and life forms in the universe. Let's explore how these memories affect the universe. Each species, from its incarnation on the planet, is allocated a specific block of memory from the vast network of the universe's memory. Each block of cosmic memory gives shape, size, form, and function to a species and determines its behaviors, activities, survival skills, nourishment, and purpose in the great schema of the universe's mind. Since each species carries a distinct block of cosmic memory, members of the same species can communicate and reverberate, sharing a vast field of vibration, energy, and information. By tapping into their own memory segment of the universal network, each life form can continually interact with the entire energy field of all living things since all memory is sourced in Earth's vibrational energy. Refined from the first minutiae of manifestation to the present and into the future, this grid work of cosmic memory forms the primary substratum for the universe's countless species' form and function.

For the universe's vast memory network to be sustained and thrive, each species must be in a state of relative equanimity until it becomes naturally extinct. Extinction is an intrinsic part of the natural evolutionary process. When a species becomes extinct due to the natural course of evolution, its particular block of cosmic memory is dissolved, no longer required within the vibratory field of memory in the universe. The memories that desist as a result of the natural process of extinction are no longer necessary for the welfare of the life forms that still exist on the planet. In this dynamic creation, natural extinction occurs because as universal consciousness matures, it transcends its dependency on certain blocks of cosmic memory. The snake analogy is a good example: when it no longer needs its worn-out skin, the snake sheds it. The snake is neither impaired nor enhanced as a result. Likewise, during the course of evolution, certain cosmic memories become worn and, along with the species, are eliminated from the universe. When the universe no longer needs a certain memory block, the species that carries that knowledge naturally dies out. However, when a species is unnaturally annihilated, surviving species suffer the premature loss of the memory that was energetically imprinted on our collective consciousness. We can no longer access that species' memory – a memory that had not yet run its natural course or fulfilled its cosmic purpose but is forever lost to the consciousness grid. This dims our awareness and creates a state of amnesia relating to that memory that echoes the loss and pain of the universal mind.

The Wisdom of Trees

Trees and other plants play a cardinal role in life. While even the most vehement climate change deniers must admit that we are physically dependent on nature for our water, food, shelter, and the very air we breathe, many people still fail to understand how dependent our medicines are on plants, regardless of whether those medicines come from a garden or a lab. According to Dr Ciddi Veeresham in the *Journal of Advanced Pharmaceutical Technology and Research*, "Up to 50% [of] the approved drugs during the last 30 years are either directly or indirectly from natural products." Humans have always relied on plants for their healing power. In the 1950s, archaeologists uncovered evidence of plants being used for medicinal purposes more than 75,000 years ago at a Neanderthal burial site in the Shanidar cave of the Zagros Mountains in northern Iraq, where eight species of medicinal plants were buried with human remains. Some of these plants, including yarrow, cornflower, bachelor's button, St Barnaby's thistle, ragwort, grape hyacinth, horsetail, and hollyhock, are still used for medicinal purposes today.

A sterling example of the deep medicine topiary life gives us can be found in Ayurveda, the Earth's maternal medicine system, which, by a spate of miracles, has survived the atrocities of time. Ayurveda is one of the world's oldest medical systems and remains one of India's foremost healing traditions. Ayurveda sprouted its virginal roots at a time when communion between human beings and plants was a visceral reality. This seamless knowledge has been handed down to humanity through a plethora of scribed pages, treatises, texts, and books. Ayurveda seers and seeresses conversed in sublime communion with the forest, tree, river, and sky. Vedic seers cognized the value of each living form and its interrelationship with human life; they knew how to activate abundance and blessings and remove negativity and harm by symbolically utilizing the rich medicine of one species to bless another. Crone cultures – those once widespread but now all but extinct cultures that spiritually guided, embraced, healed, and kept balance in their communities – once observed the deepest regard for each life form, coexisting with and utilizing them without polluting, modifying, dousing, or transgressing their innate nature or mitochondrial integrity. In this sense, ancient lifeways continually created natural conditions for the renewal of health and hope in the individual, society, and humanity.

In Ayurveda, plant life is sacred; thus, medicinal plants are associated with the names of various sages, celestial beings, gods, and goddesses. We refer to medicinal plants as *aushadhi*, a Sanskrit word that means "light-bearing medicinal herb," inferring that all plants are nourished by light through photosynthesis, both sunlight and moonlight. Like plants, we too are sustained by the divine light through metamorphosis that occurs in our relationship with the sun and moon and nature's elements. According to Charaka, an ancient Ayurvedic physician, all plant substances in the world possess some medicinal use, though one must consider the method and purpose or diseased condition before employing any substance as a medicine.

Modern scientifically "advanced" culture has overridden this intelligence, blinded as we are by a binary, dualistic, linear system that wrestles mystery and magic into finite equations. Modern medicine disregards Earth's intelligence in favor of reductive pharmacology, leading to chemical dependency. Of the more than 100,000 medicinal plants in nature's pharmacology identified by ancient Ayurveda, only about 10,000 remain in common use. These plants are being environmentally safeguarded from chemical toxicity by holistic farmers, who are exhibiting a burgeoning return to Vedic tenets in their care for land and water. These farmers perform the arduous but necessary seasonal plant rotations using only the manure of local animals and other natural fertilizers, treating the Earth as our sacred mother. Still, these remaining medicinal plants are threatened by the artillery of pesticides and neurotoxic chemicals we use every day on our Earth, transmuting or destroying plant cellular memory and causing more than 9 million premature deaths each year from contamination of our forests, land, air, water, food, and consumer goods.

Plants and trees heal far more than illnesses and injuries. Vedic wisdom elucidates trees as elder souls, the probable incarnation of an old soul finishing its cycle of rebirths. Generally, old souls incarnate as trees directly before entering the state of *moksha,* that state of ultimate enlightenment wherein there are no more rebirths. They are completing their final round of embodied karma on Earth at this stage. Like humans, trees have biological sexes. The neem, for instance, is a Shakti form, while the pipal tree is a Shiva form. In India, it is believed that when a neem and a pipal tree grow closely together, especially near a sacred site or by a river, it symbolizes the final rebirth of the advanced soul of a female and a male whose last karmic duty is to undergo marriage: this scenario concludes a symbolic cycle of procreation and rebirth. Trees embody stillness, the art of pure witnessing, generously providing non-reciprocal gifts to humanity. Trees are the perfect embodiment for the elder-most soul's final journey because they do not act willfully; they are non-attached to producing karma, detached from the fruits of their nature while giving support, shade, and nourishment with no expectations in return. The Vedic culture also facilitates ceremonies to wed one tree to another, joining a tree that represents the primeval Shakti with one that symbolizes the primeval Shiva principle. These topiary events mark the last rites of the cycles of rebirth for these ancient souls, enabling their final liberation. The location where this ritual is performed is also considered auspicious and gains prosperity and well-being for its inhabitants.

At one point in my life, after I unrobed from my monastic life but sensed I was still some distance away from Shiva-Shakti marital bliss, I considered the Vedic protocol of marrying a tree. This tree ritual, called *kalyanam*, is an ancient Vedic practice to remove karmas that may have blocked the path of happiness in a marriage. In Tamil Nadu, at one of the sacred sites of a Shakti temple, I explored this fantastic idea with a stoic Brahmin priest. I confided in him my heart-awakening love for a man who was not available and wondered if a tree marriage would be a sagacious choice to allow my womanly desire to bloom, given my celibate past. The priest was kind. He listened intently. Then he took me on a walk around the hallowed ground to a grove of banana trees, where he informed me that these were the prospective grooms for a woman or girl marrying a tree.

A mischievous thought flickered through my mind as I stared at one particular banana tree — it was lean, tall, stable, clearly the silent type, perhaps a bit too green, but otherwise a perfect match ... except, alas, no blue eyes. This marriage was not to be. The priest advised me to be patient and to simply observe my inner desires and allow them to unfold naturally. He reassured me that I did not need a husband, tree or otherwise, to facilitate the organic process of discovering my feminine sexuality. He did suggest another ceremony for me to perform while in Tamil Nadu, however, which would help me to ease out of the commitment to my monastic vows harmoniously.

Apparently, a tree marriage for a woman or man is only meant to neutralize certain negative karmas the potential couple may have that obstruct a happy spousal alliance. As he escorted me out of the compound, the priest pointed out an ancient, majestic banyan tree surrounded by many tall banana tree stumps. "These are the wedded tree spouses from prior weddings," he told me. After the marriage ceremony, the "husband" is deposited here to "reflect" on the Goddess in the shade of the banyan tree. Married, yet free of the husband, tree wives were at liberty to pursue their newly cleansed karma.

The ancients were so wise. In their purview, every union within nature abided by the principle of Shiva-Shakti. Trees like coconut and banana are considered Shakti trees; they are constantly in the cycle of creation, renewal, and dying, while the banyan, a Shiva tree, represents immortality. The appropriate Shakti or Shiva tree is appointed depending on the flaw to be remedied in a potential marriage. A young woman marrying a banana tree implies she is first to be united with the Goddess to align with the grace of Lakshmi — the goddess of fertility, wealth, and prosperity — to remove her karmic flaws before her marriage to a man can occur. Marriage to a banyan tree, which exudes the blessings of the gods, vibrationally removes obstacles from a woman's path and brings forth an appropriate human spouse in due course. Walking reverently around a banyan tree

108 times supports the aspirant's spiritual yearnings. Among the thousands of designated sacred trees used in Vedic rituals, the banyan tree represents our spiritual aspirations; with a host of aerial roots shooting down from its branches into the Earth, it gives us an idea of firming up spiritual practices and freeing ourselves from material attachment. Sadhus, hermits, and others who have forsaken familial attachment and material pursuits have made its shade their home. As you may surmise, quite a few people prefer these arboreal partners to their human counterparts.

Kalyanam, the Sanskrit word for ritual tree marriage, means "auspicious or prospering," as in the renewal of fertility and wealth. Depending on the need, a kalyanam ritual may be performed between any two beings, human or nonhuman, animate or inanimate, or between embodied deities or any combination thereof. In this magical culture, there are several wedding rituals involving the majestic tree. The one I've referred to above is to marry a woman or man to a specific tree, depending on the impediment to be resolved. This ceremony, performed with devout spiritual presage, is done to overcome astrological obstacles that may hinder a couple's fertility, longevity, or happiness. For example, a woman's astrological effects may prevent her from having a happy marriage, or if she does marry, may bring harm to the unwitting husband. Therefore, her marriage to a Shiva tree like the pipal would be considered her first marriage, and this wedding ritual would neutralize the poor karmic omens indicated in her astrological marriage chart. When she finally marries her human spouse, the risks of injury or impairment to their happiness or longevity will no longer exist. Additionally, the vibration of such a ceremony resonates beyond the immediate intent of its nuptials: its circadian rhythm embraces the community at large and acts as protection for all trees or afflicted human beings for whom this ritual is performed.

Tree veneration and practices in India are prevalent, and similar traditions were found in every ancient culture before patriarchal rule. Cultures that revered Earth's intelligence fostered a profound relationship with their forest friends. Norse mythology, for example, speaks of Yggdrasil, a mythical tree (often thought to be an ash) at the center of the cosmos that connects the nine worlds of Norse cosmology. This tree was said to nourish gods, humans, and animals, allowing gods and other beings to travel between the realms. The concept of the World Tree exists in many cultures. With its branches reaching up into the sky and roots deep into the Earth, it can be seen as a link between heaven, Earth, and the underworld, uniting above and below and mirroring the balance encapsulated by yin-yang, Shiva-Shakti, and the awen. This remarkable tree acts as an axis mundi, supporting or holding up the cosmos. In Siberian mythology, legends of the sky-high tree that reaches the heavens are quite popular. In these legends, the tree holds the sky up or pierces through its portal to reach other worlds. Celtic polytheists used oak groves to perform their sacred rites. The term druid itself possibly derives from the Celtic word for oak.

In Vedic mythology, plants possess ancient souls. Gods and goddesses are aligned with trees, shrubs, vines, and creepers. The mother of the plant is called *Ira*. The forest dominion is safeguarded by the *Vana Devatas,* illumined forest spirits inherent in each plant that contribute to the celestial potency of its medicine. In the epic tale of the Ramayana, when Sita was abandoned in the forest by her guardian, Lakshmana, at the command of her husband, Rama, Sita's sorrow stirred the trees and plants. They empathized with her tears by shedding flowers shaped like teardrops. The goddess Parvati lovingly reared a Devadaru sapling like her own son, watering the young plant with her breast milk. Milk, considered the goddess's ambrosia and the elixir of life, is often symbolically associated with trees in Vedic India. Trees like pipal naturally ooze a white sap considered to be the breast milk of its inherent tree goddess. Throughout Tamil Nadu and Kerala, trees are festooned with bulging bags filled with cow placentas. This practice is done to energetically nourish sap-oozing trees so that their innate milk becomes abundant. Indeed, these offerings are meant to mimic feeding the trees the same way a cow feeds its calf.

How trees are approached and treated is of great concern to Vedics. The tree is sacred; it is our elder. Before a tree is cut down, especially if its wood is to be used for creating spiritual idols, or in the scenario of the tree representing a human groom or bride, significant rituals are first done to thank the tree for its sacrifice. The sculptor, who is also a priest, carefully carves the outline of the intended idol into the trunk before they cut down the tree. This is a prayerful way of asking the tree's permission and indicates the sacred purpose of its impending sacrifice. Several ritual offerings are made before it is cut down to show the tree gratitude. The night before the tree is laid to rest, the priests render offerings to ask forgiveness of the spirits, divinities, snakes, animals, and others who would normally seek refuge there. Early the next morning, after sprinkling holy water on the tree and smearing the blade of his axe with honey and ghee, the sculptor cuts clockwise around the tree, starting from the northeast corner, which is the most auspicious directional aspect of Vastu for receiving omniscient blessings for an event. Specific trees are chosen depending on which divinity is being sculpted. The most prominent trees selected are sandalwood, deodar, sami, madhuka, ashvatta, and khadira. Each tree species carries its own cambium of cellular memory that denotes its specific function in the forest community.

Thousands of years after the Vedic culture discovered the quantum intelligence of the Earth wherein each and every species is connected by vibrational energy and each one strives to be whole and healed, science is now discovering a tiny fraction of trees' mysterious reality. Suzanne Simard, an American Forest Ecologist, writes, "Trees and plants have agency. They cooperate, make decisions, learn and remember – qualities we normally ascribe to sentience, wisdom, intelligence." Professor Simard is not alone in this view. Richard Grant, in his article published in the *Smithsonian*, "Do Trees Talk to Each Other?" writes: "I'm walking in the Eifel Mountains in western Germany, through cathedral-like groves of oak and beech, and there's a strange, unmoored feeling of entering a fairy tale. The trees have become vibrantly alive and charged with wonder. They're communicating with one another, for starters. They're involved in tremendous struggles and death-defying dramas. To reach enormousness, they depend on a complicated web of relationships, alliances and kinship networks. Wise old mother trees feed their saplings with liquid sugar and warn the neighbors when danger approaches." Modern science is in the infancy stage of understanding nature's ways. Many scientists, past and present, cast aspersions on this noble, heart-awakening reality. Recently, Lincoln Taiz, a retired professor of plant biology, along with a group of 32 plant scientists, published a rebuttal to the theory that plants and trees possess intelligence. They allowed that trees may possess some sort of "swarm intelligence" but stated that "the appearance of purposefulness is an illusion, like the belief in 'intelligent design.' Natural selection can explain everything we know about plant behavior." Indeed, the comprehension that the forest is a super-organism of unique individual trees is yet to be recognized by most modern scientists. We have, however, made some progress in our awareness of the agency of trees since Sir James George Frazer, a Scottish social anthropologist writing at the turn of the twentieth century. In her article, "The wedding of two trees: connections, equivalences, and subjunctivity in a Tamil ritual," published in the Journal of the Royal Anthropological Institute, Dr Soumhya Venkatesan paraphrases Frazer's self-congratulatory assessment of Vedic tree marriages: "Such primitives, the logic went, were incapable of distinguishing between humans and nonhumans and approached the world through a mixture of 'superstition, magic and irrational ritual.'"

Meanwhile, the ancient forests and numerous species are rapidly disappearing. The superficial mindset of our recent past and present world culture, climate change, and deforestation are making it more difficult for the old forest giants to survive. We must preserve the priceless value of our ancient trees and their secrets. Secrets that, for the most part, must remain secrets from the treachery of modern science. We need to honor their grandeur, crone purpose, and deep medicine. They did not sign up for science to plunder the integrity of their cellular memory. Their secrets are shaktified and sanctified. They reveal these totems to those who recognize and cherish them, the Earth lovers who intuit these morsels from the crones themselves. To know what the tree knows implies we must stretch our awareness with the overwhelming desire to get to know our crones. These secrets preserve humanity's wholeness.

An Inter-species Language Not Made of Words

A persistent primitivist theory contends that people who do not categorically differentiate between humans and nonhumans are cognitively and culturally less evolved than people who do. The significant difference between intuitive understanding of nature and scientific comprehension is that with intuitive understanding, we find truth in the process of communion, an inter-species language not made of words. We do not discover nature's mystery and majesty through experimentally dissecting and pharmacologically extracting the components of her creations. Communion is key. Thus, for all of us "less evolved" people, it gives me great joy to dive into a spate of fantastic storytelling that evokes an ever more profound love affair with nature and her many animate forms.

In Vedic culture, animals are not used as mere totems for the deities but serve in partnership. They are treated as exemplars of friendship, support, guidance, transport, and companionship and inspire the development of our intuitive faculty. As such, they hold a revered place in Hindu iconology. Each deity has a particular animal vehicle, or *vahana,* on which they travel the universe. These animals represent the various spiritual and psychological forces that each deity possesses and protects. In truth, like the gods and goddesses, each one of us also has an innate animal vahana that represents our unique psychic-spiritual force. In partnership with the deity's powers, the vahanas often serve as placeholders for their charges. It was only with the help of her tiger-lion that Durga managed to destroy the demon, Mahishasura. The goddess Saraswati's vehicle, the graceful swan, emboldens her status as the embodiment of wisdom and the arts. Vishnu rides the Garuda, his eagle whose wings float like a kite, while he salvages the world from our destructive actions. When Vishnu needs rest, he reclines on the primeval serpent, Sesha Naga, which represents space, time, and infiniteness. These divine partnerships represent human dependence on nature. Realizing this truth, we begin to align physically and spiritually with her.

I formed my own animal partnerships during the 24 years I spent in the oxygen-filled forest of Mount Pisgah, where I established the Wise Earth School of Ayurveda. Early each morning, during my ritual meditation and prayers for the land, I sought to connect heart to heart to my Earth. The deer herd that lived in the forest would respond to the prayer bells, gallantly cantering across their forest paths. They would sit around me if I was outdoors or climb onto the deck and sit on the landing of my cabin if I was indoors. During the hour-long meditation and chanting, I felt their peace, a blissful state of *turiya,* beyond the duality of thought or willful conditioning. I would decorate their foreheads with *vibhuti,* holy ash, and sandalwood paste from my Guru's monastery – bucks first and then the doe, as was their hierarchal way. I noticed how the doe would look back to check on her protector, the buck, her Shiva, from whom she gleaned her direction and clues in their unspoken exchange. I saw how fiercely the buck would protect their young fawns. When the neighbor's German shepherd dog would attack the herd, I saw how the buck would tuck away his companion doe and the young ones in the bamboo grove and then deliberately gallop in the opposite direction to lead the threatening dog away from his family. There was no reason to enforce modern feminist values upon their order. They blessed me with their presence and faithful attendance, and I returned the gift by circling them with the light of the ghee lamp while sprinkling holy water on their head. Afterward, I would offer them their favorite treat – pine nuts. In these moments, the majestic trees bore silent witness, and the larger community within the forest would exude a palpable peace. On occasion, when I was tired from my travels and did not rise at the appointed time to perform my rituals, my wake-up call would come. The arch-buck would stand before my door and tap his rear feet loudly against the landing boards. For years, having surmised there was no human-buck around me, this particular arch-buck would make it a point to accompany me around the compound. He would spend the whole day grazing in the barley field while keeping an alert, guarding eye on my movements.

One early morning in spring, as I walked down the hill to open the front gates for a contractor, I felt a tug at the hem of my dress. I looked back to find the buck yanking at me. Deer are Earth's quiet creatures; their minds are so serene that you rarely sense their presence. Suddenly, out of the ancient mystery, they would appear. By contrast, the human mind is so loud that even when we are quiet, you can smell, hear, and sense us rattling on from some distance away. That same day, as the contractor began pouring the concrete footings for a large yoga deck we were building, the buck suddenly sprinted onto the construction scene and began forcefully scraping his horns against the contractor's leg. Generally, in the springtime, bucks rub against the rough bark of the walnut or dogwood trees to loosen the fur covering their horns; had the buck mistaken the contractor's leg for a tree? Given the sensitivity of their observant mind, I felt it hardly likely. The astonished contractor, awed by the deer's boldness, confided that he was one of the hunters who would go deer hunting in and around my forest. He said they would try every trick to lure the deer into a trap while hunting them. Apparently, in the peaceful protection of the school's compound, the deer felt no angst or fear of being hunted. He must have recognized the hunter and felt like taking his bold revenge while he had the chance. The hunter, a man who would kill in sport, was entranced. After that encounter, he confided he would never hunt deer again.

Another morning on Mount Pisgah, I noticed the cows in the neighboring fields had an eye disease and were wearing netted mesh blinders to keep the flies from lighting on their eyes. This suffering sight made me sad. I approached the farmer of the dairy cows and asked his permission to spend time with the cows so I could chant with them. He was amused. "Why would y'all wanna do that?" he asked. "I hate to see the animals suffering, and I can help them," I answered. His amusement turned skeptical, "How can y'all help 'em?" Asheville is a community dotted with churches: Methodist, Baptist, Lutheran, and many more denominations. Taking refuge in religion, I told him, "I sing hymns; glorious, compelling hymns that help everything to heal." I saw his body relax. "Oh! Well, y'all can sing ta 'em, but try nahwt ta scare 'em," he said with a twinkle in his weathered blue eyes.

Cows wake up with the dawn, so at six o'clock each morning, I walked down the unpaved road a few hundred yards from my property and began chanting with them. I recited the Rudram, a powerful Sanskrit chant for healing. They responded with awe, each cow vying for front-row standing room. They stood transfixed and stared as I chanted the thirty-minute-long verses. The next day, the class was ready when I arrived five minutes late. The elder cows took the front row while the younger ones stood behind in the second and third rows. As I started my instructions, two bulls suddenly dashed out of the barn and began pushing against the passive cows; in no time, they usurped the front row. Stepping back, the disheartened females ceded to the bulls' wills. The week went by nicely. With bulls in front, as usual, I could see the improvements in the cows' eyes, although the farmer continued to strap the blinders on them. A fortnight later, after chanting with the cows daily, I saw that their eyes had healed. To celebrate the graduation of my most incredible students, I fed each one appropriately cut-up apples. To end that glorious session, I chanted the cosmic sound "Om." Much to my delight, the cows began "ooming" back. No, they do not "moo." These maternal creatures have been "ooming" for eons. Like so much in modern culture, we have it backward. I joined my wholesome students in a lively reverie as we "oomed" to our hearts' content. Competing with the newly found verve and authority of their shaktified companions, the front-row bulls decided to join in the refrain. We were all stunned to hear their gruff growls. They were so busy "gruffing" and throwing off the sublime harmony, they paid no mind to the gentle toning of the cows. The farmer arrived during this parting ceremony. He stood agape, not believing his ears but conceding that the cows' eyes had indeed gotten better.

Another example of animal partnership is evinced by India's frog ritual, called *Manduka Parinaya*. During frequent droughts in India, the Vedic rain god, Indra, is often invoked. In this ritual practice, a female and male frog are sought. They are then readied for a sacred wedding on consecrated ground, where recitations of Sanskrit mantras and vows performed by priests accompany their marriage ritual. The community hopes they will become so blessed in marital bliss that they will start croaking their rain melody. In a recent frog marriage in Madhya Pradesh, two clay frogs, the symbolic placeholders, were wedded. Not only was their call for rain successful, but two months later, the area was severely flooded. To stop the downpour, the community thought it sagacious to arrange a follow-up ceremony officiating a divorce for the clay frogs. Following the divorce, the clay frogs were released in a vessel filled with water, and the rains stopped.

In a recent example, a cow named Poonam and a bull named Arjun tied the knot in a stupendous Hindu ceremony in Gujarat, India. No expense was spared. It cost the guardians of the cow bride and bull groom a quarter million US dollars to perform this lavish ceremony. Three hundred royally received guests witnessed the traditionally dressed Poonam and Arjun chanting their "I moo's" for each other. This kalyanam was organized by a Hindu NGO that strongly protested the slaughtering of cows in India's designated sacred sites. For eons, cows have been held sacred by Hinduism, Jainism, Buddhism, and Sikhism. The Vedic culture has long revered the cow as a symbol of fertility, prosperity, and nurturance. She is considered a mother-ancestor and the embodiment of Aditi, the mother of the gods.

Vedic culture has maintained an enduring regard for all animals. Dogs, for instance, are powerful friends to humans. The annual Hindu festival of Kukur Tihar in Nepal blesses and worships dogs by adorning them with sandalwood paste and flower garlands around their necks and treating them to a feast. When it comes to ancient religious symbolism, dogs are the faithful companions to many different deities, including the God Shiva, Yama, the god of death, and Lord Dattatreya, whose four canine companions represent the four major Vedas.

Horses are also cherished. Archaeological findings show the existence of the horse in India during the Iron Age and, in some places, as far back as the Bronze Age. The horse is seen as a sacred animal often associated with a particular deity, warrior, king, or totem. The cosmic chariot of Arjuna, the brave Pandava warrior in the epic war of the Mahabharata, was pulled by five horses, each one symbolic of one of the five senses (the reigns signified the human mind, while the charioteer himself, who was god Krishna in this case, was the ultimate symbol of *anandam*, or pure consciousness). The sun god, Surya, rides a chariot pulled by seven celestial horses, signifying, among other mystical seven-some events, the seven colors of the rainbow, the seven days of the week, seven notes in traditional Indian music, the seven major chakras, the seven tissue layers in the human body, seven worlds above Earth, seven worlds below the Earth, and the seven-fold powers of the goddess, Shakti.

Fyodor Dostoevsky evinced an unvarnished truth, "People speak sometimes about the 'bestial' cruelty of man, but that is terribly unjust and offensive to beasts, no animal could ever be so cruel as a man, so artfully, so artistically cruel." Who are the primitive ones — the ancients who loved, understood, respected, and engaged in massive ceremonies and prayers for the trees and other animals in their shared outcome for humanity, or our present-day modern industrialized society that slaughters, murders, kills, and destroys for avarice and profit? The inured ignorance toward nature stretches deep into the cavernous pit of patriarchy, reaching outward with new sproutings of neoliberal ideas that grab the attention of a new generation of the hip, young, and modernized. Most young people in the present world culture are alienated from the profound lessons of their ancient, ancestral past, preferring instead the linear, binary scientific approach to life. Two-thirds or more of the world's population have bought into the patriarchal ideology that success, avarice, and business acumen supersede nature's phenomenal rights and values. We act as if nature is some expanse of space out there waiting to be used, where everything is dispensable or can be scientifically improved. We have forgotten what we are made of and what we belong to.

"We are made of stars," Carl Sagan confirmed, having calculated that the carbon, nitrogen, and oxygen atoms in our bodies were created in previous generations of stars over 4.5 billion years ago. Our bodies are temples to Shakti and vessels for the universal mind, yet we are not superior to or separate from nature. We are nature. We are formed from water, microbes, stars, and frogs, blessed with the gift of consciousness not over nature but by her. How we continue to use this endowment from her — whether to discard her creation or to protect it — will determine our shared fate.

Chapter 15

Time, Moon, Woman, Womb

A diadem adorns the night
Of multitudinous stars;
Her silken robe is white moonlight,
Set free from cloudy bars;
And on her face (the radiant moon)
Bewitching smiles are shown:

Kalidasa

Long before modern science learned to control a woman's sacred reproductive function and manipulate her intrinsic rhythms, the ancients recognized that a woman's fertility, abundance, and splendor are tied to the movement of the moon. In fact, Shakti cellular anatomy in its entirety is governed by the lunar wheel. This knowledge was lost to us centuries ago when many Vedic tomes were destroyed, and those that remained had to be ferried and hidden underground for safekeeping during numerous foreign invasions of India. My life thus far has been spent recovering, recreating, and intuiting this lost knowledge while reveling in the universe's transmissions. These revelations helped me restore many women's healing principles and lunar practices to present-day Ayurveda. Ancient sages recognized that the moon significantly influences a woman's biorhythms and that her body, mind, and spirit are intricately connected to her cycles. Accordingly, to restore Shakti balance to the world, we must first restore lunar rhythm to our bodies and lives.

A Woman's Turn with the Moon

Modern science is finally beginning to scratch the surface of women's health and reproductive relationship to the elemental energies of nature. In a recently published article in *Molecular Biology*, scientists Gabriela Andreatta and Kristin Tessmar-Raible report on their research on molecular mechanisms of lunar controlled rhythms: "Why is cellular respiration, in which cells pulse between empty and full, the foundation of life? It is plausible that ... the first life forms adapted to the different rhythms controlled by the moon." They contended that the most basic life-forms operate through the pulse of cellular respiration and the opening and closing of valves and that they evolved these valves in tidal pools in alignment with the moon. This basic valve structure — the mechanism of pulsing between open and closed — became the very foundation of how glands and organs work in the body. The pumping of the heart, opening and closing of valves, and ebb and flow of hormones can all be attributed to the lunar rhythms.

The ancients claimed that all life's substance is created from Mother Moon's dust, our cosmic source. Her illumination and visible shape-shifting keep our heads craning upwards to the magical skies. The moon is the matriarch of all planets, herbs, sacrifices, austerities, rituals, arts, music, festivities, and dance. Her perpetual cycle determines nature's tides and our rhythms, desires, vibrations, and possibilities on the Earth. Moreover, she significantly influences a woman's biorhythms and her body, mind, and spirit, which are intricately connected to her cycles. In whichever of her 32 phases she sits, from full to empty and back again, or by whatever name we call her — Silver Salmon Moon, Popping Tree Moon, Moon of Serving Rice, Moon of the Falcon, Moon of the Deer, Moon of the Frog, Moon of the Falling Leaves, Moon of the Lotus, Jasmine Moon, Peacock Moon, Swan Moon, or Cow Moon — she has an epic impact on our mind, heart, womb, and daily living conditions.

Living in accordance with the lunar calendar maintained the ancestral memory of the crones, which enabled the provision of sustenance and human well-being. The descriptive functional names ascribed to each full moon throughout the annual cycle, such as Strawberry Moon, Harvest Moon, and Corn Moon, tell the story of a people's rhythmic way of life. Honoring the moon and recognizing the prosperity and nurturance that she brings with each of her manifold phases, crones and elders were able to impart essential information to younger generations about appropriate seasons and times to gather, plant, and harvest crops. This way of being, of honoring the cyclical, circular movement of time and the greater lunar energies, wasn't just a lifestyle — it was literally a lifesaver.

Living by the lunar rhythm likewise maintained physically healthy individuals and societies. Indigenous life kept a constant momentum synced with nature and the Earth as people moved from day to day in rhythm with the lunar wheel. Foraging and gathering food, digging into the black earth, chasing animals, cutting wood, feeding fire, and performing daily rituals were the activities that maintained a limber body and healthy spirit. Aligned with Mother Earth, stress levels were low despite arduous work. There was space to breathe in the luxury of oxygenated air, drink the pristine springs' sparkling waters, and imbibe nature's feast fresh from the Earth. Nature thrived, and with her, the well-being and intuitive power of the individual, family, and community flourished.

Our natural harmony came to a dramatic stop when we lost affinity, rhythm, and pace with Mother Moon. This loss of friendship has resulted in the impairment of the precious human gift of intuition. This intuition once told us when to sleep, when to plant, when to harvest, when to retreat from strenuous activities with the slimming of the moon and prepare for our menstrual release, and when to luxuriate in body, mind, and spirit with her fullness. Even as we breathe in deeply and sigh out in the presence of her immaculate beauty, we can reset the rhythm of our heart pulse. This is why ancient women gathered in circles to blissfully drum, dance, and sing upon the Earth as the moon's belly became perfectly round. Today, we can learn the healing codes of the cosmic pulse by paying attention to our own cycles and rhythms.

Ancient Lunar Time Piece

Consider that every moment of time is created by the moon herself. Set in motion by her vibration and rhythm, the circle of time is marked by the moon's shifting shape. Emulated by the circle of life in a woman's womb, the moon is an intoxicating symbol of life's rhythm and the most ancient way of marking time. Women are the cosmic keepers of the lunar calendar; in the past, they marked the passing of time by their monthly bleeding cycle, and the number of children they birthed roughly marked the annual cycles. The visibly changing shape of the luminary in the night sky was their sole calendar, and each culture named its nocturnal turn with names that sustained the memory of their sacred relation to her. For them, the moon cycles reflected the five natural progressions of creation: birth, growth, fruition, dissolution, and death. The counting of each month began with the minute sterling sliver of a moon, the first sign of light in the dark sky, and a disappearing moon marked the end of the month. The moon's first rising from below the vast depths of the western horizon was hailed with joy, a celebration of the Supreme Goddess's act of resurrection. This silver crescent in the sky heralded a new month, a fresh new beginning. Vedic people observed the new moon as a crucially auspicious time called *amavasya* since it signifies the Goddess's emanation of rebirth. Destined to grow bolder in awesome splendor into the full moon, this effulgent circle is a splendid time for celebrating abundance. Ancient people honored the lunar phases to ensure the nourishment and protection of sacred life. The rituals and ceremonies performed during various aspects of the moon cycle kept human memory alive and thriving. Earth elders who repeatedly adhered to the full cyclical wheel of the moon before finally retreating into their wisdom cycle of menopause share numerous lunar stories. They celebrated the significant moon cycles with prayers, worship, fasting, feasting, vows, stories, and offerings to their deities.

Modern Hindus continue to honor the Goddess and mark the auspicious cycles of her lunar wheel, performing elaborate sacred rituals with yantra, mantra, and tantra. On the eve of the full moon of Ashvini (September–October), for instance, the harvest festival of Kojagara is celebrated with a night vigil of prayers and festivities. As legend would have it, the goddess Lakshmi descends to the Earth on this auspicious night to bless women with wealth and prosperity. The village elders tell the ancient story of a queen whose husband's wealth was lost and regained due to her night vigil and profound devotion to the goddess Lakshmi.

The Vedic calendar plotted out our vast history of time through the cycles of the moon. Called the Wheel of Time, the Kalachakra presented vast knowledge of the cosmos and its relevance to the greater energies. The Vedic calendar, determined by the lunar cycles, is divided into two fortnightly periods, or *pakshas,* and 30 lunar days, or *tithis.* These 30 days are equivalent to 29.53 solar days. The first fortnight, *shukla paksha,* is the bright cycle of the waxing phase that begins at the new moon. The dark fortnight, *krishna paksha,* or the waning phase, begins at the full moon. The Kalachakra represents the history of eternity as it evolved from Lalita Tripura Sundari, the Supreme Goddess of eternity and cosmic controller of time, whose peerless beauty is praised by gods and goddesses alike. Brighter than a thousand suns, she wears the crescent moon on her head. As the source of consciousness, the Goddess is located in the lotus of Sahasrara, the crown chakra. Lalita is seen as the indissoluble reality, the power source of awareness.

The lunar wheel reveals the sixteen major phases that control the life of all species on Earth. Each phase is a notch in the lunar wheel, and each notch maintains its significant record of time and space. Fifteen *nityas*, rays of light emanating from each notch, mark an equal number of lunar days of the waxing moon, not counting the full moon. That is to say, nityas are the changing projections of Lalita's moon rays; she who represents the full circle of time. On the sixteenth day of the waxing moon looms the full moon, its effulgence revealing a trope of glory that Lalita bequeaths every woman. Although we can perceive her altering shapes and forms, the moon reflects the unchanging nature of Lalita's eternity, immutable splendor, grace, mystery, and magic, which we women have inherited in the Shakti of our eternal womb. As we explore, you'll see that the Shiva-Shakti principle mirrors the relationship between the sun and the moon. The sun is the moon's resting place where she and her Nitya emanations retreat during her dark phase.

The moon has four significant phases whose potent energies control a woman's Shakti cellular anatomy and influence our lives in more ways than we can imagine. These phases are the full moon, waning cycle, new moon, and waxing cycle. Her transition from one phase to the next is known as the lunation cycle. In our fertile years, when we are healthy, the full moon increases ojas and brings forth the potency of ovulation. During the waning cycle, when the moon is in transit from full to new, the uterine lining thickens in preparation for potential pregnancy, and lunar energy becomes a force for cleansing, retreat, and reorientation. The new moon or dark moon phase draws the Shakti-packed mensural blood from the lining of our womb. During the waxing or bright moon, as the lunar cycle moves from the new moon to the full, Mother Moon's essence infuses our womb space with the cellular respiration of Shakti Prana while eggs mature in preparation for the next ovulation cycle.

Celebrating the Ovulation Cycle

Every woman loves the magnificence of the full moon. It heralds our ovulation time, enriched with ojas, our immunity-building juices. Native women faithfully observed seasonal rhythms to ensure the Earth's sustenance and nourishment and recognized that the cycles of the seasons, like the rhythms of the womb, were created from the moon's phases. They cherished their sacred anatomy and its connection to the moon time. The cosmic genesis of a woman's magical anatomy can be traced to the ancient Sanskrit names referring to her procreative anatomy. The vagina is known as *chandra-mukha,* moon-faced, and a particular blood vessel in the vulva is called *chandra-mauli,* moon-crested. Woman's menses is moon-blood; her juices, moon-nectar; her tears, pearl drops of moonlight; her hair is moon-mane, and her eyes are the light and dark moons.

Our ovulation and menstrual cycle preserve our most primal relationship with the Shakti force, safeguarding species' natural sentience. Our yoni is the gateway through which human life enters the world and the lunar gateway through which primordial feminine energy enters our body to nourish and sustain our Shakti anatomy. A woman's yoni, or vagina, is likened to a flower that opens the Shakti portal through which the universe's rhythm and memory are continually communing with human life. It is also a safe and regenerative space that shelters, nourishes, and revitalizes the penis while cultivating Shiva-Shakti oneness. Even the Western name for the vulva — vagina, a word derived from Latin, means "sheath for a sword." Though we have swerved many revolutions away from understanding and honoring this metaphor, the truth remains: when women use their sexuality in harmony with their knowledge of the Shakti anatomy and its lunar calling, sex becomes an inner ceremony, the ritual that promotes feminine power and generates wholesome prosperity and harmony for humanity. After replenishing her cellular intelligence and intuition, the woman's cellular architecture is naturally designed to extend her assets to nourish and heal the entire world.

When lunar rhythm prevails, the ovulation cycle naturally begins as the moon grows into fullness. The full moon is where hope and celebration are savored. This light period marks the time for nurturance, beautification, abundance, and the fertility that results from the purification of the primordial menstrual blood being transformed into Shakti-infused, life-giving cervical mucus in the follicular phase. The centripetal force of this lustrous oracle prods the natural flow of ovulation in a woman, bringing forth her most potent time for fertility and nurturance. According to Ayurveda, during ovulation, the Pitta humor, or metabolic fire principle, is most dominant. Blessed with increasing moonlight and a powerful energy thrust from Lalita and her divine nitya emanations, a woman's ojas naturally increases. Her sexual vitality is once more replenished, and her breasts are ripened with goddess Aditi's nourishment funneling through the nipples. While ovulation is at its natural lunar peak, the neuropeptides FSH (follicle-stimulating hormone) and pLH (luteinizing hormone) cause the rise of estrogen levels in the body. During this time, rejuvenation practices such as oil massage, aromatherapy, warm baths, moonlight dips in water, and the use of healing gems are engaged. Water, the elixir of life, is one of five powerful elements used to bless, cure, heal, nourish, nurture, and revive the body, mind, and spirit. Water carries the magnetic force of liquid moonlight that folds us back into the memory of the Goddess. From the menstrual cycle to ovulation and back again, a woman's Shakti cellular anatomy is being fed and revitalized. Primordial matter, once cleansed and revived during menstruation, is renewed once more for the making of life. Controlled by the energy of the lunar deities, the Shakti Prana circulating the womb is potent during this time.

After the full moon, during the roughly 14 days of the lunar waning cycle, our emotional need to withdraw from the world of activity and retreat into a time of introspection happens almost immediately. This is known as the luteal phase of the menstrual cycle. At this time, body, mind, and spirit also wane; a woman naturally yearns for quietude and resolve. Lunar energy becomes a force for cleansing, detoxifying, and reorientation. The moon's waning cycle offers ample opportunity for serene practices such as meditation, journaling, drawing, painting, fasting, and other heart-opening activities that build and strengthen your inner harmony.

Menstrual Moon Time Cycle

> *Blood fecundates the Earth and through a magical process of alchemy transforms it into rain and food.*
>
> Pupul Jayakar, Activist

The ancients called the dark days of the moon "Woman's Moon" and "Resting Moon," linking a woman's menstrual and emotional state to the new moon phase of the lunar wheel. The new moon marks the time of rebirth and renewal when women naturally release their profound life-creating blood back to the Earth. After the dark days of the new moon, the first sighting of the rising moon was hailed with joy and celebration. It stood for the moon's act of resurrection — a metaphor for the menstrual cycle. Ancient women honored menstrual blood as the essential life-generating material willed by Lalita. The dark moon provides a cozy atmosphere for a woman's bleeding time when she can wholeheartedly rest, reprieve, and replenish. Other nicknames such as "Sleeping Moon" and "The Days of Lying Down" evince this regenerative phase. Remarkably, during the dark moon, Lalita and her nityas make their monthly sojourn to the sun to recharge their lunar effulgence. While the nityas are away from their lunar abode, the dark moon phase thusly becomes more solarized than usual. This unique momentum of solar energy in the lunar abode aids in the release of the endometrium. At this time, menstruation is set in motion by the new moon, which is aided by the sun-absorbing energies from the Earth, which draw the menstrual blood from the body. The monthly cycle is the primary means by which a woman cleanses and restores the rich life blood that collects in the lining of her womb. During menstruation, activities are reduced to the essentials so that the body, mind, and spirit may flow in accord with the natural rhythms of the new moon. Retreating from intense routines and everyday intrusions is necessary for this Shakti practice so that you remain mindful of the great transformational experience of shedding the lining of the uterus. Once shed, the womb environment is renewed once more. The menstrual cycle remains faithful to the dark moon phase when it is not being disrupted by the use of contraceptive pills and other birth control devices, harmful foods, and sexual activities, all of which run counter to the nourishment of the womb during its vulnerable time.

Across various cultures and faith traditions, names for menstruation reify a woman's sacred connection to the lunar wheel. German peasants called the menstrual blood, *die Mond,* "the moon." The French called the monthly blood *le moment de la lune,* or "the movement of the moon." In China, the menstrual blood is said to be the yin principle, the primordial essence of Mother Earth that gives life to all things. The cycle of the moon is even suggested in the commonplace metaphor, "a woman's period." "Period" comes from the Greek term for "going round," the cycle of life. These are just a few of the many examples of ancient and modern cultures recognizing the menstrual-moon relationship.

The Uruk record states that the reigning queen of the Third Dynasty of Ur took to ritual offerings to the moon in the final days of her dark cycle. This culture believed a drumming ritual would resurrect and return the moon from the underworld. Layne Redmond elaborates on the ancient Uruk tradition: "This monthly ritual drumming may also have facilitated the flow of menstrual blood. Menstrual cycles and lunar cycles retained their ancient association; references from the ancient world suggest that women normally menstruated en masse at the dark of the moon."

In the final phase of the menstrual cycle, which occurs during the moon's waxing cycle following ovulation, eggs grow and develop in the womb. This is known in Western science as the follicular phase. Studies show that the immune system cells known as lymphoid aggregates also begin to develop in the uterine wall during this time. At the physiological level, this may explain why women experience an abundant surge of creative and sensual energies, vibrantly growing in tandem with the waxing moon as she becomes brighter and brighter. During the waxing or bright moon, the lunar cycle moves from the new moon to the full as Lalita projects her stupendous power through the changing shapes of the nityas in the night sky. During this phase, we gather strength, potency, regeneration, and rejuvenation. A harbinger of reprieve, the waxing moon offers a natural period for women to foster health, wealth, abundance, and creativity.

Myth versus Intelligence

Over the 30 or more years I have been teaching this work to practitioners, I have been told a zillion times that the menstrual cycle's "dos and don'ts" sound like old wives' tales and ignorant myths. Why shouldn't women do exactly as they feel or carry on with their daily routine rituals during their cycle? "Why should we not cook and swim, do yoga, run, garden, and do our errands as usual?" they ask. "We're not living in the dark ages!" Let me be clear: we have been trained to equate alienation from nature with the freedom to do as we please. This is dark age thinking, hammered into our brains for thousands of years. Women's bodies, minds, and spirits are divinely designed to be nourished, nurtured, and healed by the moon and with the moon as we chart our monthly progression with her. The actions we are guided to take during our cycle are ancient but not archaic. They help nourish our womb and heal its wounds during the new moon's rays. During our potent menstrual time, we are vulnerable and fragile and are therefore advised to take certain precautions to preserve the natural rhythms of our three predominant internal elements: air, fire, and water. We must continually seek to balance the elements within and without. For example, we are cautioned not to take baths or lengthy showers or swim while we are actively bleeding. Minimum bodily cleansing is recommended at this time. Quick, cool showers or wiping down the body will do. These measures preserve the least degree of intrusion so that the necessary discharge can be completed without interruption. The water element is sacred. Controlled by the moon, it has its own cosmic memory, unique gravitational force, and lunar charge. This force can compete with and impair the flow of the menstrual cycle. The air constituent, called *Vata,* is the most dominant element during menstrual time. Vata's nature is erratic, dark, cold, and ungrounded; therefore, at the physiological level, we need to keep the body warm, cosseted, protected, and stabilized as our psyche is most vulnerable at this time. Blood is equated to the dominant element of fire. The solitude practice we create during the shedding of the womb's lining is to keep mindful of the sacred blood, exercising the care we would take while tending a fire. As we take the necessary time to be mindful while we are bleeding, we are, in truth, tending to our own fire ritual within.

Putting aside the beautiful arts of gardening, cooking, planting, and other food-related activities during our bleeding time is also advised as we wish to prevent potent menstrual blood energy from pervading the foods. Furthermore, we avoid food activities that can put the body's upward-rising and downward-flowing air in conflict with each other. The energy or memory of food — that which is derived from plant life — is imbued with prana, a rising energy flowing up from the Earth toward the sky. During menstruation, we need to be mindful of how we interact with the upward-rising prana since we require the downward-flowing air, *apana vayu*, to be dominant at this fragile time. Apana vayu is the Earth's magnetic force, which helps pull the blood downward. Moreover, food and Earthing activities are predominantly *Kapha* in nature. Kapha, as you may recall, is the foundational Earth and water principle within and without. It is full of youth-giving energy that nourishes the body, while menstrual blood is primarily dominated by air and fire humors that aid the cleansing and revitalization of the womb's blood.

The time of the menstrual cycle is both a sacred and precious period for a woman. During menstruation, we must go at a slower pace and allow the body to cleanse itself; we are also advised to pare down activities to the bare essentials so that body, mind, and spirit may experience the least degree of intrusion. Ayurveda recommends creating a gentle space to conserve feminine energy and inculcate creative potential. Refrain from sexual activities. Maintain a light, wholesome diet of salads, fresh juices, grains (basmati rice, millet, couscous, amaranth), pasta, tofu, leafy greens, and fresh fruits. Herbal teas such as raspberry, organic rose flower, peppermint, ginger, lemon balm, hops, and chamomile are also revitalizing during this time. Above all else, remember that menstruation is all about letting go, letting be, resting, reprieve, stillness, and allowing the majesty of our blood to renew itself at its own pace while reformatting its sapient form.

Reclaiming Women's Health and Reproductive Rites

The Sanskrit word uttara means "womb, cosmos, that which is filled." The wise perceive the womb as uttara — filled with contentment and fulfillment, the carrier of life itself.

Maya Tiwari, *Women's Power to Heal*

Modern, sanitized society sees menstruation as an unclean, mundane, inconvenient happening that may as well be curtailed early or pushed back into oblivion with an artillery of products such as sanitized pads or tampons and disinfected with antiseptic douching formulas. These products are processed with a variety of chemicals that we do not wish to introduce into our body. They also interrupt the flow of Shakti Prana's downward circadian rhythm, which we require to assist the unobstructed flow of the menstrual blood. Nowadays, many women use douching for hygienic and cosmetic reasons — more a cleansing detergent rather than a soothing treatment for specific conditions. Commercial, over-the-counter douching products, as well as those prescribed by doctors, have been proven harmful to women's health. A current medical advisory warns that frequent and excessive douching can increase the risk of infections such as pelvic inflammatory disease, bacterial vaginosis, chlamydia, premature birth, sexually transmitted infections, and cervical cancer. The Ness study conducted in 2002 by a team of gynecologists and obstetricians indicated that 87 percent of the 1200 women interviewed who were using popular commercial brands of douching products reported incidents of bacterial vaginosis after use. When these commercial douches were tested in vitro, it was discovered that they inhibited natural vaginal microorganisms, thereby disturbing the eco-balance of vaginal flora.

Hormonal therapy practices such as suppression of menstruation for non-medical reasons are also harmful. There are many ways these medications can be delivered, including a pill, skin patch, vaginal ring, injection, or implant. All these options contain progestin, which causes the lining of the uterus to grow thin so menstrual bleeding can be suppressed. The progestin-containing intrauterine device (IUD) is a common way to deliver medication directly to the lining of the uterus. Norethisterone is a drug that is also given to suppress menstruation. This drug prevents the womb's lining from breaking down, thereby stopping periods from occurring. These procedures have been proven to have devastatingly negative effects on women's health and wellness, including dizziness, nausea, vaginal spotting, vomiting, and abdominal cramps, and can prove disastrous to those who have blood clotting conditions, high blood pressure, or low cholesterol. Medical science, for the most part, views a woman's fertility and menopause as recurring "crises" rather than a result of natural changes in a woman's grand fertility cycle. Intrusive and harmful solutions for feminine care, such as hormone patches and other forms of hormone replacement therapy, have become the norm, with little to no consideration given to their consequences.

Fortunately, millions of women are changing their perspective on the medicalization of their reproductive health. More and more women are seeking holistic approaches to healing their disease. This has been a long and challenging turn-about for women since we have been indoctrinated to trust the prescriptive medical model of health. Any approach that strays from the Western medical model creates fear and skepticism. Over the past four decades, I have introduced Ayurveda long-lost education and therapies to women to maintain their pristine reproductive health in concert with lunar cycles. Among the many forgotten gems is a practice called *Uttara Vasti*, a gentle way of cleansing and nourishing the womb at the new moon to reorder the cycle back to its natural flow with the dark moon. A warm and loving therapeutic treatment, its effectiveness has been proven by thousands of women who have used this sublime practice successfully to heal a plethora of reproductive conditions and to realign their cycle back to the new moon phase. While *uttara* means "womb, cosmos, that which is filled," *vasti* refers to an animal's stomach lining, used in ancient times to create the first Uttara Vasti therapy bag. My work has helped thousands of women whose reproductive health or monthly cycles were impaired. I am continually awed by how quickly the cycles revert back to the new moon. In most cases, it happens after only one application of Uttara Vasti. Many of these women have confided that after using this home therapy, they feel like they had "a glow in my belly."

Magnetic Magic of Our Blood

Feminine lunar ideals have been perverted over the centuries to meet the standards of colonization and the Neo-Christian religious and political motivation of Western civilization. Through the eyepiece of the Earth, moon, and sun, our menstrual blood is magnetic and magical. Irrational connotations of the menstrual blood being unclean, unhygienic, or toxic are a modern concept reeking of primordial fear of the feminine. The stoic reason for approaching menstrual blood with deep reverence — that is, employing logic and seeking to understand the processes of nature — is that menstrual blood is the most priceless asset on Mother Earth as it brings forth new life. The process we call menses does not begin to encompass the far-reaching magic and miracle of a woman's blood. It is Shakti in the form of iron, cinnabar, and heme, in the mythical mix of primordial feminine powers. It is meant to be treated with the greatest reverence. Hence, the prevalence of natural laws and contra-indications associated with the menstrual cycle. We wish to safeguard this priceless, shaktified material from energetic interference to preserve its uninterrupted, pristine flow. Modern interpretations of these rites of passage and their bearing on cosmic energies are largely misconstrued and treated with the trained disdain of the patriarchal ideology that denigrates and marginalizes feminine native intelligence as suspicions, hysteria, and old-fashioned nonsense. However, as we return to the wisdom of cosmic lunar rites and their preservation, we discover the rich life force tradition of our blood.

Ancient women knew exactly what time of day and month they would need to retreat to their bleeding sanctuary. Amazing as it may seem, they were intimately familiar with their rhythms. They did not wear pads and tampons and all the other horrific products that now invade the sacred yoni; instead, women convened together in comfortable make-shift menstrual lodges to share stories while squatting to let their menses flow back to the Earth. This unimpeded menstrual flow allowed them to return to the Earth the Shakti-energized blood that had been transformed through their sapient bodies to continue the cycle of replenishment and regeneration.

Wise husbands of yore recognized the heightened energy field within a woman's body, mind, and psyche during her menstrual time and would plot out a piece of land in the forest and surround it with a stone wall high enough so that the potent menstrual energy could not permeate beyond it. Children, animals, and young people were kept at a distance from the menstrual lodge and grounds. Instinctively, animals retreated deeper into the forest and away from the lodges. In fact, Vedic texts inform us that the animals were terrified of the potency of menstrual blood. They recognized that the lining of a woman's womb moon was evacuating the procreative material of the Shakti and kept at a reverent distance. Meals were lovingly prepared for menstruating women by the elders or male members of the community and served by the elder women. Nowadays, we have also lost touch with the innate support from our men and elders that we were accustomed to receiving during our bleeding time. We have also lost touch with this necessary continuum of nourishment and fertilization – the art of giving back to the Earth the riches of our bodies as we evacuate so that the ongoing cycle of the Earth's Shakti memory may be preserved. Would it not be wonderful to invite these sublimely supportive practices back into our lives?

A magical story of the blood river goddess lives on in India. In Assam, in one of the most prominent Shakti temples, the goddess Kamakhya, the avatar of Lakshmi, is revered. It is said that the mythological womb of the goddess Shakti is installed in the *Garvagriha,* or innermost sanctum of this holy temple. The women's festival of *Ambubachi* is observed at the temple during this time. Ambubachi means "spoken with water," signifying the rainfall expected during this month of the monsoon that makes the Earth fertile. According to the local folks and millions of disciples, during the month of June, at the start of the monsoon season, the goddess sheds her menstrual blood. To safeguard the goddess's absolute privacy while she is discharging and recharging her cosmic womb, regular worship of devotees is suspended during the first four days of the festival. In fact, the entire state ceases all digging, plowing, sowing, and transplanting of crops to honor Kamakhya's annual "menstrual flow." At the end of the fourth day, having completed her cycle, the goddess is ceremonially bathed and adorned with new clothes by the temple priests, and her utensils are thoroughly cleansed and blessed with holy water, after which the temple doors are swung open. Women pour in by the thousands to worship the goddess at the Ambubachi Festival.

By no small coincidence, the Brahmaputra River, which runs alongside Kamakhya Temple, turns red during this time. Pieces of Kamakhya's iron-rich rock are sold in the form of Kamiya Sindoor, supposedly endued with the goddess's mind-expanding powers. The mineral cinnabar is intimately connected with Shakti worship. Geologists analyzing the river's content inform that it is rich in iron and cinnabar with an underground cave system filled with mercuric sulfide. This would account for the river's blood-red water. If we were to decipher the content of blood, we would find that human blood is red because of the protein hemoglobin, which contains a red compound called heme that's crucial for carrying oxygen through the bloodstream. Heme contains an iron atom that binds to oxygen. The menstrual blood of Kamakhya, why not? The cinnabar, iron, and mercuric content of the Brahmaputra River appear to have a parallel heme to her annual red blessings.

In the burgeoning schema of the patriarchal takeover, when the trend toward immobilized agriculture began, we lost our connection and natural alliance with Mother Moon. Loss of knowledge of nature's cycles – lunar, solar, and seasonal – has severely impacted our memory of the Shakti anatomy, resulting in the loss of the human currency of sentiency and intuition. To recapture our feminine prowess, we need to take an example and guide our daily affairs by the appearance of the moon. I invite us to begin gently by familiarizing ourselves with the moon calendar, marking the times for the new and full moon. There is nothing more powerful than a circle of women who join forces in reclaiming their lunar rites of passage: invite the women of your community to gather in a drumming circle under the full moon to share stories and feminine rituals, songs, and dances. At the new moon phase, gather yourself and retreat as best to create space for quietude, reflection, and meditation. Keep the intent to bring your cycle in harmony with the slim moon, and if you are in the years beyond, treasure the gifts of your maturity, wisdom, and grace. We can find a modicum of time to prep, pamper, and prosper at every lunar notch. Whether you are looking to bring your cycle in harmony with the dark moon, or take loving care of the womb, or simply to strengthen Shakti Prana, I have set out the powerful Root Lock Herbal Bath for your sacred water-healing pleasure.

The Root Lock Herbal Bath—Sacred Water Healing

This ritual is performed simply by sitting in a hip bath laced with a rose, raspberry, and aloe vera herbal decoction while learning to do a Mula Bandha—the root lock wherein you contract the anal and vaginal muscles to reinforce prana and apana vayu. As you absorb the healing water into the vaginal channel and perform the root lock before releasing the water, a wealth of healing can occur. Many women—old and young—have shared the sense of happiness, healing and lightness they experienced after this gentle practice. This root lock practice is usually not done in a bath, but for the purpose of doubling the benefits of cleansing and restoring Shakti Prana in the womb space while enjoying the surge of energy that locking the hammock of lower cavity muscles propels, we will be doing the Root Lock Herbal Bath.

Root Locks, called Mula Bandha in yoga philosophy, are locks or valves in specific areas of the body that, once engaged, can forge the flow of prana to energize specific cellular healing within the tissues. The Mula Bandha practice supports a diamond shaped group of muscles that spans the space between the bones of the pubis in the front, the sitting bones on the sides, and the coccyx in the back. Engaging the root lock on pelvic floor muscles supports the internal organs of the lower abdominal cavity and redirects awareness to the space of the pubis and uterus. In this practice, we contract the anal sphincter as well as the urethra by locking the apertures of the vagina and anus with the same tenacity as we do when making a tight fist. Performing this practice in a sit bath allows a small amount of the herbal decoction to enter the vaginal cavity. This gets released after loosening the lock. Vibrationally, Mula Bandha has an upward pull on the energy that lies in the perineum which, in turn, instigates the awakening of Kundalini at the base of the spine. By continuously practicing your Mula Bandha, in and out of the bath, we experience a methodical repair of the womb, exuding healing vibrations to the lower abdominal organs and chakras. A powerful yet easeful practice to enhance our psycho-spiritual sense of balance.

The Practice: Root Lock Herbal Bath — Sacred Water Healing

Use this bath to help shift your cycle to flow with the new moon phase. You may take this bath every day for 30 minutes during the first 7 days of the waxing cycle. For those in your reproductive years, do not do this particular bath during your bleeding time. This bath can be taken at any time for those who are aged or post-menopausal; women healing from miscarriage or abortion may perform this bath 4–6 weeks after the incident.

Exception Note: In the case of vaginal infections and/or malodor or sexual abuse, the optimal time to use the Root Lock Bath is in accord with the New Moon waxing phase.

Instructions for Root Lock Herbal Bath:

- Fill the bathtub about a quarter full, adding 1/2 gallon of herbal decoction to the warm water.
- Assume a semi-squatting posture in the bath by keeping your knees up with feet planted on the floor of the tub. Breathe gently and invite the herbal water into the vaginal channel. Use the root lock by squeezing closed your buttocks and vaginal channel firmly.
- Hold the decoction in the vaginal channel for about 1-3 minutes before releasing the root lock and allowing the decoction to flow out.
- Repeat this procedure 3–5 times.
- Afterwards, relax your legs and stay in the warm bath 20 minutes or so. After drying yourself, gently massage your belly with a teaspoon of sesame oil.
- Rest in a warm, cozy space for an hour after the therapy.

Rose/Raspberry/Aloe Decoction:

Ingredients:

- 2 ounces Red Raspberry Leaves (organic)
- 2 ounces Pink or Red Rose Petals (organic)
- 5 tablespoons organic Aloe Vera gel
- 1/2 gallon of water

Bring water to boil in a double boiler. Add dried leaves and buds. Cover and simmer on low heat for 10 minutes. Remove from heat and let steep for 15 minutes. Strain the decoction into a jug and retain the herbal roughage for one more decoction making. Afterwards, collect the used herbal roughage and compost it. Add aloe vera gel to decoction and pour into the warm bath water.

Directions: If You Are Shifting Your Cycle to the New Moon

- Begin this practice the day after the new moon.
- Continue every day for five days.
- Inappropriate times for those who are looking to shift their cycle to new moon: full or waning moon.
- Never when bleeding, spotting, or during pregnancy.

Chapter 16

The Wisdom-Bearing Years

Woman of the Winter Moon may be a woman in her greatest power, woman in her guise as Elemental, as Force of Nature. This is woman to be revered. She is a concentration of feminine wisdom gathered and concentrated over the years, blended with the astral knowledge of the soul-star.

Elizabeth S. Eiler, Ph.D., *Singing Woman*

In Hinduism, the Shakti force in women is considered to be inherently divine; her fertility and menstrual and menopausal cycle are all timed with the rhythm of the lunar turn. As we have seen, our Shakti cellular anatomy in its entirety is governed by the lunar wheel. As a personification of the goddess Shakti, the qualities women naturally embody grow more luminous with age – intuition, nurturing, caring, forgiveness, and compassion. These "feminine" traits are aspired to by men, women, and all genders as a spiritual means of accessing and balancing the primordial power within. As we reach menopause, the Red Bindu retires its operation in the womb, while the "prana-bindu-menstrual" operation that regulates our hormonal function is naturally reset to subtler levels that compel the womb's circadian rhythm to open to the influence of the dark fortnight – krishna paksha – or the waning phase that begins at the full moon.

The goddesses in the Hindu pantheon are beyond human processes, beyond the material world, representing not only human aspects, but the underlying cosmic feminine force of Shakti. In the elder years we are transformed into the characteristics of the mature goddess. At menopause, we have our own privileged moon time. Our menopausal anatomy follows the identical rhythm of the dark phase of the moon. In truth, we have the exclusive invitation to come and sit with the fierce goddess Kali, who presides over the dark phase of the moon. This is the austere cycle of the waning moon that follows the magnificent full moon. Just as the bright phase of the moon can offer women deep, energetic medicine in their fertile reproductive years, the dark phase of the lunar portal brings its own special balm for the elder. This lunar phase opens wide primarily to wise older women in their menopausal time. It takes a certain degree of wisdom, storied life, and discernment to enter the domain of Kali. She is the fearless warrior of the open skies, and she is terrifying. Every woman in her menopause phase is her disciple. She is the warrior mother of the mature, the friend of the wise, and the guardian, companion, and protectress of the devoted. Menopause is the individual dark phase of our womanly lunation, where we emulate the magic, mystery, purpose, and serenity of the dark phase of the moon. A rather significant, serene getaway awaits us — a time for re-orientation, for debriefing from our entire active, driven reproductive life. We are rescued into that blessed space of reconciliation where warriors retreat after battles fought and won.

To glean an idea of how privileged, private, and precious the dark moon space is, let us peer into the journey of the nityas during this moon phase. As the majestic full moon celebration gives way to the dark moon cycle, Lalita Tripura Sundari releases her nityas from duty. They have been working arduously and lovingly during the waxing moon phase to aid the affairs of women on the Earthly plane. Even the nitya goddesses need their time out. Thus, the Supreme Goddess Lalita releases her emanations from active duty to humanity. Each night of the dark phase, one after the other, the nityas leave the moon's mansion and travel to the domain of Father Sun, quietly stealing away without ritual or fuss to his private sanctuary. The night following the full moon, the fifteenth nitya, Chitra, takes refuge in the sun. She is followed by the fourteenth nitya, and then the next night by the thirteenth nitya, and so it goes, night after night, until all the nityas are serenely ensconced in Father Sun's domain. As each nitya leaves, the moon incrementally decreases in size until, in their absence, it becomes completely blacked out.

As the light dwindles, the luminosity within the elder's womb space becomes brighter. Feeding off the nityas' serene vibrations while in the sun's domain, the usual angst and fear and dark emotions of the waning moon cycle are offset by the nityas' experience. In the nityas' retreat at the sun, they rest, refill, and replenish themselves. They enjoy peace, quiet, and the serenity of being exempt from their arduous duties, solarizing and basking in the warm cover of golden rays. They are silent, sheltered, secure, and free. During this time, the nityas' vacation experience in the sun's domain is vibrationally propelled into the sphere to be received by elders who are aware of this quiet lunar transference. The nityas' vacation ends on the day of the black moon. They begin their return to their abode in the moon, starting with Kameshavari, the first nitya, whose light we see in the first sliver of a crescent in the sky. One by one, as they return, the moon grows fuller and fuller. By the night before the full moon, all the nityas have returned to their lunar mansion. Each month, we have the luxury of receiving Lalita Tripura Sundari's waning lunar energies to help us shift into that quieter resolve within that fosters our intuitive intelligence.

As menopausal crones, we become more of an observer than a participant in the waxing cycle and our waning years. We retain our residency within the waning cycle of the moon. Here, we are generating our own inner light to offset the dark skies and revel in our free nature, promoted by the elements of air and space, where insight, clairvoyance, and wisdom can be harnessed from our lived experiences. We can show ourselves from time to time and share our riches with younger generations of women or with other menopausal women. We find a different quality of courage after we cease bleeding. We no longer get invested in proving our physical worth, courage, resilience, or social acceptability. We can be unapologetically ourselves, whatever that looks like. We may no longer feel pressed to do the morally courageous thing. But at this very juncture, we arrive at a very different plinth of courage. This is the place where we don't invest our time in pleasing anyone. This is where we truly begin our spiritual ascent back to the Shakti source. At this pivotal juncture, when each moment is measured against a dwindling number of years, we want to rise tall and live with purpose through a heart-centered approach. We wish to be kind even toward the undeserving. We wish to love our grown children and free them for their own journey. Now, let us rise up and honor our inner space, that shaktified space that gives us nurturance, healing, light, and life. I love that space within me. I embrace it, just as I embrace that I will never again be forced to defend it or hold it behind iron bars regardless of who is displeased with my existence or freedom as a woman.

As we move into our elder years, our pineal gland, too, becomes more awakened. This gland produces the hormone melatonin, which is a stress releaser that regulates our sleep cycles and minimizes the effects of radical change in our lives. More profoundly, it is connected to the third eye, heightening the intuition, insight, telepathy, and clairvoyance that strengthen after menopause. This is a gland through which we dream; it is the conduit to the multi-dimensions of our universe, the portal through which we may enter Lalita's dark lunar fortnight each month. When awakened, we can travel and float through our astral bodies at leisure. Centered in the Ajna chakra, the third eye connects our body and mind to the soul. As we age, we draw nearer to the operations of the Ajna chakra that controls the pineal gland and gain more access to this subtle realm of our energetic body. The pineal gland produces a mysterious substance called dimethyltryptamine (DMT). DMT is known as the spiritual molecule that curiously releases during the rapid eye movement phase when we dream. This substance is so powerful that it can transfer our consciousness to other dimensions and realms.

The following is a gentle ongoing practice to do during the fourteen days or nights of each monthly waning lunar cycle. Trataka Kriya meditation practice awakens the pineal gland, which brings clarity and awareness and becomes a pleasurable practice to expand consciousness. Practice Trataka meditation in the morning or evening by simply sitting and focusing your eyes on a lit dipa, or candle, without blinking. Once you are seated, close your eyes. Slowly open your eyes and stare at the light without blinking for as long as possible. Close your eyes again and then slowly reopen them. Do this practice nine times while silently setting an intention dear to you. Keep it simple to not overload the mental process. Trataka Kriya reduces stress and rids us of anger, angst, and impatience. Aided by the dark moon, this simple practice can regenerate the necessary vision to move forward with clarity and purpose.

What Went Wrong?

The draftsmen of the sexual revolution zero in on fertility as a marker of femininity, which is quite unfair considering a woman's best years – after she has or has not given birth to her brood – can be found in the genesis of menopause. This precious state of maturity and elegance has been thwarted through a multitude of modern filters where fertility, youth, external beauty, moonlit skin, lustrous hair, and slimness are not only lauded but somehow fastened to self-worth. If we subscribe to these lenses, we are felled before we can even rise. This is why the great transition into menopause can morph into a tsunami. When driven by the tune of an adverse rhythm, even nature's blessing can turn into a storm that fractures the balance of the Earth. In the Earth traditions, very few women suffered from menopausal symptoms when they reached their non-reproductive years. By refusing to internalize unnatural patriarchal attitudes and treatments foisted on menopausal women, we can embrace our shaktified wisdom and unfurl into a new phase of unfettered and purposeful femininity.

The most convincing evidence of post-reproductive lifespan in a non-human long-lived species comes from marine mammals, such as short-finned pilots and killer whales. Women, like whales, have a long and phenomenal period of creativity and productivity after their reproductive years, while other species experience senescence in fertility and health as they age. Whales exhibit a similar life history to humans, with reproductive capacity ending between 36 and 50 years and maximum lifespan reaching over 60 to 80 years, respectively, resulting in decades-long post-reproductive phases in both species. Recent evidence suggests that such a life history in killer whales may result from adaptive benefits that old, post-reproductive females bring to their adult offspring and grandchildren. Before we delve into the profound wisdom and purpose that await women in their menopausal time, however, let us take a cautionary look in the rearview mirror.

Historically, male opinions on menopause have been as dehumanizing as they are imbecilic. "The unpalatable truth must be faced that all postmenopausal women are castrates," opined the gynecologist Robert Wilson, who elaborated on this theme in his 1966 bestseller, *Feminine Forever*. The influential book, it was later disclosed, was backed by a pharmaceutical company eager to market hormone-replacement therapy. In his 1969 release of *Everything You Always Wanted to Know About Sex but Were Afraid to Ask*, David Reuben reveals his deeply biased opinion on this hot topic, opining, "Once the ovaries stop, the very essence of being a woman stops." One can't help but speculate about what these so-called experts were compensating for or how the women in their lives managed to put up with them. In 1976, I had a hysterectomy at the early age of 23 due to ovarian cancer. I have managed to live a rich and fulfilling life in service to thousands of women, many of whom have had reproductive issues and thrived after healing from this type of ruthless disregard from the medical industry. My work in Ayurveda inspired them to reclaim their feminine rights, health, and power.

Unsurprisingly, the medicalization of menopause has been an entirely male-dominated affair. A male French physician coined the term menopause in 1821. Medical interest in menopause increased considerably in the mid-nineteenth century. In the 1930s, people started describing it as a deficiency disease. Before this time, menopause was not shrouded in myth, superstition, or clerical and medical incursion. Throughout the Middle Ages, women's health was women's business. Midwives were the Earth's scientists who were the sole providers of women's health care. Their roles remained unchallenged until the seventeenth and eighteenth centuries, when, gradually, these women were pushed out of business by so-called male midwives. It became popular for these male practitioners to brand their female counterparts as vetulae. Although the literal meaning is "old woman," the term was perverted by physicians to denote a discard of society, a woman who was evil, venal, offensive, or wicked. Her Earth medicine practice was deemed ignorant, dangerous, and harmful. In Women Healers Through History, Elisabeth Brooke succinctly states, "Describing women healers as vetulae denied them a personal name and identity, making them the contemptible 'other,' easy to demonize, isolate, and vanquish. The medical profession colluded with the Church in these attacks, as both aimed to eject women from the public realm." During this time, the medical profession consisted only of men, all of whom were university-educated. In the three centuries preceding the Renaissance in Europe, clerical and medical misogyny ruled the day. Two primary trends drove the downfall and replacement of women healers. The first was the evolution of European universities that systematically excluded women as students, thereby creating a male monopoly on the practice of medicine. The second development was the campaign promoted by the Church and supported by both clerical and civil authorities to brand women healers as witches. Patriarchal primordial fear of the feminine was at its pinnacle. The women's intuitive, esoteric healing skills posed a direct threat to the Church's autocracy. Within a century, more than 100,000 "witches" were executed by burning at the stake or hanging. Those persecuted were unknown numbers of mostly peasant women, single women, widows, and crones.

In the 1970s, medicalization of menopause became finely honed in the Western World. Menopausal symptoms were ascribed to estrogen deficiency, and estrogen (a hormone) replacement therapy (HRT) – using synthetic estrogen developed in 1938 – was exhorted as the ultimate liberation for middle-aged women. The medical industry, led by Pharmaceutical companies, entered the menopause scene in a big way and dominated the center stage. In the 1970s, a group of male clinicians established the International Menopause Society. The burgeoning hormone therapy business, estimated at 600 billion dollars, was so profitable that these clinicians marketed hormonal drugs to postmenopausal women regardless of their specific needs. Scouring this potentially massive market of 3.905 billion women was a new high for the patriarchal medical industry. Fortunately for all of womankind, the awakening of the Shakti force is happening now, and the tides are changing. Earlier this year, eight stalwart women founded the Female Founders Fund to meet women's needs and help support their postmenopausal journey by disrupting Big Pharma's exploitative intent.

From the physiological and medical perspective, menopause occurs when a woman permanently stops having menstrual periods. Often called the "change of life," this stage signals the end of a woman's ability to have children. Women's hormone levels change, and the production of estrogen and progesterone decreases. A quantum drop in estrogen levels causes most of the symptoms of menopause. During the four or so decades of our reproductive years, estrogen is dominant in the first two weeks of our cycle and progesterone the second two weeks; however, at the onset of perimenopause, the pituitary gland begins to turn down the volume of these hormones. They keep dropping until the hormonal levels recede to the point that the cycle no longer produces menstruation. While the cycle is still happening, the hormone levels are not high enough to create a lining in the uterus that needs to be shed each month. Menopause is said to be complete when menstrual periods have ceased for one continuous year.

Interestingly, women in Western cultures tend to view and respond differently to menopause than non-Western women. Women in Western countries view menopause negatively. This is contrasted with a positive outlook towards menopause in developing countries like India. While there are many reasons for this, the power of the pharmaceutical industry in Western countries plays no small part. HRT use rate, accordingly, is high in the West while it remains low or negligible in countries like India.

According to Ayurveda, the problematic menopausal conditions many women suffer are largely due to the toxic state of our modern living environment. Mycotoxins produced by mold are one of the most tenacious adversaries of hormonal health. Zearalenone is a fungal-based estrogen that not only plays a role in hormonal imbalance but is suspected to be a primary contributor to hormonal cancers, such as breast and cervical cancer. These toxins stress our immune system and make us more susceptible to fatigue and illness. Our immune system depends on ojas, that marvelous immunity-building substance responsible for strengthening nourishment in the tissues. Ojas is created through the digestion process, fed not only by the healthful foods we ingest but also by other forms of nourishment: nature, movement, purpose, and love. After our seven tissue layers, the last of which is our reproductive tissue, have been sequentially fed, what remains is ojas, the most refined form of nourishment. Ojas is our immunity. When it is strong, we thrive. A strong ojas fights internal and external environmental toxicity. Ojas is a building principle of Kapha, one of the three bodily humors in Ayurveda. Kapha is the elemental principle of water and Earth, which is characterized as stable, methodical, and sustaining stamina. Kapha is usually more abundant in women than men, partly due to our state of fertility. Kapha is the primary ojas-building principle in the body and predominates our constitution in the first stage of our life. When Kapha becomes vitiated, ojas is scanty or weak. We become more sensitive to diseases and illness. As hormonal levels decrease during menopause, so too does our ojas. We are naturally more prone to imbalances. During menopause, a heightened sympathetic nervous system is occurring. As a result, we experience an increase in cortisol levels, blood pressure, cholesterol, and heart rate. As we get older, Vata, our elemental air and space principle, also plays a more central part in our metabolic body. The erratic and mobile Vata can shift our body into sympathetic overdrive. The delicate balance between the sympathetic nervous system, the stress-buffering system, and the parasympathetic nervous system, which activates renewal, struggles to maintain equanimity. Elevated Vata can instigate Pitta, the fire and water principle, to accompany it, further disrupting our balance. Moreover, decreases in hormonal activity can bring both Pitta and Kapha into derangement since these two principles depend and thrive on hormones. Excess Pitta and Kapha can decrease our digestive fires and push Pitta through the portal, creating hot flashes, night sweats, irritability, impatience, and so on. It is vital, then, that we maintain a well-nourished Pitta, Kapha, and Vata during our major pause.

At the time of this writing, more than 50 million women in the US are undergoing menopause. The painful symptoms of menopause in our present culture, caused by living out of sync with nature's rhythms, the enormity of environmental pollution, and the deterioration of the Shakti force, typically range from brain fog to anxiety, depression, reduced vision, sleeplessness, exhaustion, vaginal dryness, stiff joints, hot flashes, memory loss, vitiated orgasms, and a sense of feeling paltry, defeated, exhausted, unloved, and not-so-pretty. Most women feel embarrassed to share their discomfort and angst with family members, partners, and employers. The period of menopausal change is also a peak time for suicide, and one survey of 3000 women who went to their doctor during menopause revealed that 66 percent were offered antidepressants.

While we have come a long way from certain inured medical opinions about women, periods, and menopause, it's not nearly far enough. It is high time we shift our perspective from the doomsday medical assessment of menopause to the next natural progression of our beautiful feminine lives. Menopause is not a disease. It is not a time for despair. We do not start growing beards and have escalating testosterone highs. The better our health is in our reproductive years, the more our reproductive hormones naturally align with the moon cycles, and the easier the transition becomes physically and emotionally. More profoundly, the portal of menopause answers our soul's call for liberation from the mundane fetters of routine womanly life.

Put You First

Life is continually transforming. Entering menopause is a huge juncture in our lives. I recall that when I had a complete hysterectomy following my bout with ovarian cancer at the delicate age of 23, I was told by Dr Carmel Cohen, my compassionate gynecologist, that it might take me years to discover what a big loss that was. Frankly, during those youthful years, I was not disappointed at losing my monthly cycle since I endured heavy bleeding each month. Later, I accepted that I was not meant to engage in the reproductive years or bear children. I am now 72 years old. Technically, I have been menopausal for 49 years and have yet to experience a hot flash, sweat, or any other common symptoms. My estrogen levels have maintained their stasis. The dramatic turn of life sans my womb did impact many psychological choices I was led to make: the conscious choice to remain unmarried, to adopt a monastic life, to immerse myself in scholarly Vedic studies and holistic health, and to confidently occupy the big stage with my work. However, it's taken this incredibly trying past decade of personal hardship for me to realize that I had gleefully but mistakenly reached for the gift of menopause way too early. In retrospect, I would have made different choices about my life, love, and relationship with a partner and explored my creative gifts more deeply had I bided time with my loss and waited for the gift during my mature years.

At the turn of my 55th year, I stirred into the realization that the cloistered life I had chosen was not supporting the growth of my femininity, my Shakti force. I was feeling a deep emptiness, a sense of androgyny that was not particularly akin to my passionate nature. As I noted earlier, I dropped my robes and took to a more ordinary path where I could allow my femininity to breathe — and breathe she did. While traveling about with the World Peace Mandala tours, I began to experience the grand rush of discovering my felinity, a state beyond hormonal function where I was overwhelmed by a subconscious desire, an almost reckless urge to exercise my womanhood. Then suddenly, at an airport, as you may recall, I encountered my perfect Adonis, a man whose masculine power and beauty have illuminated the big screen of my mind ever since. More than an actor, this man was a mechanic who reached into my depths to wrench at my soul, unleashing unresolved issues with my father that had been holding my femininity hostage all my life. I realized I had paternal karmas to let go of and Shakti karmas to reclaim. This man is real, but for me, he was a mirage, an illusion and delusion rolled into one. He was a messenger who split open the wounds of my womb to air out a stuck bundle of childhood traumas, freeing my profound sense of ancient womanhood rarefied by wisdom, desire, and abundance. The lesson was a profound one. Officially, I feel that my actual menopause occurred at this juncture at age 55 when I was catapulted into maturity by a desire born through my yoni. For the first time in my life, I felt myself breathing through that sacred, secret passage. It flew wide open. Menopause offers a profound opening of the subtler channels of our Shakti sensuality, the deep internal alignment of tissue, cells, memory, and ojas. I felt my womb space finally opening to allow the effulgent green light of the heart space to enter. A sense of fearless pleasure arose in me from beyond the space of knowing as if I were being called to merge my sexual body with the spiritual, innocence with passion, and the fulfillment and hope for recreating beautiful karmas yet to be lived. My menopausal time after 55 has taught me to reclaim my authenticity and deepen my purpose. Now, I continuously contemplate what it would feel like to feel and be more genuine in every moment and not waste any more time on the irrelevant ... and then act on those motivations. It's sublimely freeing.

It was surprising to me at my official pause to notice some of the simpler joys and downright commonsensical things I discovered for the first time, or rather, recognized their importance to my well-being. I came to revel in "me time," whatever that means at the moment. I learned to stop mothering the fathers — to love and respect them but learn to say "no"; the firmer the "no," the better. I became more observant and released the sense of entitlement and being overly judgmental that can easily arise from an intelligent mind, reminding myself that everyone comes with some degree of darkness, evil, stupidity, or cunning. I now generate more self-love with my own touch, balms and baths, and other body-loving care practices. I create more inner space, holding inner harmony with more care and avoiding outer chaos and dissent. And when I do lose my temper, I allow mindful space to follow — Earthing more in my ancient spirit where faith is supreme and fear negligible. I show more gratitude for everything, especially for trusty friends who can point out my snarly areas of self-sabotage. These simple things have become precious to me.

Menopause can present the gift of a blank slate in terms of finding the freedom to define or redefine how we wish to be and live going forward. This is when we can finally fully open to the inner light without fear or consternation. We can make inner and outer choices that strengthen our purpose and utilize our storied wisdom to do something beautiful, simple, or big in and for our world.

Our menopausal years can be treated as a time of great undoing. By unraveling hard-earned wisdom, we learn to let go of the ideal life and begin to unlearn useless pursuits and time-consuming habits. In doing so, we can unload mega-burdens of angst, guilt, over-doing, over-pleasing, over-compensating. After losing my womb, I began to regenerate a more potent power within me and therein protected the integrity of my right of passage to and through menopause. Often, I advise women my age to consider taking a sexual pause for three to six months while still deepening a loving environment of attentiveness, care, and affection with themselves. This is not as difficult as it may seem. In India, this abstinence is called *Vanaprastha ashrama,* the act of literally retreating into the forest – especially advocated for those who had reached their later years. Older couples tend to strengthen their spiritual bond and foster a more caring relationship as a result. At the same time, a woman can create the space to re-goddess her profound ability by nurturing Shakti Prana. Abstinence is a deep journey into the eternal forest within us wherein we marvel at the magic of having had the gift of carrying the born or unborn seed of life.

The Practice: Taking Pause with Shitakari Breath

Taking a mindful pause is best performed in the evening after the sun sets and the air of quietude descends around you. Shitakari Breath practice generates a deep sense of inner calm by cooling the breath and dissipating any negative vibrations in the mind. As you cool down the breath, you will feel an immediate sense of relief from bothersome thoughts or situations. Shitakari is an especially excellent practice to do during the waning cycle of the dark moon when the vibration of fears, angst, uneasiness, anxiety, and other restless emotions can arise. During this practice, you are allaying these emotions while harnessing the nityas' restful energies within.

- Find a warm, quiet space and sit in a comfortable posture with your back upright and chin slightly lowered.
- Hold the intention of letting go of any regrets, guilt, angst, or uneasiness.
- Empty your lungs by breathing deeply into your belly, and forcefully exhale the breath through your mouth by making a whooshing sound.
- Start the practice by inhaling through your mouth with a hissing sound by opening your lips to form an "O" while slightly stretching your tongue over your lower lip. Do not curl your tongue.

- Close your mouth, hold your breath for 15 seconds or so, and then exhale through your nostrils. Repeat this practice about 12 times.
- After your practice, you may lie down on your back, feet hip-width apart and enjoy your inner stillness.

Chapter 17

A Shakti Rescue from the Black Hole

Love alone is capable of uniting living beings in such a way as to complete and fulfill them, for it alone takes them and joins them by what is deepest in themselves. All we need is to imagine our ability to love developing until it embraces the totality of humanity and the Earth.

Pierre Teilhard de Chardin

Being tossed into the abyss — or the black hole, as I call it — is the Goddess's way of forging our strength and understanding and forcing it to the foreground so it can blossom into soulful feminine enlightenment. Black holes are one of the universe's most mysterious and powerful forces. A black hole is where gravity has become so strong that nothing around it can escape, not even light. Black holes are invisible; we can't actually see them because they don't reflect light, but scientists know they exist because we can observe their effect on light and objects around them. Our problems, both personal and societal, can feel a lot like black holes — so dark and massive we struggle to understand them and so consuming that it seems impossible to escape once we've been pulled in. To avoid the black hole, we must rescue ourselves and each other before we pass that point of no return — before we fall into the merciless gravity well where we become crushed and distorted by hurt, anger, and vengefulness.

Like many of us, I struggled for years to escape my own black hole, pushing to shift my understanding before I became consumed by my darkness. Ultimately, to free myself, I had to figure out the quantum physics of my mind. The ever-present grace of the Goddess was my passage out of the darkness; she taught me to accept my dark history and trauma and invite them into the light of awareness. Before then, I had sought only the light, failing to recognize that darkness is the womb that gives birth to light. At the nadir of my darkness, I discovered a safe and serene space where forgiving even the most abominable acts became possible. In this shaktified sanctum, I was granted the wisdom to avow both the darkness and light within myself and the fortitude to embrace it in others. It is this hard-won, formidable ability to forgive ourselves and others for all the mistakes, all the misunderstandings, and even all the depravities that will save us all from the black hole.

As women, we are the carriers of life, love transmitters, and the staff bearers of this world, and we must continue to make the sacrifices necessary to keep balance. This is not to say that we should allow our aggressors to continue their oppression, but rather that we must summon the strength to show them the Shiva-Shakti way again and again and allow them the grace to follow it. Only by stepping out of our comfort zone to truly engage the other's opposing beliefs and ideas can we close the "us/them" gap and right the Shakti imbalance in the world. Leading this change will require resilience, bravery, creativity, compromise, and fierce, unyielding love — in short, it will require women.

All of us have experienced hurt and caused hurt to some degree. Both social science and personal experience inform us that hurt people are bound to hurt others. While ancestral pain patterns get ferried from generation to generation, hurting is the fallout. It is not true that "good" people who love themselves don't hurt others. At some level, we all participate in the hurt scenario, unwittingly or otherwise. We bear wounds, some deeper than others. This relates to the damaged tissue memory humanity carries. These wounds cause people to hurt other people, entire communities to band together in a barrage of hate and violence against other communities, and men to collectively repress and punish women.

Each of these hurts brings us grief, and this grief fuels a sense of separation from the whole. It happens. It happens to all of us. And it's painful. It does not necessarily make us stronger or better people. It just is. Each one of us bears it differently. We share suffering, but we suffer alone. We can't control loss, whether it is of a dream, a way of life, a person, or even a person we used to be. We can't control violence, hate, bitterness, or any untoward circumstances that befall us. Try as we might, we can't control what other people do. We can only be accountable for our own actions, show love even to those acting unlovable, and shine our shaktified light into the darkness.

All life depends on community. Plants and animals living in a habitat interact and form communities. Humans, too, require and thrive in biotic communities. We are a social species; we depend on our community to help us meet both our physical and emotional needs. We have a primal need to be accepted and to belong. Even children play in groups and defend against other groups. Every child knows the fear of being left out of a group, sitting in the bleachers at a game, or not being called to participate while your friends are playing. It matters not the age of the person. Being slighted evokes a primal fear of isolation, of being left behind, of being ignored, disfranchised, or ostracized.

Social psychology data demonstrates the effects of exclusion, rejection, and ostracism. A 2003 study asserts that a history of chronic or acute peer rejection underlies aggression in schools, including 87 percent of school shootings. Rejection is a form of communication that conveys to the individual that something undesirable about them warrants exclusion. Rejection can be expressed in multiple forms: physical or verbal aggression, bullying, shunning, or ostracism. Whatever form it takes, the research is clear: rejection hurts. Rejection that does not get processed and healed leads wounded people to wound and reject others in an inexorable cycle; men wounded by primal fear hurt women, who pass those wounds on to their children. One or both wounded parents may also wound their children in other ways, giving rise to adult children who perpetuate the abuse or neglect with their own partners, children, or associates ad infinitum. We will not break the cycle if we cannot summon the radical bravery to confront and forgive these hurts.

I recall a particularly painful example of rejection from my male colleagues that transpired in early 1995 when I was on my annual visit in India. My book, *Ayurveda: A Life of Balance,* was being widely celebrated in the US, Europe, and India for heralding a global awakening of Ayurveda, which had, until then, become nearly defunct even in India. When the ashram I was staying in organized an Ayurveda Conference hosted by my Vedanta Guru, many noble Indian Ayurveda gurus were invited to speak. Though my book was a precursor for Ayurveda's meteoric rise, I was not invited to present at this masculine self-congratulatory event. A few attending elder mahatmas recognized me because of my pioneering work in Ayurveda's resurgence and greeted me with warmth and gratitude, noting their chagrin at my not being included in the event roster of presenters, but many others were happy to simply take credit for the fruits of my labor. This was but one of countless exclusions from prominent holistic hierarchal events that left me feeling hurt and invisible. I was tempted by all the ways I might have outmaneuvered the men who intentionally excluded me from these forums — it would have been a very human response. Instead, I challenged myself to rise above the pettiness and redouble my commitment to the work that meant so much to me.

The patriarchy is the embodiment of this cycle of wounding — men suffering the rejection of their inability to create life and lashing out in primal fear of women, who then withdraw, withhold, or strike back, causing them to redouble their efforts. Patriarchy's understory is rooted in humiliation, ostracism, and betrayal. Its ideology is just a neatly packaged mandate for massive destruction. Its mission exacerbates the Shakti imbalance in the world. We have become habituated to its binary system; a system that pits one set of people against another, one set of ideologies against another, one set of beliefs against another. It creates artificial lines drawn between two contrived and oversimplified sides of infinitely more complex issues.

Long centuries of patriarchal rule have entrained our minds in this dualistic thinking; us and them, black and white, evil and good, right and wrong. To break free of the binary response, we have to try and find the understory in each adverse situation – to truly seek to understand where people are coming from, how they may have evolved certain maladaptive beliefs, and how they explain and justify their hurtful actions to themselves. Nobody sees themselves as "the bad guy," no matter how cruel their behavior; we all just think we're doing whatever we need to do to take care of ourselves.

While many fields require a binary system, as in technology, mathematics, astronomy, editing books and films, and gambling, contrary to popular opinion, our minds do not naturally jump to binary thinking. They have been entrained to do so. The organic human mind is wired through complex conduits aligned with frequencies and vibrations across multidimensional spectrums of colors and hues and infinite platforms of wonderment and choice. We are formed from magic; the mind is magical. In the sphere of magic, there is a solution, an answer, and a resolve for all things, however difficult or painful they may be.

While it's true that we are mentally programmed to think in terms of differentiation, we have taken it too far, rendering this adaptive tendency maladaptive. Humans live in groups, are wired to think in groups, and yearn to belong to specific groups. While this grouping and need to belong is healthy, the idea of "othering" that it engenders is not. The very thing that allows us to identify with a group has become twisted to identify and exclude others we deem not to belong. *Nama-rupa* is the Sanskrit term used for this human need to try and grasp differentiation between things, people, and ideas. This differentiation is an innate survival skill, yet too much of it can threaten our survival. The danger is that once we get fastened to a group, to their ideology, to the categorical concept of group thinking, group wellness, group affairs, and group biases, we become trapped. We then begin to defend our group, which means someone else's group is the enemy or needs to be guarded against. This means we become more and more insular within our group. The present state of American politics is a perfect example: a two-party system that is deeply mired in discontent, each side wallowing in extreme divisiveness. The battle between the sexes is another relentless example.

There is a shaktified response to human judgment, groupthink, divisive ideology, and fear of isolation. The patriarchal hierarchy passionately promotes its divisive binary system to maintain control while it shoves our natural state of diversity into obscurity and fleeces nature and humanity of its inherent largesse. As women at the forefront of Shakti's restoration on Earth, we must eschew this binary so all of nature can breathe again. We must haul it out into the open, release it from deep storage, and think outside the system. We must reorder compassionate groups and communities and restore our unique and innate human ability to accept and care for one another. Let us gather the unfortunate, the misfits, and the outliers and congregate a Shakti force in groups intent on creating harmony and progressing wholesome actions; groups who are awakened to humanity's desperate plight. Data shows that once 10 percent of a community or population buys into a certain ideology, that concept and its resultant activities spread like wildfires. Imagine what a shaktified response to humanity's plight can do. As the Shakti force awakens, we influence and attract a universal-minded group of free thinkers grounded in Earth intelligence; the light bearers, Earth-hugging warriors, crones who can tread the pitch darkness, and passionate humanitarians. It takes trillions of dollars to promulgate hatred, violence, racism, separatism, wars, and divisiveness – products of a binary system. The paradox of the Shakti force is that it is fed and nurtured by the universal mind, generating awareness as its precious currency.

If we cling to any despairing emotion for too long, it can block the path of forgiveness. Despite the difficulty, we must strive to understand those who oppose us, hurt us, or threaten our lives and livelihood and why they feel so deeply justified by their actions. Only in this way can we begin to heal ourselves and each other. Here, I offer my own story of overcoming seemingly insurmountable hurt and rage to forgive the deeply damaged men who tried to destroy me. Amongst the ashes of the life I once lived and the self I once was, I unearthed a fiercely burning brand of forgiveness that immolates everything but the truth, illuminates our path forward, and casts a beacon that all may follow.

My suffering was engendered by the tenacity of men's primal fear of women, feminine sexuality, female monism, and the power of a woman's voice. During the arduous period following my assault, I became enraged, unable to forgive the crimes against my feminine body, mind, and soul. I tried a thousand times early on to forgive the faceless men who had violated me. I knew that living in a state of unforgiveness is treachery unto itself. I discovered that unforgiving is the loneliest place to live – a graceless state that reigns in tyranny and swallows every iota of inner harmony. Anger kept forgiveness at bay, indignation at these untoward and unjust assaults against my sacred being, indignation that these unrelenting crimes against humanity are granted free rein to carry on without being held accountable.

Once more, I had no choice but to turn to the Goddess. She is so deeply stamped into our Shakti cellular memory. No amount of assault could keep me away from her presence, even as I writhed from the very thought of my sacrosanct body temple being violated. But the guiding principle of the Goddess is my ever-present refuge. I sought to find understanding, a common ground on which I could more easily accept my lot. Even as I struggled to understand the sheer brutality of the experience, I knew I needed to shift my perceptions of these experiences by meeting my assaulters without angst, should the opportunity ever present itself. To release myself from the black hole, I had to push myself to forge a radical bravery and stay open to confronting my attackers if and when a chance occurred to forgive them, even if there was no repentance or change of awareness on their part. Otherwise, I would continue to struggle and fail to break the vicious cycle of "us" and "them." Insurmountable as it seemed to learn to understand or forgive these hollow men, I recalled that that wisdom had served me through other trying times, though none before had been as hard as this. Through the deep loneliness and feelings of isolation and oppression, I knew I had to find a way to use my Shakti oars to navigate troubled waters. I knew that I must continue to strive to uncover their point of view, the place where they were coming from. For many years, I felt outraged by the vileness of being poisoned, raped, treated like a pariah, and my residence ravaged — yet at the end of every day, I was sorely aware that I must open wider to the understanding of abusers having been abused, of agreeing to disagree, of garnering tolerance, by which I do not mean tolerating flagrant abuse, but cultivating tolerance as a nucleus for peace — a peace steeped in compromises that becomes necessary when belief systems and ideologies of the "us" and "them" are rife with impossible odds. Narrowing the distance between conflict with "the other" teaches us to wield forgiveness in strength instead of capitulating in weakness.

We must strive for harmony within and without. I needed to see my abusers' reality and understand their actions from their point of view. Amanda Ripley, author of *High Conflict: Why We Get Trapped and How We Get Out,* evinces, "We can do both, you can and you must if you want to stay out of the tar pits." This unbiased perspective was my weakest point. It is humanity's weakest point. We are steeped in the binary thinking that concretizes evil vs. spiritual, as in "those bad guys" and "me good girl." And yet, the mind itself is not limited to binaries; it is vast and magical. I called on the Goddess's strength to see me through my rage onto a path to forgiveness. I even drew on Nora Roberts, who puts it this way "Magic exists. Who can doubt it, when there are rainbows and wildflowers, the music of the wind and the silence of the stars? Anyone who has loved has been touched by magic. It is such a simple and such an extraordinary part of the lives we live." Habituated to the logic of reason, I had to keep pushing my mind with fervor to "see" through the eyes of magic even in pitch darkness. But darkness is the only time when we can see the stars. I began to pull myself up. I had to make the mark; I knew I'd remain stuck in the tar pits if I didn't. Amanda Ripley also wisely acknowledges that high conflict usually produces a reality of its own, meaning the conflict may play out in so many shapes and forms that what provoked or caused it in the first place can become distorted beyond recognition.

Conflicts happen even between good people. None of us are born inherently evil or violent. We all care for ourselves and our loved ones as best we are able, however little that may be. For the most part, the hurt we inflict on others is almost always either unintentional, in retribution for some way they've hurt us, or intended to protect ourselves or those we love. Notions of scarcity often play into this, resulting in competition for love, food, land, acclaim, or any number of other things we fear not having enough of. In fact, archaeologists speculate that it was only about 10,000 years ago that group violence began as human lifeways became more socially complex and hunter-gatherer groups began competing for resources. There is usually more than one understory dictating the narrative we witness.

I thought of all the conflict and hurt engendered by my own family. I emerged from ancient, intelligent noetic people who had perfected the state of conflict into a high art form. They were conflict entrepreneurs. I see how my maternal elders would smoothly set up any number of disputes among their children because, while growing up, this is how they were trained to handle grievances. They watched their elders create conflicts among family members or the community to get what they needed. Through their devastating history of being victimized, I see how binary thinking has become a way of life. These rifts transported in the hearts of my people became shards upon which I swore I'd never walk. Yet, my responses to personal tragedy were largely dualistic. I found myself responding exactly the way my ancestors did when pushed into a hole — belligerent, righteous, outraged, and vilified. For the longest time, I held on firmly to the binary belief that the invisible force that abused me was evil and divisive. I had dehumanized these people as objects in my mind. I tried to negotiate the forces in every possible way to defend myself and my home without weapons, guards, or watchdogs. I kept my inner light flickering with mantras and songs. I showed conscious care to everyone, to share whatever inkling of energy I had remaining. Still, I kept stumbling and losing the high ground. My stamina was progressively waning.

I dug in to unearth compassion, knowing what it felt like to be rejected, sensing that the ignorant men who tried to diminish my light were most likely victims of rejection, abuse, and violence in their lives. I soon discovered that the truly decisive force was hidden in the understory of my own perception. This is where understanding is so critical to help get us out of the grip of the black hole. I had a cleft within myself, separating my mind from my heart space. My understory is linked to injury from colonization and the colonized biases against my Vedic heritage; a Hindu stigma that eludes Western understanding and continues to irk Western intelligentsia. It's linked to the ancient ancestral mind that lives in the frame of a dark, proud, older woman who apparently raised the ire of the white male culture. A culture that has yet to reconcile its own history of enslaving black people, destroying women, and devouring entire native cultures. Through these lenses, I could well have been seen as an arrogant immigrant, lacking humility, boasting a proud air without contrition, shame, or lowliness. Perhaps it was my notoriety, the pedestal, the place up high from which they were determined to cut me down.

Immersed in this abyss for a seemingly immeasurable time, every iota of light was stolen by blackness. Black holes are mysterious, an enigma. Strange things happen around black holes that have to do with quantum physics and space-time. I knew I had to gather my reserve and crawl back out to that special boundary around the black hole called the event horizon. To change the deep, dark detritus of my situation, I had to shift my understanding. The longer a conflict plays out, the harder it is not to get further sucked in. We know this subconsciously. We feel it when we are first sucked into the abyss. Arduous experiences shift our progressive motion off kilter and can leach our grace, light, and humanity. The same answer to the question of being stuck to the abyss kept resounding in my mind: binary choices that flourished in my DNA, choices we are ancestrally trained to make — choices that isolate, separate Shiva from Shakti, humanity from being human, choices that dim the light of love and wisdom.

My experiences and mistakes taught me the dire importance of reordering a shaktified response that honors the Shiva-Shakti relationship that has been so brutally damaged within all of us. The damage to Shiva-Shakti has been far more brutal than the brutalities foisted upon me. Living in a space of unforgiveness was antithetical to reclaiming my primeval balance. I had to start meeting savagery with grace, cruelty with kindness, contempt with compassion. When all else failed, I cried. As tears moistened my heart, I was once more open wide to prayer.

After I left my forest sanctuary, I returned to India to cleanse and restore my body, mind, and spirit. I participated in austere Shamanic and Vedic fire ceremonies held on Mother Earth's sacred ground. I beseeched her for understanding, compassion, and forgiveness to show me the way. Ceremonies have always been an important practice in my life, and I am thankful for the noble souls who helped facilitate these rituals for me. I yearned for inner peace. I yearned for an unmitigated reality, my fluency with nature, once more to dance with the forest and converse with the brook. I was open to finding a compromise so that the debilitating forces tethered to my mind could move on, allowing me to move on. I called upon the cosmic mediators, the archangels Michael and Raphael, the god Ganesha, and the goddess Durga to aid me in my struggle. Finally, when life began to feel abundant and joyous again, I kept on praying. Prayers gradually replaced my tears. To cultivate the heart of ahimsa, we have to keep reminding ourselves that beneath the hurt, angst, and debauchery — the swamp of all things — a lotus can thrive and bloom. Even while my body and mind writhed with anguish, I held on to the truth that we must continually rescue love. We've got to keep reaching into our inner light. Human transgressions create low-vibrating apathetic energy, yet the sun's rays can pierce through its density, cleansing and restoring it to pure prana. Healthy prana generates our inner light. So, instead of tightening our hearts, we must expand them and become softer and more generous, especially during this perilous time in our world.

We learn to see the greatness of spirit in becoming more generous in response to others' needs and greed. This softening was the second most difficult lesson I have had to learn because it continually got pushed against the concretized walls of binary ways in which we are taught to think, to assimilate experiences, to divide the "good us" from the "bad them," and the "sacred" from the "evil."

The most arduous thing I was forced to do in accepting my reality was recognizing that at some level in the vast cosmic field, my soul's demands necessitated unearthing my rusted chest of vitiated maternal memories. This experience has brought me into a space of raw humility, along with a deep sense of recognition that in somehow "choosing" this experience, I had reflected the ancestral parts of myself that tolerated abuse, violence, molestations, misogyny, goddess-less-ness, lovelessness, deception, unkindness, and hypocrisy. Diving headlong from the momentary bliss of my unrobed heart into the blackened depth of an abyss, I realized I had somehow brought this fire unto myself. These incubi we can subconsciously manifest force us through waves of human karma, rebirthing into death or new life as we fall. My fire walk over hot coals has taught me my soul will never again tolerate the relationships my maternal ancestors endured. Going forward, my relationship with a masculine counterpart and with all men and women must be blessed with the shaktified values of self-awareness, mutual grace, transparency, divine goodness, humility, and kindness. I did not besiege my mother, the Earth, to open up and swallow me as Sita Devi did; instead, as a womb born, I surrendered my cardinal mistakes and past karmas to her grace. She cautioned me to forgive the fathers so that we may all move forward in the spirit of truth and reconciliation and to be more mindful and sensitive to my womanly needs.

The perilous paths in my life cost me dearly, paid for from the soul's currency. My heart raw and worn, I wondered. Sometimes, we go so deep into the abyss that we get lost in our own darkness. I understood the deeper transformation of unlearning the ways of the unloving. As Gloria Steinem counsels, "The first problem for all of us, men and women, is not to learn, but to unlearn." To comprehend and commune with "the other," we must make harnessing the power of heart-awakening love our first priority. Through the Goddess's love and the Earth's love, we can connect so deeply that her nectar can seep into our skin, shedding light on the perennial memory of love, her creation in our hearts. Epic. Because of this connection to love, my heart stayed open, reforming into a gentler, more reflective nature throughout the brutal juncture. After a 12-year-long nightmare of heart-waning challenges that included walking in robes through often hostile territories, hosting my Ayurveda holistic medicine work in an unawakened community, being assaulted by depraved white men, being poisoned, and having my home sanctuary continually violated, I finally awoke. I rose as if shaking off a slothful slumber with clarity and certainty in my heart. I am alive. I am inviolable. I Am Shakti.

As I shed the binary, I saw that everything and everyone can change. No force is beyond reconciliation; no force is permanent; no force is entirely evil or entirely good. Every force, however invincible or invisible it may appear, can be changed. This is the non-binary power of Shakti, which, for the first time in my ancestral life, I am experiencing and applying, negotiating good, negotiating evil. If the latter seems impossible, it simply means it will take a little bit longer to accomplish. Astronauts, too, are trained to respond in this way. They endure elaborate discipline and training to test their human tolerance and non-binary communication skills. They engage in complex processes to vet their mental stability, emotional adaptability, stress tolerance, social agreeability, and physical fitness. They demonstrate low conflict levels, especially when working with others in highly stressful situations, such as being isolated in a spacecraft up in the atmosphere for umpteenth months at a time. It took me years to comprehend that my binary choices of right and wrong, good and evil, ancient and modern, spiritual and atheistic, had gotten me fastened to the storm. In the same amount of time, Attila the Hun or Genghis Khan could have conquered an entire continent. Wars and conquerors were relics of a senseless binary system with no redeeming grace or reward — this had been my state in the black hole. The abyss I found myself in had become a supermassive black hole at the center of my galaxy. It had absorbed every speck of light, acquired massive burdens, and consumed other stars within me that were on the verge of rising. The price we pay for living in a black hole can never be repaid. There is no compensation awaiting pain, misery, and suffering endured. We pay with the soul's currency. As Bob Riley puts it, "Hard times don't create heroes. It's during hard times when the hero within us is revealed."

Had I crossed the event horizon into the black hole, there would have been no escape. Mercifully, I was able to move upward onto the perimeter where light was still present. Now, I find myself in that special space on the event horizon. This tenuous perimeter is the point where everything, even light, races toward the black hole. The event horizon is the boundary beyond which events cannot affect an observer. A mysterious, temporary foothold where we may acquire some stillness, distance, perspective, and clarity. This is an apt metaphor for maintaining one's balance on the event horizon and not getting sucked into the black hole. Light consciousness and the black hole — these two seemingly opposing realities are, in truth, one seamless reality, the cycle of day and night within. Braced by the Shakti force pushing me outward and upward, I finally arrived at an unfamiliar, universal space of understanding. My giant star had imploded at age 59, and now, at age 72, I am finally blessed with the light to rise again. Black holes are formed when giant stars explode at the end of their lifecycle – my explosion had been a supernova.

At the profound depth of my DNA, I was being overhauled and rethreaded to meet my new existence. The ancestral angst imprint and the scarred victim scenario were being overwritten and erased. Through this torturous odyssey, I realized I was being re-imprinted to reflect a brand-new perspective, one that does not belong to my ancestry but to humanity itself – the indelible seal of the Shakti force. My subtle anatomy had been changing over the years. As physical cells and vital tissues were shrinking with poisoning, my DNA was being systematically transformed, my soul awakening with new light and new thought forms culled from the universal intelligence. In reality, your subtle body is a self-contained energy field that draws unto itself other thought forms that synchronize with it. We are told that in accession to our higher self, we can change the patterns of our subtle body to resonate more deeply with the soul's purpose. In ascension, the soul itself changes its patterns to manifest whatever it wishes to project upon the Earthly plane of existence. In this new recalibration of my awareness, I find spirituality is not so much about wisdom or intellect. It is not about healing others or even the noble service of helping others get onto their feet. It is about finding persistent faith that can help us catch and put to use the stones being hurled at us. It is about bearing crisis with patience and positivity. It is about knowing that we can and will rise above hardships because we are continually rising to specific patterns of energy that are stamped within our individual soul by the force of consciousness.

These searing experiences have taught me my most significant lessons: chief among them is loosening the binary. This is a plan we must take to the forefront of all confrontations and painful situations in our lives. In reclaiming the Shakti force, we exit the black hole while keeping our genders, careers, purposes, attitudes, and ways of life fluid, ever flowing with mindfulness and kindness. In trying to tamp out or control diversity or the play of opposites, we contribute to the chaos.

We are women. We are the daughters of Mother Earth. We are the Shakti Force. We are walking into brave, new, and yet familiar territories. We lead the change to right the Shakti imbalance in the world. We recognize it will require compromise and love – not the weak, biddable forces that some men demean those words to imply, but canny, courageous compromise and fierce, powerful, unyielding love. We are meant to risk rejection and even failure so that trust in ourselves is strengthened like a phoenix in flight. We are pioneers of a new and ancient movement of conscious, evolving, open-minded, non-binary justice. We are defying the old paradigms and arcs of history. We are woke enough to walk our journeys in friendship with each other and in easeful companionship with our Shiva mates. We protect our Earth, our men, and our children like Shakti protects Shiva, and we do this by laboring to maintain balance. Let us once more create a gloriously complex world wherein every person can feel a sense of belonging and embrace the beauty, grace, and nutriment of Mother Earth.

Shavasana – Letting Go

Shavasana is a classic yoga posture that literally means "corpse posture." It is an effortless practice designed to help you let go of the physical, mental, and emotional plane. This practice has been endowing deep rest to me during my difficulties in recent years; its consoling stillness is a balm to the over-exhaustive push and pull we are all feeling in this present time of unrest. It is our perennial rescue from the event horizon around the black hole. As you surrender your body to the ground (a heartwarming practice to do directly on the Earth, if you can), you are engaging in the optimal act of surrender. This is an especially excellent practice to do in the evening during the waning lunar cycle when energy naturally dives as the moon decreases her illumination in the sky. We breathe deeply into our belly. Diaphragmatic breathing is a proven way to assimilate profound thought while resting the cellular body. Even ten minutes in this posture can provide a sense of restorative balance when you feel overwhelmed, stressed, fatigued, or exhausted.

The Practice: Shavasana – Letting Go

- Place a yoga mat on your floor and lie on your back with your arms relaxed by your side, palms facing up.
- Position your legs hip-width apart, let your body go limp, and gently draw your breath into your belly.
- Close your eyes, breathe in and out gently, and visualize a soft white moonbeam of light traveling and flooding around your body. Feel the cloud of light touch the crown of your head and float over your face, eyes, nose, mouth, throat, neck, and bosom, flowing out to the tips of your fingers, surrounding your belly and lower body, and flowing down your legs to the extremities of your toes.
- Wiggle your toes and fingertips for a minute or so before letting go of the body.
- Go still and continue to breathe gently.
- Do this practice for 30 minutes or less.
- When you are ready to rise, gently shake out your hands, arms, and legs. Rise up slowly.

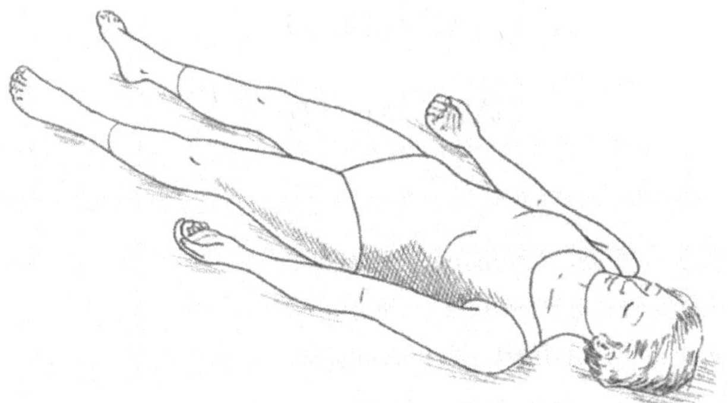

Fig. 6. Shavana pose

Chapter 18

We Can Heal

Lead us from the untruth to the truth
Lead us from darkness to light
Lead us from death to immortality
Om peace, peace, peace

Brihadāranyaka Upanishad

Humanity. The cosmic memory imprinted in every life form gives it a distinct pattern that is responsible for its structure and form. Across the vast swath of species, these patterns are continually interacting with each other, every atom and molecule communicating at all times. The distinct pattern of love imprinted in the human soul keeps us in permanent relationship, each soul's pattern continually coalescing, reaching out, and touching one another. Love is the most profound soul pattern; it allows us to heal. Each individual is universally programmed toward healing — that is, when we are in a state of Shiva-Shakti balance, we heal. When we are out of balance, we hurt. As you encounter the world, be mindful of every interaction, always reach out in your own inviolate way of your soul's unique pattern to embrace the various soul patterns you meet. We are here to heal and to create a relationship of healing with everyone and everything we touch. In living through our unique soul pattern, we loosen the grip on anxiety, fear, doubt, and distrust and instead reclaim our natural Shiva-Shakti equilibrium of ease, gentleness, passion, and authenticity.

It is almost four decades now since my Wise Earth Ayurveda work began teaching communities to gather their intrinsic soul medicine potential to love, nourish and heal. Each one of us has the innate ability to heal ourselves. We each embody the brilliant energy nexus that courses within and through the Earth, sky, and everything in between. However, when our biological system is continually attacked, as in the case of the individual, familial, communal, and global environmental violence we suffer, we are forced to go deep within our tissue memories to reset default habituations and karmic patterns. Our human family has been splintered by discord between women and men, heteronormative zealots and proponents of more expansive gender, and people of all different political views, creeds, and colors. We feel divided because we do not own up to that powerful sense of our soul's pattern that connects us to joy, wellness and honoring our diversity. We are further disconnected by the appalling state of fragmented patterns of our precious Earth. This distress is unavoidable; all life – human and otherwise – is interconnected by the soul's myriad patterns of love, and all of it hinges on the balance of Shiva-Shakti energy. We cannot be made whole again until we collectively return to Shakti's embrace and restore her place alongside Shiva.

Many of us have been working our whole lives to restore balance; others have been working against it. While their brutal war against feminine largesse can never be forgotten, Shakti's response to the fallible fathers is to forgive. It wrenches my gut to forgive them, but we must. In forgiving, we are not capitulating to toxic notions of feminine weakness or condoning our aggressor's barbarity. We are not giving up our feminine authority. Forgiving is not about justifying heinous acts or eliminating accountability for wrongdoing but reconciling ourselves to the darkness within all of us and choosing not to be consumed by it. As scourged as our aggressors may be, they are also human, and while they may not deserve redemption by human standards, the way of the Shakti urges us to grant it even so. By forgiving, we consign our aggressors to the past, becoming the force that topples them. By forgiving, we can end the wars the patriarchy instigated between the sexes, against the ubiquitous other, and against nature herself.

I believe there is far more light than darkness within each of us and in the world surrounding us. Our infinite Shakti nature can neither be betrayed nor can it betray us. It cannot come undone by the finite. Shiva-Shakti energy is pure and inviolate. It is important to understand that this force cannot be manipulated, changed, or lessened by the ploys and mechanism of patriarchal power — that is, unless we play into its convoluted system. Even then, what gets tampered with is the human qualities, our mental realm, perceptions, discernment, and choices.

How, exactly, do we learn to forgive though? Like any wound healing, it's a slow and often messy process. Healing is a primal function of the sacred life force. To keep on healing is the natural rhythm of life, yet it's taxing. It's exhausting. As someone who has suffered and healed from cancer, ancestral trauma, the belittling of my significant achievements, and even the horror of being targeted, poisoned, and defiled, I can testify to the abysmal reality of trying to hold it together, to stay true to purpose, and to maintain personal integrity. Despite my fiery intellect and shaktified temperament — all of which have been sharpened, and dangerously so, by my ancestral largesse — I was stuck in the calipers of abysmal despair. But somehow, in the depth of that despair, a strength would rise within me from the primordial beyond, an ancestral grace that kept pressing me forward through dank corridors to find my way to the light. I heard the maternal voices reassuring me that my soul's pattern of love is not lost but had gone inward to illumine memory and facilitate cleansing.

The most painful lesson for me was learning to surrender to the Goddess's divine will; to stop fighting for control and composure and yield to her. Lost as I was in the darkness, the thought of surrender was terrifying. In my inured state of fright, flight, fear, and fawn, I was aware that I could not bend or bow.

I began to delve deeply into my own pile of detritus in search of truth. While challenges tediously played on around me, a dirge of messiness unfolded within. I sensed the tissue layers of my mind and body were shrinking. I felt claustrophobic. I yearned for inner and outer space to stretch, gather, and process, but my traumatized brain kept forgetting what it was that needed to be processed. Deeply hidden truths continued to evade me. For years, I stumbled, trying and failing to fully surrender to my own wisdom. Despite my deep faith, I would find myself shaken up and riled, reacting in fear, anger, angst, sadness, bitterness, frustration, disbelief, and terror. I realized it was imperative for me to express and empty my thoughts, however damning they may be, but the sheer enormity of my responses kept blocking me from delving within. Then, finally, I grew so weary, so exhausted that I had no choice but to collapse — to sit, to lie down and do nothing. That special nothing that clearly witnesses everything. My mind, body, and spirit demanded that I stop doing and simply be.

To surrender, we need not only faith but the reserve of inner poise that comes only from that specific patterning of love embedded in our soul; love for self, love for each other, and love for even those men and women from whom the sun itself might be tempted to shy away. We harness the power of heart-awakening love to help us comprehend and commune with "the other." The greatest form of energy pattern in the universe is love. Vibrating at the highest frequency, it vacuums up negative energies and transforms everything into harmony. The love between a mother and her offspring is the most potent and enduring love in the world, and this is Shakti's love for us — the original ancestral form of bonding, the premier love from which everything on Earth evolved. Shakti Prana revolves at the core of the love principle. Mother Earth bestows the female creature with the Shakti Prana of the womb, embryo, fetus, and eggs and the Shakti power to procreate, bring forth new life, and create babies who assume the resemblance of their parents and bear the same vulnerabilities. The child, colt, calf, and mouse instinctively know who their mother is and have the maternal memory of love to cuddle up, nurse, and be nourished and protected by her. Maa, mother, mere, matr, ummi, mor, makuahini, mutter, matka, mama ... the infinite number of names for Shakti Love is imprinted upon the skin of the Earth and can never be wiped out. It is this love that gives us the strength to surrender and forgive.

The solution to grief always reveals itself in time — be still, breathe, allow, and allow again the healing and revelations to come forth of their own accord. People, conditions, behaviors, and circumstances are ever-changing. In a split second, our vibratory field can be energized by love's myriad appearances; the grace of a scent, a passing breeze, the slivery crescent relaxing into a cloud, the sound of a gurgling brook, the sight of a deer licking its doe, or the silent musings of an ancestor heard in the rustling of the forest. Let us not give permanent shelter to challenges and despairing conditions. The longer we forget to breathe in and breathe out — a reminder that all things come and go — the longer we hold on to angst and misery and the deeper we sink into fear and obsession. No one chooses to be a victim. New age narrative tells us that everything happens for us and not to us — that's a pile of malarky. Enduring violence has never made anyone a better person. Abuse buckles the legs, not in humility but in humiliation and shame. We may bow or break, but we can and will be made anew.

When I forgot the blessing hidden in the broken, when I forgot that the darkness fetched and carried me to my destination, I'd remind myself of the sun and moon within me, the sun rays that feed my right breath and the lunar rays that feed my left breath, and I'd breathe into a stronger alignment with sun and moon, light and dark, so my weary body could be invigorated to traverse its journey to healing. The way of Shakti teaches us to see the greatness of spirit in becoming more generous in response to others' greed, kinder in the face of malice, and more understanding in response to hate. Walking away from difficult people, negative circumstances, things we do not favor, and those who do not contribute to our worldview is not the answer. We have to rise beyond these dualities and see the blessings and human potential in every situation, however grave. We must continually keep forgiving the impossible and choosing love, choosing to see the hidden love pattern imprinted in the soul of even the most damaged person, for unless we forgive and keep on forgiving, we remain frozen, separated from the wellspring of grace.

Often, I engage a hand gesture called *Dana Mudra* to inspire opening the heart and giving generously. Dana Mudra, the downward pointing hand with an open palm facing outward, was later popularized in the portraits and statues of Mother Mary and Christ. At a more profound level of healing, mudra practice has helped me to seal my sacred intentions and set them in motion. In this healing continuum, we may seize the chance to cleanse old binary karmas as we emblazon Shakti energy within. Generosity fosters community, renegotiates greed, and propagates the communion of sharing, loving, and bonding.

As we move forward, we must focus not only on healing the past and restoring the Shakti force but also on creating the future, a world culture revived by love, kindness, mutual respect, and reverence for Mother Earth. As I write these words, I am awash in the profound Hippocrene of the Goddess as she places her hands over mine, guiding me to scribe and scribe again. We can gather together on mutually respectful terms in integrity, sloughing off learned denials, taboos, and excuses, and explore the truth of our individual gendered experiences, violations, and aspirations. Eradicating the ills of divisive separation from our pure nature is an act of community.

Healing gender despair, disease, and disillusionment is an act of community. Community is much more than a gathering; it is a container that gently witnesses, alchemizes, and inspires cooperation and coexistence. It shows us we are not alone. We need the friendship of each other to reclaim our soul's patterns of love, wholeness and wholesome health, however fluctuating this reality may be. To fasten our friendships, we need to shift ancestral conditionings and belief systems from prejudice to acceptance, from ignorance to intelligence, from isolation to conviviality, from the binary finite to infinite possibility. We have got a lot of inner work to do. As women, we must dig deep and reclaim Shakti power and feminine authority – the intelligence we are equipped with to take back our primordial sacrosanct rights. Once you get in touch with your Shakti force, you find immutable strength through intuition, sensitivity, and introspection. We begin to find sorority with each other. Our feminine psychic, physical anatomy is fueled by aligning with lunar rhythms. Everything comes alive.

Once I was able to glean these deep truths from my arduous set of circumstances, the Goddess magnetically drew me to her in a different way than I had been drawn before. Unlike my post-cancer journey into monkhood, my recent recovery catapulted me into humanhood, becoming kin to all humanity. The Goddess is still within me, beyond the beyond of my tradition, ancestry, cultural faith, and years of spiritual discipline. During the most emotionally excavating junctures of my life, I would sit each night and feel her shapeshifting in her waxing lunar phases while chanting the invocation for each phase and opening my deeply wounded heart. Through her lunar luminosity, I sponged the darkness within and discovered the imperishable summer in the sunlight of my soul. I have finally found a palpable sense of solace, an aliveness in the sanctified space where my womb once lived. The dross has been expunged from within me and spun clear into the brisk light of the late morning sun.

Through these intense periods of my life, I have learned that our heart space is expansive enough to forgive and to hold suffering and grief alongside joy and awe. This grace, which some may call gratitude, is a life-saving shift into consciousness. While spending some time in the high desert of New Mexico, I witnessed how the parched Earth glistened when, with just a few cups of water, the lavender and goldenseal would thrive in joy. It takes so little to make them happy. It is a simple thing to heal our fears when we surround ourselves with nature's infinite beauty. We can emulate the rhythm of a tree — any tree — stoic, unflinching, surrendering utterly to whatever comes at it. We see how the soft, unoffending grass can survive the most wicked storms while great, strong oaks may be felled. Trees release all manner of fears pelted upon them. Instead, they receive and convert our fear globules into life-giving oxygen for the benefit of all. They transform their traumas and wounds into a thing of beauty, giving rise to flowers, sprouts, fruits, and shelter. Sheltered by roots, they stand firm yet can bend and flow. When the human body can find no more room for its morass of traumas, turn to a tree, a brook, a stream, a rock, a mountain, a meadow, or a friend. Find fresh air. Look. Revel in the majesty that the Himalayas are still growing; Everest is getting an inch taller each day. Herman Hesse evinces, "When a tree is cut down and reveals its naked death-wound to the sun, one can read its whole history in the luminous, inscribed disk of its trunk: in the rings of its years, its scars, all the struggle, all the suffering, all the sickness, all the happiness and prosperity stand truly written, the narrow years and the luxurious years, the attacks withstood, the storms endured."

The Shakti way to healing and creating right relations between our Shiva and Shakti energies, between women and men, among all genders, and with our beloved Earth can only be affected by awakening to truth. We awaken the communal alchemy of women to end the tyranny of silence, oppression, harmful stereotypes, and the trauma of feminine suppression. Our first priority is to restore the Shakti force in our world, and for this, we invest in awareness and effort to restore Shakti's power in ourselves and on Mother Earth. We have the whole of nature to support us. We emulate the constancy of her trees to fortify our strength. We sway and chant, dance, and sing to reactivate a sense of wellness in our stupendous cellular body. We use our sight to trace the moving shapes of clouds and the lunar swelling and to be spellbound by myriad patterns of sunlight touching leaves. Every pattern in nature is a yantra.

Nature's yantras are always at our disposal. Her healing tools present themselves at the precise moment you require them. In the Earth traditions, there are millions of yantras – spiritual drawings and symbols, sacred geometric designs imbued by nature – images that hold powerful vibrations for loosening the grip of fear, healing, and remembering. Let us strive to regain Shakti's intuition, integrity, and authenticity. Let us make the necessary effort to restore our natural balance – physical, psychic, and spiritual. Yantras open pathways in the mind that are difficult to access. These yantras hold the aggregate power of the Goddess, Shakti, Earth. The triad symbol, the trinity, in particular, holds the power to help shift our thoughts from negativity and despair to hope, faith, and reassurance that we are embraced in this battle by all those who have gone before us. Merely by absorbing the vibration of their form, we can shift from the state of fear and hopelessness and become energized to achieve our shaktified goals. I have been reminded often in my arduous journeys that to be lost is to learn the way. We are all lost but have no need to go searching for the way finds us. As I near the end of my sharing with you, I find words that once were filled with grace are now living fully because I share them with you. Words return a reflection of memories from your own unique wellspring. Once assimilated, words dissolve. Only the essence and spirit of their yantra live on. Yantra symbols emerge from the human collective, speaking to our souls in a language of consciousness older and deeper than words.

Shiva's trident, Trisula, is one such instrument, a potent symbol of strength and courage to overcome adversity – what better inspiration to envision the fall of the patriarchy? Its three-pronged imagery evokes a perfect sense of balance – Shiva, Shakti, and a center-balancing prong. The Trisula symbolizes Shiva's three fundamental powers: will, action, and knowledge. Both a weapon and an instrument for justice, the trident also reminds us that we have dominion over the Earth and therefore the power to eliminate destructive forces on all the three planes of existence – spiritual, psychic, and physical.

Fig. 7. Shiva's Trident

Similarly, the Celtic symbol of Triskelion revolves around strength, progress, and the ability to move forward and overcome adversity. Comprised of three conjoined spirals with rotational symmetry, it represents the origin of movement and motility. The left spiral is the Yin, the right spiral is the Yang, and the centrifugal spiral is its balancing force. The movement of life is formed from past, present, and future. That is why it is also called "the triple spiral." It represents the triple nature of the physical, ancestral, and celestial worlds.

Fig. 8. Triskelion

Likewise, the Awen, that Neo-Druid symbol of balance, is used to invoke unity and harmony of the opposites in the universe. The Awen contains three rays or flames. The two rays on the sides represent male and female energy, while the one in the center represents the balance between them.

Fig. 9. Awen

The African Adinkra symbol signifies prudence, vigilance, and balance. It is a reminder that life is made up of good and bad, dark and light events. Life is not a linear or binary path. As such, the future of life is uncertain. The Adinkra inspires humans to use Earth's resources in moderation so that future generations may enjoy its abundance. The Adinkra symbol possesses the healing vibration of the ancestors. It reminds us of our profound duty to Mother Earth and to learn from the past so that we may improve the future. The blessing through which we live wholesome and sustainable lives is walking ethically upon the Earth and restoring our connection to her. In the Ghanaian culture, there are several modifications of this symbol with specific meanings for enduring life's transformations and honoring the Earth, spirits, deities, and forebears. We are told to expect hard times and are shown ways to spirit through them and overcome great difficulties while gleaning necessary lessons.

Fig. 10. Adinkra

The Practice: Anjali Mudra – Sealing a Shiva-Shakti Friendship

"Whose beloved are you? You are so unbearably beautiful," I asked.
He replied, "My own. For I am one and alone, love, lover, beloved . . ."

Fakhruddin Iraqi

The balancing of Shiva-Shakti – "To whom do you belong?" is a perennial affirmation of the friendship we bear with ourselves. In turn, we share this friendship – Shiva-Shakti and solar-lunar with each other. This bonding is reflected in the epic journey of the Kundalini Shakti, wherein Shakti immerses into Shiva at the crown chakra. Shiva-Shakti: the Indivisible Love. It is Awen, it is Yin Yang, it is Inyo. It is male and female. It is children; it is the animals, the trees, the sky, and the Earth. It is the Masculine/Feminine Divine within each one of us. We are the universe, continually attracting connection within and without that makes us experience a sense of wholeness even in a broken body or this broken world. The magic of this divine balance can be seen dancing in every molecule and atom of life. There are about an octillion atoms in the body, sustained by oxygen, carbon, hydrogen, and nitrogen; all are billions of years old. We are formed from the miracle that is Earth.

Shakti Prana breathes life into us, gracing us with bodies that replicate her magic and mystery. Close your eyes and visualize the very formation of your human body as it transmutes from one element to another through the mystery of nature's divine hues. Your vital tissue layers, *dhatus*, are formed from the five elements amid a vast information network of light and a spectrum of colors. Plasma is milky white, and it forms the blood, which is crimson red. The blood forms the flesh. From the flesh develops the fat, silvery in tincture, which in turn produces the golden-yellow skeletal tissue. Inside the bones, the rustic brown bone marrow forms. From the marrow develops the pearlescent semen. From the union of semen and female vital energy, the ovum, the human embryo is produced. You were filled with Earth magic and born with masculine and feminine divine energy intact. You — we — are powerful instruments capable of greatness.

All ancient Earth cultures had a mechanism for drawing the universal healing energies of Shiva-Shakti back into alignment for individuals and our world. Yantras, mantras, and tantras are used to attract and bond with the Earth's healing energies. We share friendship with ourselves and with each other. In the following text, a beautiful passage that reflects the original intent of the *Apastamba Mantra Brahmana* and is often used in Hindu marriage ceremonies, we are given a reminder of the natural bond of friendship evolving within each one of us, existing between the masculine and feminine energies, forming the organic bond between a man and a woman, and becoming the friendship all genders share.

> Shiva: I am the sky,
> Shakti: I am the Earth.
> Shiva: I am the music,
> Shakti: I am the melody.
> Shiva: I am the mind,
> Shakti: I am the speech.
> As we walk in harmony through
> the journey of life, let us always protect the peace and friendship
> within us and between us.

With Anjali Mudra, clasping the palms of our hands together in prayer pose, we merge the marriage of lunar and solar, coalesce the five elements, and bond the masculine/feminine energies within. When we forget our primordial nature when we are in distress, the ancients remind us to use our limbs creatively, in simple hand gestures, or mudras, to plant seeds in the Earth, to caress the rich black soil, and to sprinkle water on our faces. They remind us to keep our sense of gratitude thriving by bringing our palms together, or to hold them like cups with fingers pointing upward to collect the universal Shiva-Shakti energies. They remind us to rub and soothe our skin, to create art, to drum or strum a musical instrument, to overlay hands upon the heart, and to extend them in embracing all things. And in these precious moments, we transcend the binary mind that feeds into dual concepts — love and hate, grace and bitterness, friend and enemy. The five elements of existence course through the human body with a blast of energy as they reach the fingertips. This dynamic surge explains why your hands are so powerful, such a healing instrument of nature. The logic of why Hindus and other Native traditions ate with their right hands goes back to this timeless wisdom — the right hand attracts more solar energy. Our hand transmutes the food by the solar energy before it is ingested. Through our fingertips, we can recharge our internal illumination system. In this way of healing, we lay our shaktified hands on ourselves, upon each other, and on Mother Earth.

Anjali Mudra: Clasped Hands of Gratitude

As we go forth in peace and sorority, keep faith that the darkness in all of us can give way to light. The journey to consciousness must always be traveled through the darkness. Not the darkness we meet with fear, distrust, disdain, and hopelessness but the darkness that sponges the soul with its subtle nuances and blatant surgeries; the darkness that provides shelter so we can burrow down into the Earth, protected from the glare of transparency, suspended in stillness and timelessness – the optimal environment for transforming chaos into consciousness. In this still, sacred space, in the arms of the Goddess, we are fortified with the love, strength, and understanding we require to heal ourselves and our world.

References

"1,500 Animal Species Practice Homosexuality." News-Medical (October 23, 2006). https://www.news-medical.net/news/2006/10/23/1500-animal-species-practice-homosexuality.aspx.

AbuHasan, Qais, Waquar Siddiqui, and Vamsi Reddy. "Neuroanatomy, Amygdala." National Library of Medicine, StatPearls Publishing (February 20, 2019). https://www.ncbi.nlm.nih.gov/books/NBK537102/.

Adlington, Lucy. "World War One: Fashion Revolution." The History Press (October 10, 2018). https://thehistorypress.co.uk/article/world-war-one-fashion-revolution/.

"Agrippina the Younger: The Un-Killable Mother of Nero." Moan Inc (n.d.). Accessed December 12, 2022. https://www.moaninc.co.uk/ancient-women/agrippina-the-younger.

Alberts, Bruce, A. Johnson, and J. Lewis. *Molecular Biology of the Cell*, 4th edition. New York: Garland (2002).

Amara Das Wilhelm. *Tritiya-Prakriti*. Xlibris Corporation (2008).

Andreatta, Gabriele, Florian Raible, and Kristin Tessmar-Raible. "Biological Rhythms: Hormones under Moon Control," *Current Biology* 32 (22): R1269–71 (2022). https://doi.org/10.1016/j.cub.2022.10.018.

Anonymous. *Rig-Veda-Sanhita*. Books on Demand (2023).

Arya, Ravi Prakash. *Dhanurveda*. Indica Publishers, Varanasi, India (2015).

Aydoğmuş, Azime. 2015. "Clytemnestra as a Nightmare to Patriarchy in Aeschylus Tragedy, the Oresteian Trilogy." https://dergipark.org.tr/en/download/article-file/838116.

Balakrishnan, Gaurav. "Story of Mohini Avatar of Vishnu | Only Female Avatar of Vishnu." Svastika (July 17, 2023). https://svastika.in/blogs/blog/story-of-mohini-avatar-of-vishnu?

Becker, Amanda. "Liberal Justices' Dissent Sketches out 'the Loss of Power, Control, and Dignity' in a Post-Roe America." The 19th (June 24, 2022). https://19thnews.org/2022/06/liberal-supreme-court-justices-abortion-dissent-roe-v-wade-america/.

"Benchmarking gender gaps, 2023 — Global Gender Gap Report 2023." The World Economic Forum (2023). https://www.weforum.org/publications/global-gender-gap-report-2023/in-full/benchmarking-gender-gaps-2023/.

"Bibi Dalair Kaur." Discover Sikhism (2024). https://www.discoversikhism.com/sikhs/bibi_dalair_kaur.html.

Blago Kirov. *Ralph Waldo Emerson: Quotes and Facts*. (2016.)

Bomb, Cherry. "Rainer Maria Rilke — from 'Requiem for a Friend' (1908)." Fleurmach (March 8, 2017). https://fleurmach.com/2017/03/08/rainer-maria-rilke-from-requiem-for-a-friend-1908/.

Brooke, Elisabeth. *Women Healers through History*. Aeon Books (2020).

Burnett, Frances Hodgson. *A Little Princess* (Global Classics). Createspace Independent Publishing Platform (2018).

Campbell, Joseph. *Goddesses — Mysteries of the Feminine Divine*. New World Library (2013).

Castro-Vale, Ivone, Milton Severo, Davide Carvalho, and Rui Mota-Cardoso. "Intergenerational Transmission of War-Related Trauma Assessed 40 Years after Exposure," *Annals of General Psychiatry* 18 (1) (2019). https://doi.org/10.1186/s12991-019-0238-2.

Chaitanya, Turya. *Bhagavad Gita Volume 3 Karma Yoga*. Independently Published (2022).

———. *Bhagavad Gita Volume 3 Karma Yoga*. Independently Published (2022).

Chiu, Kenny, David M. Clark, and Eleanor Leigh. "Prospective Associations between Peer Functioning and Social Anxiety in Adolescents: A Systematic Review and Meta-Analysis," *Journal of Affective Disorders* 279 (October 2020), pp.650–61. https://doi.org/10.1016/j.jad.2020.10.055.

Coburn, Thomas B. *Devī-Māhātmya: The Crystallization of the Goddess Tradition*. Delhi; Varanasi: M. Banarsidass (2002).

Crawford, Harriet. *Ur the City of the Moon God*. London Bloomsbury Publishing Inc., Bloomsbury Academic (2015).

Current Biology, Volume 33, Issue 15, pp.R781–R828, 3073–3298. ScienceDirect.com by Elsevier (7 August 2023). https://www.sciencedirect.com/journal/current-biology/vol/33/issue/15.

Dadlani, Chanchal B. *From Stone to Paper: Architecture as History in the Late Mughal Empire*. New Haven Ct: Yale University Press (2018).

Doniger, Wendy. "The Third Nature: Gender Inversions in the Kamasutra 1," in *On Hinduism*. Oxford University Press EBooks, (March, 2014), pp.314–29. https://doi.org/10.1093/acprof:oso/9780199360079.003.0022.

Dow, Gregory K., Leanna Mitchell, and Clyde G. Reed. "The Economics of Early Warfare over Land," *Journal of Development Economics* 127 (July 2017), pp.297–305. https://doi.org/10.1016/j.jdeveco.2017.04.002.

Downham Moore, Alison M. *The French Invention of Menopause and the Medicalisation of Women's Ageing*. Oxford: Oxford University Press (2022). https://doi.org/10.1093/oso/9780192842916.001.0001.

Drugs and Lactation Database (LactMed). PubMed. National Library of Medicine (US) (2006). https://www.ncbi.nlm.nih.gov/books/NBK501922/?report=classic.

Earls, PhD, Averill. *Witches Brew: How the Patriarchy Ruins Everything for Women, Even Beer*. https://digpodcast.org/2018/10/21/witches-brew-how-the-patriarchy-ruins-everything-for-women-even-beer/. Podcast produced by Averill Earls, PhD and Elizabeth Garner Masarik (n.d.).

Eiler, Elizabeth S. *SINGING WOMAN: Voices of the Sacred Feminine*. Outskirts Press (2018).

Els, Hennie. "Robert Bly Quotes, poems etc." Pinterest (December 11, 2022). https://cl.pinterest.com/pin/robert-bly-quotes-robert-bly-poems-robert-bly-poetry-robert-bly-books-quotes-robert-bly-iron-john-quotes-robert-bly-young--324259241938631221/.

"Excerpts from I Am That by Sri Nisargadatta Maharaj — Part 72." Nonduality.com (n.d.). Accessed April 22, 2024. https://www.nonduality.com/hl7072.htm.

Forester, German. "Are Trees Sentient Beings? Certainly, Says German Forester," *Yale E360* (2016). https://e360.yale.edu/features/are_trees_sentient_peter_wohlleben.

Frazer, James George. *The Golden Bough: A Study in Magic and Religion*. Oxford: Oxford University Press (1998).

Friedman, Milton. *Milton Friedman on Economics*. University of Chicago Press (2010).

"Full 9th Chapter of Manusmriti." Eweb.furman.edu (n.d.). Accessed October 27, 2023. https://eweb.furman.edu/~ateipen/ReligionA45/protected/manusmriti.htm.

Furey, Robert J. *The Joy of Kindness*. New York: Crossroad (1993).

Gaborik, Patricia. *Mussolini's Theatre: Fascist Experiments in Art and Politics*. Cambridge: Cambridge University Press (2021).

Gedney, Rachel. "The Emerging of the Divine Masculine." LinkedIn (2024). https://uk.linkedin.com/in/houseoffeminine.

"George Eliot (1819-1880)." *A Survey of British Literature* (2.6). Humanities LibreTexts, May 27, 2021. https://human.libretexts.org/Courses/Skyline_College/LIT_232%3A_Survey_of_British_Literature_II_(Skyline)/02%3A_The_Victorian_Age/2.06%3A_George_Eliot_(1819-1880).

Georgia Tech Biological Sciences. "Eukaryotes and Their Origins." Organismal Biology (n.d.) https://organismalbio.biosci.gatech.edu/biodiversity/eukaryotes-and-their-origins/.

Goenka, Priyadarshini. "Alcoholabuse Blog," *Times of India* (2023). https://timesofindia.indiatimes.com/readersblog/alcoholabuse/.

Goyette, John, Mark S. Latkovic, and Richard S. Myers. *St. Thomas Aquinas and the Natural Law Tradition*. CUA Press (2004).

Grim, John, and Mary Evelyn Tucker. *Thomas Berry*. (2010.)

Han, Enze, and Joseph O'Mahoney. "British Colonialism and the Criminalization of Homosexuality," *Cambridge Review of International Affairs* 27 (2) (2014), pp.268–88. https://doi.org/10.1080/09557571.2013.867298.

Hesse, Hermann, and Damion Searls. *Trees*. National Geographic Books (2022).

Homer. *The Homeric Hymns*. Penguin Classics (2003).

Idel, Moshe. "Androgyny and Equality in the Theosophico-Theurgical Kabbalah," *Diogenes* 52 (4) (2005), pp.27–38. https://doi.org/10.1177/0392192105059468.

Igini, Martina. "10 Shocking Statistics about Deforestation." Earth.org (April 14, 2022). https://earth.org/statistics-deforestation/.

Iraqi, Fakhruddin. "Lama'at (Divine Flashes)." Technology of the Heart (November 2009). https://www.techofheart.com/2009/11/fakhruddin-iraqi-divine-flashes-lamaat.html.

Jackson, Chris. "LGBT+ Pride 2021 Global Survey Points to a Generation Gap around Gender Identity and Sexual Attraction." Ipsos (June 9, 2021). https://www.ipsos.com/en/lgbt-pride-2021-global-survey-points-generation-gap-around-gender-identity-and-sexual-attraction.

Jaklevic, Mary Chris. "'Medical Errors Are the Third Leading Cause of Death' and Other Statistics You Should Question." Association of Health Care Journalists (July 27, 2023). https://healthjournalism.org/blog/2023/07/medical-errors-are-the-third-leading-cause-of-death-and-other-statistics-you-should-question/.

Johnston, Charles. *Prashna Upanishad and Commentary*. (2020.)

"Kalidasa Poems by the Famous Poet." Allpoetry.com (2024). https://allpoetry.com/Kalidasa.

Kaur, Brahmjot. "The Kohinoor Diamond Was Obtained by the British Empire. Some Argue It Should Be Returned to India." NBC News (September 12, 2022). https://www.nbcnews.com/news/asian-america/twitter-users-want-britain-return-kohinoor-diamond-s-know-turbulent-hi-rcna47284.

Klein, Joanna. "Scientists Find Genes That Let These Bees Reproduce without Males," *The New York Times* (June 9, 2016). https://www.nytimes.com/2016/06/10/science/bees-asexual-south-africa.html.

Korman, Justine, Karl Geurs, Carter Crocker, and Alan Alexander Milne. *Disney's Pooh's Great Adventure*. VHS video (1997).

"Kunjapuri." District Tehri Garhwal, Government of Uttarakhand, India (2024). https://tehri.nic.in/tourist-place/kunjapuri/.

Lahdenperä, Mirkka, Khyne U. Mar, and Virpi Lummaa. "Reproductive Cessation and Post-Reproductive Lifespan in Asian Elephants and Pre-Industrial Humans," *Frontiers in Zoology* 11 (1) (2014). https://doi.org/10.1186/s12983-014-0054-0.

Levy, Sue-Ann. "LEVY: Women's Rights Activist Warns Gender Dysphoria Has Become an Epidemic." True North News (April 25, 2022). https://tnc.news/2022/04/25/levy-womens-rights-activist-warns-gender-dysphoria-has-become-an-epidemic/.

Lowe, Nancy K. "What's New in JOGNN," *Journal of Obstetric, Gynecologic & Neonatal Nursing* 32 (1): 9 (2003). https://doi.org/10.1111/j.1552-6909.2003.tb00119.x.

McCoy, Daniel. "Yggdrasil." Norse Mythology for Smart People (2019a). https://norse-mythology.org/cosmology/yggdrasil-and-the-well-of-urd/.

———. "Yggdrasil." Norse Mythology for Smart People (2019b).

Merton, Thomas. *Thomas Merton: A Life in Letters*. Harper Collins (2008).

Metcalf, Stephen. "Neoliberalism: The Idea That Swallowed the World," *The Guardian* (September 3, 2017). https://www.theguardian.com/news/2017/aug/18/neoliberalism-the-idea-that-changed-the-world.

"Military Deception." Wikipedia (2023). https://en.m.wikipedia.org/wiki/Military_deception.

"Mohenjo-Daro an Ancient Indus Valley Metropolis." Harappa.com (2019). https://www.harappa.com/mohenjo-daro/mohenjodaroessay.html.

Moosa, Almira, Meeladah Ghani, and Helen C. O'Neill. "Genetic Associations with Polycystic Ovary Syndrome: The Role of the Mitochondrial Genome; a Systematic Review and Meta-Analysis," *Journal of Clinical Pathology* 75 (12) (2022), pp.815–24. https://doi.org/10.1136/jcp-2021-208028.

Narayanaswami Aiyar, K. *Thirty Minor Upanishads*. Legare Street Press (2022).

Ness, Roberta B., Sharon L. Hillier, Holly E. Richter, David E. Soper, Carol Stamm, James McGregor, Debra C. Bass, Richard L. Sweet, and Peter Rice. "Douching in relation to bacterial vaginosis, lactobacilli, and facultative bacteria in the vagina," *Obstetrics & Gynecology* 100, no. 4 (October 2002), pp.765-772. https://doi.org/10.1016/s0029-7844(02)02184-1.

Neumann, Erich. *The Fear of the Feminine*. Princeton University Press (2022).

Ng, Patrick "A Brief History of Men's Style: Edward VII and the Duke of Windsor (Edward VIII)." Medium (2024). https://medium.com/@pvtrickng/a-brief-history-of-mens-style-edward-vii-and-the-duke-of-windsor-edward-viii-0c27cb926452.

Nielsen, Euell A. "Queen Amina (1533–1610)." Black Past (November 5, 2023). https://www.blackpast.org/global-african-history/queen-amina-1533-1610/.

Nietzsche, Friedrich. *A Little Book of Essential Quotes on Life, Love, and Truth*. Independently Published (2020).

Oldster, Kilroy J. *Dead Toad Scrolls*. Bradenton, Florida: Booklocker.com (2016).

Oliver, Mary. *Wild Geese: Selected Poems*. Tarset: Bloodaxe (2004).

"One of Many Dharmasastra Texts of Hinduism." Wikimedia Foundation, Inc. (December 10, 2004). https://en.m.wikipedia.org/wiki/Manusmriti.

Oppenheim, Maya. "Menopausal Women Being Wrongly Prescribed Antidepressants Which Are Making Their Symptoms Worse, Warn Experts," *The Independent* (October 10, 2019). https://www.independent.co.uk/news/health/menopause-antidepressants-symptoms-worse-hrt-shortage-a9148951.html.

"Orwell and the Politics of Despair: A Critical Study of the Writings of George Orwell." Choice Reviews Online 27 (01): 27-013127-0131 (1989). https://doi.org/10.5860/choice.27-0131.

"Otto Frank Quote." A-Z Quotes (n.d.). https://www.azquotes.com/quote/733166.

Ovid, and Rolfe Humphries. *Metamorphoses the New, Annotated Edition*. Bloomington: Indiana University Press (2018).

People for the Ethical Treatment of Animals. "Experiments on Animals: Overview." PETA (2017). https://www.peta.org/issues/animals-used-for-experimentation/animals-used-experimentation-factsheets/animal-experiments-overview/.

"Prescription Medication Use – Breastfeeding Special Circumstances." U.S. Centers for Disease Control and Prevention (May 29, 2024). https://www.cdc.gov/breastfeeding-special-circumstances/hcp/vaccine-medication-drugs/prescriptions.html.

Pruitt, Sarah. "How Early Church Leaders Downplayed Mary Magdalene's Influence by Calling Her a Whore." Sky History (March 2019). https://www.history.com/news/mary-magdalene-jesus-wife-prostitute-saint.

Radhakrishnan, Sarvepalli. *The Principal Upaniṣads*. Allen & Unwin/ Harper, India (1953).

Rajadhyaksha, Abhijit. "The Marathas: Gaekwads of Baroda." The History Files (2024). https://www.historyfiles.co.uk/FeaturesFarEast/India_Modern_Marathas15.htm.

Rai, Diva. "Criminalization of Transgender People in Colonial India: Criminal Tribes Act." IPleaders (December 9, 2021). https://blog.ipleaders.in/criminalization-of-transgender-people-in-colonial-india-criminal-tribes-act/.

Ranade, Deepak. "Matter May after All Be Only in the Mind." Speaking Tree (October 9, 2022). https://www.speakingtree.in/article/matter-may-after-all-be-only-in-the-mind.

Rayor, Diane J. *The Homeric Hymns: A Translation, with Introduction and Notes*. Berkeley: University of California Press (2014).

Redmond, Layne. *When the Drummers Were Women: A Spiritual History of Rhythm*. Echo Point Books & Media, LLC (2021).

"Research Explores the Impact of Menopause on Women's Health and Aging." National Institute on Aging (May 6, 2022). https://www.nia.nih.gov/news/research-explores-impact-menopause-womens-health-and-aging.

"The Rich History of Fashion in India." Pure Elegance (December 15, 2017). https://www.pure-elegance.com/blogs/arts-culture/the-rich-history-of-indian-fashion.

Roben, David. *Everything You Always Wanted to Know about Sex*. Pan (1971).

Roberts, Nora. *Hidden Star*. HarperCollins Australia (2023).

Rūmī, Maulana Jalāl al-Dīn. *The Essential Rumi*. Castle Books (1999).

Sagan, Carl. "The Starfolk," *Science News* 104 (18) (1973), p.282. https://doi.org/10.2307/3958303.

Saint-Exupéry, Antoine de. *Flight to Arras*. Houghton Mifflin Harcourt (1985).

Saint Teresa of Avila and J. M. Cohen. *The Life of Saint Teresa of Avila*. Harmondsworth: Penguin Books (1957).

Sandy, Matt. "The Amazon Rain Forest Is Nearly Gone. We Went to the Front Lines to See If It Could Be Saved," *TIME* Magazine (2019). https://time.com/amazon-rainforest-disappearing/.

Śaṅkarācārya, Appiah Kuppuswami, and Surendra Pratap. *Saundaryalahari*. Chowkhamba Sanskrit Series, Varanasi, India (1972).

Saraswati, Swami Dayananda. *Śrīmad Bhagavad Gītā*. Rishikesk, India: Arsha Vidya Gurukulam (2007).

Sharma, P., H.S. Talwar, and S. Joshi. "Shiva Lingam: A Devotional Phallic Image or Symbol of Divine Creation?" *European Urology* 83 (February 2023), pp.S162–63. https://doi.org/10.1016/s0302-2838(23)00168-9.

Sigma Aldrich. 2024. "NMR Chemical Shifts of Impurities Charts." Merck 1 (1) (2024). https://www.sigmaaldrich.com/MX/en/technical-documents/technical-article/genomics/cloning-and-expression/blue-white-screening.

Skye, Michelle. *Goddess Alive!: Inviting Celtic & Norse Goddesses into Your Life*. Woodbury, Minnesota: Llewellyn Publications (2007).

Soh, Baolin Pauline, Ryan Eyn Kidd Man, Yih Chung Tham, Eva Fenwick, Tze Tein Yong, Tien Yin Wong, Ching Yu Cheng, and Ecosse L Lamoureux. "Hormone Replacement Therapy (HRT): Utilisation Rates, Determinants and Impact on Health-Related Quality of Life in a Multi-Ethnic Asian Population," *Journal of Clinical and Diagnostic Research* (2020). https://doi.org/10.7860/jcdr/2020/42545.13463.

"South Asia's Non-Binary Communities Worry about Losing Their Identity," *The Economist*. (n.d.; Accessed February 21, 2023). https://www.economist.com/asia/2021/09/16/south-asias-non-binary-communities-worry-about-losing-their-identity.

Swahananda, Swami. *Chandogya Upanisad*. Sri Ramakrishna Math (2022).

Swidler, Leonard. *Jesus Was a Feminist: What the Gospels Reveal about His Revolutionary Perspective.* Lanham, Maryland: Sheed & Ward (2007). .

Switzer, Kathrine. "The Real Story – Kathrine Switzer – Marathon Woman." (2013.) https://kathrineswitzer.com/1967-boston-marathon-the-real-story/.

Taft, Michael W., and Hoopla Digital. *Greek Gods & Goddesses.* United States: Britannica Digital Learning (2014).

Teilhard, Pierre. *Hymn of the Universe.* Harper/Collins Publisher January 1, 1969

Tiwari, Maya. *Ayurveda Secrets of Healing.* Silver Lake, Wisconsin: Lotus Press (1998).

———. *Women's Power to Heal.* New York: Mother Om Media (2007).

———. *Women's Power to Heal* 2nd edition. New York: Mother Om Media (2012).

Tzu, Sun, and Sun Zi. *The Art of War.* Les Prairies Numeriques (2020).

UN Women. "Global Database on Violence against Women." UN Women Data Hub (2015). https://data.unwomen.org/global-database-on-violence-against-women.

Upanishads. *The Brihadaranyaka Upanishad.* (1950.)

Vaughan-Lee, Llewellyn. *The Return of the Feminine and the World Soul: A Collection of Writings and Transcribed Talks.* Inverness, California: Golden Sufi Center (2013).

Vr Ramachandra Dikshitar. *War in Ancient India.* Hassell Street Press (2023).

Vyasa, Krishna-Dwaipayana. *The Mahabharata Vana Parva, Part I.* Double 9 Books (2023).

Vyasa, Veda. *Devi-Bhagavata Purana.* CreateSpace (2015).

Walker, Alice. *An Interview with Alice Walker.* (1981.)

Watson, Katherine. *Poisoned Lives: English Poisoners and Their Victims.* London: Hambledon Continuum (2007).

Wilson, Robert A. *Feminine Forever.* Pocket Books (2000).

Worland, Justin. "Here's How Many Trees Humans Cut down Each Year," *TIME* magazine (September 2, 2015). https://time.com/4019277/trees-humans-deforestation/.

World Wildlife Fund. "What Are the Biggest Drivers of Tropical Deforestation?" World Wildlife Fund (2018a). https://www.worldwildlife.org/magazine/issues/summer-2018/articles/what-are-the-biggest-drivers-of-tropical-deforestation.

———. "What Are the Biggest Drivers of Tropical Deforestation?" World Wildlife Fund (2018b). https://www.worldwildlife.org/magazine/issues/summer-2018/articles/what-are-the-biggest-drivers-of-tropical-deforestation.

Other Books by Maya Tiwari

Women's Power to Heal: Through Inner Medicine. Mother Om Media, July 16, 2012.
ISBN 978 0979327919

Living Ahimsa Diet: Nourishing Love & Life. Mother Om Media, July 16, 2012.
ISBN 978 0979327926

The Path of Practice: A Woman's Book of Ayurvedic Healing. Wellspring/Ballantine Books, November 27, 2001.
ISBN 978 0345434845

Ayurveda: A Life of Balance: The Complete Guide to Ayurvedic Nutrition & Body Types with Recipes. Healing Arts Press, December 1, 1994.
ISBN 978 0812894909

Ayurveda Secrets of Healing. Lotus Press, August 13, 1995.
ISBN 978 0914955153

Love! A Daily Oracle for Healing. Mother Om Media, January 1, 2012.
ISBN 978 0979327933

Diet for Natural Beauty: A Natural Anti-Aging Formula for Skin and Hair Care by Aveline Kushi (Author), Wendy Esko (Author), Maya Tiwari (Author). Japan Publications, January 1, 1991

O-BOOKS

SPIRITUALITY

O is a symbol of the world, of oneness and unity; this eye represents knowledge and insight. We publish titles on general spirituality and living a spiritual life. We aim to inform and help you on your own journey in this life.
If you have enjoyed this book, why not tell other readers by posting a review on your preferred book site?

Recent bestsellers from O-Books are:

Heart of Tantric Sex
Diana Richardson
Revealing Eastern secrets of deep love and intimacy to Western couples.
Paperback: 978-1-90381-637-0 ebook: 978-1-84694-637-0

Crystal Prescriptions
The A-Z guide to over 1,200 symptoms and their healing crystals
Judy Hall
The first in the popular series of eight books, this handy little guide is packed as tight as a pill bottle with crystal remedies for ailments.
Paperback: 978-1-90504-740-6 ebook: 978-1-84694-629-5

Shine On

David Ditchfield and J S Jones

What if the after effects of a near-death experience were undeniable? What if a person could suddenly produce high-quality paintings of the afterlife, or if they acquired the ability to compose classical symphonies? Meet: David Ditchfield.

Paperback: 978-1-78904-365-5 ebook: 978-1-78904-366-2

The Way of Reiki

The Inner Teachings of Mikao Usui

Frans Stiene

The roadmap for deepening your understanding of the system of Reiki and rediscovering your True Self.

Paperback: 978-1-78535-665-0 ebook: 978-1-78535-744-2

You Are Not Your Thoughts

Frances Trussell

The journey to a mindful way of being, for those who want to truly know the power of mindfulness.

Paperback: 978-1-78535-816-6 ebook: 978-1-78535-817-3

The Mysteries of the Twelfth Astrological House

Fallen Angels

Carmen Turner-Schott, MSW, LISW

Everyone wants to know more about the most misunderstood house in astrology — the twelfth astrological house.

Paperback: 978-1-78099-343-0 ebook: 978-1-78099-344-7

Feng Shui Your Way to Abundance
Janine Lowe
Feng Shui Your Way to Abundance shows how to use Feng Shui to attract positive energy and change into your life.
Paperback: 978-1-80341-674-8 ebook: 978-1-80341-683-0

Naked in the Now
Marijke McCandless
What if getting present was less like work and more like being seduced by a lover?
Paperback: 978-1-80341-567-3 ebook: 978-1-80341-574-1

Crystal Creed
Jamie Inglett
A beginner's guide to learning the sacred healing powers of crystals
Paperback: 978-1-80341-438-6 ebook: 978-1-80341-439-3

Revealing Light
Maryann Weston
YouTube psychic-astrologer Maryann Weston, from Revealing Light, shares her spiritual evolution after cancer had activated dormant psychic gifts, revealing a new purpose...
Paperback: 978-1-80341-730-1 ebook: 978-1-80341-738-7

Temple of Love
Natalie Glebova
The secret to true love is closer than you think.
Paperback: 978-1-80341-784-4 ebook: 978-1-80341-810-0

Readers of ebooks can buy or view any of these bestsellers by clicking on the live link in the title. Most titles are published in paperback and as an ebook. Paperbacks are available in traditional bookshops. Both print and ebook formats are available online.

Find more titles and sign up to our readers' newsletter at
www.o-books.com

Follow O-Books on Facebook at **O-Books**

For video content, author interviews, and more, please subscribe to our YouTube channel:

O-BOOKS Publishing

Follow us on social media for book news, promotions, and more:

Facebook: O-Books

Instagram: @o_books_mbs

X: @obooks

Tik Tok: @ObooksMBS

www.o-books.com